DIVINATIONS

THEOPOLITICAL VISIONS

SERIES EDITORS:

Thomas Heilke
D. Stephen Long
and Debra Dean Murphy

Theopolitical Visions seeks to open up new vistas on public life, hosting fresh conversations between theology and political theory. This series assembles writers who wish to revive theopolitical imagination for the sake of our common good.

Theopolitical Visions hopes to re-source modern imaginations with those ancient traditions in which political theorists were often also theologians. Whether it was Jeremiah's prophetic vision of exiles "seeking the peace of the city," Plato's illuminations on piety and the civic virtues in the Republic, St. Paul's call to "a common life worthy of the Gospel," St. Augustine's beatific vision of the City of God, or the gothic heights of medieval political theology, much of Western thought has found it necessary to think theologically about politics, and to think politically about theology. This series is founded in the hope that the renewal of such mutual illumination might make a genuine contribution to the peace of our cities.

FORTHCOMING VOLUMES:

David Deane
The Matter of the Spirit: How Soteriology Shapes the Moral Life

DIVINATIONS

Theopolitics in an Age of Terror

DANIEL M. BELL JR.

CASCADE *Books* • Eugene, Oregon

DIVINATIONS
Theopolitics in an Age of Terror

Theopolitcal Visions 22

Copyright © 2017 Daniel M. Bell Jr. All rights reserved. Except for brief quotations in critical publications or reviews, no part of this book may be reproduced in any manner without prior written permission from the publisher. Write: Permissions, Wipf and Stock Publishers, 199 W. 8th Ave., Suite 3, Eugene, OR 97401.

Cascade Books
An Imprint of Wipf and Stock Publishers
199 W. 8th Ave., Suite 3
Eugene, OR 97401

www.wipfandstock.com

PAPERBACK ISBN: 978-1-4982-9538-3
HARDCOVER ISBN: 978-1-4982-9540-6
EBOOK ISBN: 978-1-4982-9539-0

Cataloguing-in-Publication data:

Names: Bell, Daniel M., Jr., author.

Title: Divinations : theopolitics in an age of terror / Daniel M. Bell Jr.

Description: Eugene, OR : Cascade Books, 2017 | Series: Theopolitcal Visions 22 | Includes bibliographical references and index.

Identifiers: ISBN 978-1-4982-9538-3 (paperback) | ISBN 978-1-4982-9540-6 (hardcover) | ISBN 978-1-4982-9539-0 (ebook)

Subjects: LCSH: Continental philosophy. | Political theology. | Economics—Religious aspects—Christianity. | Capitalism—Religious aspects—Christianity. | Philosophy and religion. | Postmodernism—Religious aspects—Christianity.

Classification: B105.R4 B37 2017 (print) | B105.R4 B37 (ebook)

Manufactured in the U.S.A.   10/20/17

Scripture quotations are from New Revised Standard Version Bible, copyright © 1989 National Council of the Churches of Christ in the United States of America. Used by permission. All rights reserved worldwide.

Contents

Acknowledgments vii

Introduction ix

1. The Politics of Fear and the Gospel of Life 1
2. The Politics of Indifference and the Overcoming of Capital 29
3. Only Jesus Saves: Toward a Theo-political Ontology of Judgment 74
4. The Law Exceeding Every Madness: Excess and the Law of Love beyond Capital 103
5. "The Fragile Brilliance of Glass": Empire, Multitude, and the Coming Community 136

Bibliography 181

Index 191

Acknowledgments

The arguments developed in several chapters of this work first saw the light of day in other publications.

Chapter 1: A first iteration appeared as "The Politics of Fear and the Gospel of Life," *Journal for Cultural and Religious Theory* 8 (2007) 55–80. A second iteration appeared as "The Politics of Fear and the Gospel of Life," in *Belief and Metaphysics*, edited by Peter Candler Jr. and Conor Cunningham (London: SCM, 2007) 426–51.

Chapter 2: "Badiou's Faith and Paul's Gospel: The Politics of Indifference and the Overcoming of Capital," *Angelaki* 12 (2007) 97–112.

Chapter 3: "Only Jesus Saves: Toward a Theo-political Ontology of Judgment," in *Theology and the Political: The New Debate*, edited by Creston Davis et al. (Durham: Duke University Press, 2005) 200–227.

Chapter 5: "'The Fragile Brilliance of Glass': Empire, Multitude, and the Coming Community," *Political Theology* 11 (2010) 61–76.

Introduction

One noted mark of this postmodern era is the turn to religion. Of course some religionists might object that we never left, that we never turned away from religion nor did religion ever evacuate the public forum. That religion is thought to have left under modernity, even as religionists insist we did no such thing, and now returns raises at least two interesting issues that shape the endeavor of the pages that follow.

First, the (re)turn has less to do with religionists themselves than with religion's reception by other denizens of the public forum. Specifically, it has to do with religion's reception among postmodern philosophers. Indeed, over the last few decades there has been a significant resurgence of interest in theological texts and concepts among militantly atheistic philosophers associated with the postmodern *episteme*.

This renewed recognition of religion is viewed by many religionists as a boon; yet it would be a mistake to bask in the glow of this new-found adoration uncritically. For upon closer examination, this new receptivity, this new space and time given to religion is not necessarily hospitable. Scratch the surface of any number of philosophical texts devoted to religious themes and one will discover many false friends. Thus Deleuze writes of engaging others with the intent of a monstrous procreation and Žižek is explicit in his hope to undermine Christianity by coopting it. This is of a piece with what Hent de Vries refers to as "the paradox of a non-theological, and, it would seem, even nonreligious concern with religion."[1]

Recognizing the hostile intent of many of religion's new interlocutors does not diminish the opportunities presented by the current moment nor does it mean that religionists should eschew the public stage or shy away from engagement with our most recent cultured despisers. Rather, we should welcome the engagement, and in the pages that follow, I hope it is

1. de Vries, *Philosophy and the Turn to Religion*, ix–x.

clear that I believe there is much salutary to be learned from the wisdom and insights of these new acquaintances and their (mis)uses of the faith.

De Vries suggests that what drives the current exposure of philosophy to the religious and theological is a realization that "the theological may provide us with the best, as well as both the most responsible and the most risky, access to the questions of ethics and politics in the current historical constellation."[2] Whether or not religion proves that useful to philosophy, engaging these philosophers proves illuminating for thinking theologically about ethics and politics beyond the accretions and sedimentations of modernity.

In this regard, it has been said that the church should value its heretics for the ways they prompt the church to better understand and articulate its own convictions and confessions. The same holds true for self-professed outsiders such as the militant atheists engaged in these pages. And they should be valued not the least because it is well known that the blessed Trinity has a wonderful and sometimes confounding way of speaking through outsiders—religious others, the marginalized and oppressed, devils and demons, and as my students are sometimes wont to remind me, even an ass—I assume they refer to Balaam's.[3]

As Augustine observes, pagans catch glimpses of the truth because "the mines of God's providence . . . are everywhere scattered abroad."[4] Hence the title of this work, divinations. Divination is an act of seeking, seeking signs or traces of living water, seeking truth. In this case, it is a matter of seeking traces of the divine wisdom in a manner analogous to the church's longstanding practice of discerning *vestigia trinitatis* in the natural world, except here we plumb the labyrinthine depths of the works of the likes of Agamben, Badiou, and Žižek.

Thus, this caution regarding the celebration of the turn to religion is not meant to discourage engagement. Rather, it is meant to call attention to *how* we engage these philosophers in the public forum. Which leads to the second point provoked by the recent turn to religion.

That the turn occurred even as we religionists insist religion never left, that religion never evacuated the public square in the first place, suggests something of the failure of religionists under the modern *episteme* and their way of engaging others.

Under the sign of modernity, theological claims were thought to be religious representations of common human experience, giving

---

2. Ibid., x.
3. Num 22:30.
4. Augustine, *On Christian Doctrine*, 2.40.

expression to the liminal or depth dimension of the human being in its eternal, transcendental quest for meaning. Thus the dominant theological voices among those most likely to venture into the public forum carefully stripped their theological discourse of the particularity that was thought to hinder communication and foreclose meaning. They nurtured discourse that was deemed "universal and public,"[5] immediately accessible in the sense of "reasoned discourse appealing to any intelligent, reasonable, and responsible person."[6] Moreover, they sought to carefully police the public forum, denouncing co-religionists who refused to sacrifice the particular on the altar of universal meaning as "sectarian."

Postmodernity has little patience with the totalizing commonalities of modernity. Yet postmodernity does not thereby reject any and every sense of the common. Although it runs counter to the popular narrative of postmodernity as the happy embrace of the total war of sovereign singularities, postmodernity has not dismissed the common *simpliciter* and *en toto*. As several of the thinkers engaged in the pages that follow show, there remains a dream, a hope, the work of the common. Yet, this is a common not reduced to the same.

Which is to say that postmodernity suggests that religionists no longer have to contain their particularity. Postmodernity marks a time when the particular is embraced, not effaced and dismissed in the name of an abstract sameness / common that has been unmasked as not common at all but rather largely the product of western arms and markets. Thus, the (false) humility of modern theology is exposed as being of a piece with the empire of modern socio-political forms (not the least of which is the university or the church-as-soul-of-the-nation).

In other words, the common as same gives way to the common understood as the project and product of the contingent (dare I say providential?) encounter of particulars in what, following Deleuze, we might call a disjunctive synthesis.

Thus the promise and potential for a new way of engaging others emerges. It does not require relinquishing particular claims or judgments ahead of time, as the price of admission to the public square. While a certain humility might be tactically wise, it is not obligatory or even necessarily expected. This new way is neither for nor against; or perhaps it is both for and against. It is more discerning; less *a priori* and more *ad hoc*; lest certain and more contingent, yet bolder.

---

5. Tracy, *Analogical Imagination*, 52.
6. Ibid., 131.

This returns us to the practice of divination. For what are we looking amidst the postmodern philosophers engaged in the pages that follow? Put most simply, signs of new politics.

For some time now, it has been said that we live in a post-political age, meaning primarily that traditional parties no longer function as they once did, as managing components (or power containers, perhaps, in the language of Anthony Giddens) of the nation-state. Certainly the recent election-cycle in the US suggests this is true as the traditional parties were no longer able to contain and control forces unleashed by the so-called free market.

Writing in the aftermath of World War II, Hannah Arendt already noted that political parties no longer served the nation but had become vehicles of extra-national movements. While Arendt's focus was on totalitarian movements that emerged "after politics," the signs of a new politics that comes after politics with which I wrestle are more ambiguous. On one hand, the postmodern philosophers I engage all seek a new politics after the modern politics of state and class and they all eschew totalitarianism; yet in the end it is not clear that the politics they imagine succeeds in escaping the totalizing clutches of capital and violence.

On the other hand, I engage these postmodern philosophers for the sake of articulating a theological politics that could be called a kind of diaspora or pilgrim politics precisely because it exceeds the political containers of modernity, such as class and party, states and borders. Yet it remains to be seen the extent to which this postliberal political theology, in its weakness, can actually rise to the challenge of politics—that is, can it point to a polity, a politics that actually resembles or embodies the theological claims it makes about God and the way God works in the world?

Each of the chapters that follows revolves around several concepts that are constitutive of politics, especially the political economy of capitalism: life and death and the role that fear plays in our political lives; Jewish election, incarnation, and the economic logic of debt and retribution; judgment, justice, and sacrifice; law, sovereignty, and freedom; and, finally, empire and democracy.

Immediately apparent is the fact that this divination of a new politics is forthrightly ontological. Again, against the fashionable currents of the present age, the philosophers engaged in these pages are thoroughly ontological. Following in the footsteps of Heidegger, for a time it was thought that postmodernity would also be after or post metaphysics. One thing that unites

Deleuze et al. is that they recognize, in the words of Deleuze, that "politics precedes being."[7] That is, that ontology is part of the field of struggle, that resistance to the terror of these days must be conducted not merely on the plane of programs and parties but at the level of being itself, of the constitutive power of life itself—desire—and its organization, of our very way of being in the world. Thus, each of these thinkers offers a politics of being, an ontological politics that is part of the political struggle of our day. And what we see in the process of engaging their work is what happens to the political concepts of modernity when those concepts are ontologically interrogated and reconfigured—or, in theological language, redeemed.

To be more specific, chapter 1 begins by analyzing the ubiquitous politics and culture of fear, showing how the standard account of modern political liberalism as warding off a pre- or extra-political fear is flawed. By means of the work of Thomas Hobbes, Michel Foucault, and Gilles Deleuze, I argue that liberalism thrives on the production and manipulation of fear, thus promising no end to the terror that besieges us. Then, in the constructive moment, Alain Badiou's account of St. Paul, the event, and being for life, is used to trace a politics of life, of resurrection. Specifically, using Badiou's vision of pure affirmation, I develop a non-dialectical account of Christ's death and resurrection in order to fund a politics that is finally indifferent to fear and death.

Whereas the preceding chapter drew on Badiou in a positive manner, chapter 2 shows how his politics of affirmation finally fails to deliver us from the terror of capital. Engaging his reading of St. Paul as the harbinger of a universal politics of truth over against the false or empty universalism of capitalism, I show how the ways Badiou fails to get Paul right are indicative of deficiencies in this thought with regard to the articulation of the possibilities of generating and sustaining resistance to capital. Specifically, I argue that our hope of overcoming capital depends on, to use Badiou's concepts, a different subtraction (the election of the Jews), a different universalism (the catholicity of salvation), and a different event (Christ, the concrete universal).

Chapter 3 takes up the thought of Gilles Deleuze, who rightly recognizes that the struggle against the terror of this age must be waged at the level of ontology. In a lesser known essay, "To have done with judgment," Deleuze develops an ontology of pure immanence over against the judgment of God. After considering Deleuze's vision, I will argue that only in Christ are we finally done with judgment and that Deleuze's vision of pure immanence,

---

7. Deleuze and Parnet, *Dialogues*, 17; Deleuze and Guattari, *Thousand Plateaus*, 203.

far from fleeing judgment can only subject us to the harshest judgment, one that may exceed even that of capital. Accompanying this effort will be an outline of how the practice of the end of judgment that Christ inaugurates opens a space of liberation from the bondage of savage capitalism.

Chapter 4 considers the theopolitics of law and love in Agamben, Badiou, Deleuze, Derrida, and Žižek. Each of them problematizes law in favor of some form of "excess," frequently drawing on Paul to do so. In the course of correcting their reading of Paul and Christianity on law (and incidentally but not insignificantly rescuing Judaism), I will offer a theology of law, developed from Augustine's "The Spirit and the Letter" among others (such as Aquinas), that nevertheless avoids many of the problems those thinkers associate with law, unmasking those problems to be the product of a univocal and not analogical reading of law. It is this law of love, and not a univocal antinomianism, that holds forth the promise of redemption from the lawlessness of capital enforced by the laws of the liberal political order.

Chapter 5 takes up the political questions of empire, sovereignty, exception, and democracy by means of an engagement with the thought of Agamben, Derrida, Hardt, and Negri. After considering their account of the biopolitical production of postmodern empire, I turn to their constructive visions of what comes next: the coming community, the multitude, the common and so forth. I then compare and contrast those hopes with that embodied in an Augustinian political ecclesiology, an ecclesial politics of pilgrimage, considering in particular how this theopolitics meets the hopes for a new subjectivity, a new humanity, a new kind of democracy.

As this project comes to fruition, a number of acknowledgments are in order. Creston Davis was pretty relentless in pursuing and provoking me to engage with several of these philosophers, and was more than helpful in wrestling my way through the thickets of their thought. Peter Candler and Conor Cunningham repeatedly created opportunities at delightful conferences for me to develop some of the ideas that appear in these pages. And gratitude is due to Stanley Hauerwas, whose generous nonsectarian spirit and practice has always encouraged engaging and learning from voices and disciplines far beyond the shadow of the recognizable church.

CHAPTER 1

The Politics of Fear and the Gospel of Life

Recently I was shocked to learn from my mortgage company that it was not a matter of *if* but *when* a natural disaster was going to destroy my home. This startling revelation came on the heels of the morning's paper announcing that a flu pandemic was inevitable, and a radio show featuring an expert's claim that such a pandemic would have horrific effects comparable to those of nuclear war. As I turned toward my fridge in search of consolation I caught myself just in time, recalling a recent report raising serious safety concerns about refrigerated foods, and of course there is mad cow disease, and all those bacteria and the lead leaching into the tap water from the pipes and . . . Fear abounds. From color-coded alerts and militarized train stations and airports, to runs on gas masks, Cipro, and duct tape we are immersed in what Barry Glassner has aptly called a "culture of fear."[1]

Awash in fear, armies and security forces are mobilized, secret interrogation facilities are erected, resources are diverted from more pacific needs, suspects are rounded up, civil liberties and jurisprudence fall by the wayside—all in the pursuit of one overriding and all-consuming concern: "Nothing matters more to me right now than the safety of my home and the survival of my homeland." So says a leading light among that novel political force, "security moms."[2]

Fear abounds, but so what? Who would be crass enough to challenge the legitimacy of this fear? Granted, there may be grounds for questioning the form taken by some of the concrete practices that have been promoted by this fear in response to the various and manifold threats that abound. We can, for example, debate the appropriateness of torture or the necessity of curtailing civil rights or the proper limitations of presidential powers in the midst of a war on terror, but who could challenge the underlying,

---

1. Glassner, *Culture of Fear*.
2. Malkin, "Candidates Ignore Security Moms," 11A.

primordial fear? Remembering the horror of Ground Zero, Madrid, London, surely only liberal elites ensconced in their ivory towers—sheltered (some would say "alienated") from the real world and real people by the moribund moat of academia—would dare dismiss wholesale this culture of fear and the politics it produces. And in so doing, they would expose not only the callousness of their souls toward vibrant human emotion and feeling, but also their myopia, their failure to appreciate the conditions of possibility of their own lives. This is to say, such a critique could arise only from a failure to appreciate the ways in which the modern liberal political order itself is a response to fear. Thus, to challenge the culture of fear is not only to attack a principal human emotion, but it is also to assault the foundations of the very political order that keeps terror at bay.

So we are left wondering not simply, "Is there a way beyond the culture of fear?" but perhaps more importantly, "Should we even desire an alternative to the culture of fear?" What is wrong with fear? With a culture of fear? Moreover, fear's apologists remind us, the alternative to fear is typically apathy and decadence, a culture that is lifeless and listless, selfish and slothful.[3] Whatever a culture of fear's deficiencies may be, such an alternative can hardly be celebrated as an improvement.

Any alternative to the culture of fear must address these concerns, and so they shape the account that follows. I begin by considering liberalism and fear. The dominant account of liberalism is that it is a political order designed to diffuse a pre- or extra-political fear and ward off terror, which it does by means of the construction of complex space (federalism, robust civil society, etc.). Drawing upon Hobbes, Foucault, and Deleuze, I will show that the dominant account misconstrues both fear and liberalism's relation to fear. Indeed, their analyses suggest that fear is not a primordial instinct that swells fully formed from the human breast, prior to any political discipline and immune to political manipulation. To the contrary, modern political liberalism is revealed to be not about dissipating a pre-political fear but about the production and manipulation of fear. Liberalism is a politics of fear; thus, for the denizens of liberal political orders there can be no end to fear.

The relief of our fears will require a different order, a different politics, a politics of life. What are the contours of this politics? Here the constructive moment begins with Alain Badiou's treatment of St. Paul. According to Badiou, Paul announced Christ as a truth-event that instantiates being-for-life by means of a break or rupture with the being-for-death that simultaneously

---

3. See, for example, Brooks, "Age of Conflict," 19–23; Rich, "Day Before Tuesday," A23; Brooks, "Facing Up to Our Fears," 66–69.

animates and eviscerates political liberalism. Yet, such a politics stands or falls on the truthfulness of the claim that Christ's labor was one of pure affirmation, without a shadow of negation. Can such a claim stand at the foot of the cross? This prompts consideration of Christ's work of atonement. I argue in an Augustinian and Anselmian vein that Christ's labor of atonement is not a matter of negation. Christ, and the life of fidelity to the truth-event that is Christ, is indifferent to crucifixion, suffering, and death. Thus displaced, death gives way to life, to the pure affirmation that is resurrected life. Christ gives the gift of life, a gift that founds a politics of resurrection. The final move anticipates objections that such a gift constitutes a politics at all by taking up Augustine's vision of the city of God.

I. Liberalism and Fear

The introductory defense of the culture and politics of fear follows the lineaments of what passes today for the canonical account of both the nature of fear and modern political liberalism's relationship to fear.

The Origin and End of Fear (I): The Standard Account

The intellectual pedigree of the dominant account of fear and liberalism's relation to fear can be traced back through thinkers such as Arendt, Tocqueville, and Montesquieu, and it finds expression in an array of contemporary thinkers as diverse as Elshtain, Shklar, Rorty, and Ignatieff.[4] According to this account, fear is a pre- or extra-political impulse. This is to say, it is a primordial, irrational force the cause of which lies prior to or outside of the political order. Think, for example, of the oft-repeated explanations of the motives of the terrorists who struck on 9/11 and who have since continued to inspire fear. It is said that they are persons bent simply on pure evil, as such they have neither political motive nor political goal; their aim is solely destruction, pure and simple. Thus the fear they arouse is distinctly extra-political in origin. Fear's source is similarly located by prominent theorists of liberalism. According to Montesquieu, echoing earlier thinkers such as Hobbes and Locke, fear was born of a desire for security of person and goods. Specifically, fear, according to Montesquieu, was grounded in the threat of despotic tyranny and terror. For Tocqueville, fear was a generalized or mass anxiety prompted by a rapidly changing environment that washed

---

4. The treatment of liberalism and fear that follows is drawn from the masterful study of Robin, *Fear*.

away fixed reference points and established meanings. According to Arendt, the source of fear was the radical evil of totalitarian terror, a terror that threatened the integrity of the self. The thread that unites these and similar liberal accounts of fear is that in each instance, the source of fear is located outside the properly political realm, be it in a generalized anxiety, an antipolitical despotism, or a primordial retraction from death.

If fear's origins are extra-political, the response such fear elicits, according to the architects of liberalism, is distinctly political. Liberalism is born out of fear in the expectation that the liberal political order can keep terror and its consequent fear at bay. The standard narrative of liberalism's birth is the narrative of a political order founded with the intent to ward off terror, thereby dissolving the source of fear. Thus, Montesquieu lays out a political order characterized by complex space—governing authority dispersed among separated powers with checks and balances coupled to a robust and pluralistic civil society where the self has opportunity to be enmeshed in a web of relations that can bolster it in resisting despotic intrusions. Likewise, in a similar vein Tocqueville asserts that the growth and strengthening afforded civic associations and institutions under liberalism provides the best defense against the free-floating insecurity of the masses unhinged by a rapidly changing environment. Once again, it is the complex space of liberalism's political order, the proliferation of local institutions and social hierarchies in civil society, that tethers the individual in the midst of a changing world and so inhibits the spread of fear. Finally, Arendt, acknowledging the influence of both Montesquieu and Tocqueville,[5] argued that totalitarian terror advances by means of the creation of smooth or simple space that leaves the individual denuded, isolated before power, whereas liberalism's complex space protects the individual by providing the cover of diverse civic associations such that individuals need not be so exposed before terror. Again, the consistency that traverses the various accounts of liberalism's relation to fear is clear: liberalism is a political response to an extra-political fear that wards off terror and fear by means of the construction of complex space—dispersing governing authority and providing the individual cover amongst a plethora of civic institutions and associations.

The Origin and End of Fear (II): Hobbes, Foucault, and Deleuze

In the standard account, liberalism is cast as the end of fear and civil society, in particular, as a space of liberty. This account is not without its challengers. In particular, there are those who take issue with the claim that liberalism

---

5. Robin, *Fear*, 99.

establishes a space of freedom from fear. Specifically, it is argued that far from warding off an extra-political fear, liberalism actually thrives on fear, generating and governing by means of that fear. Liberalism is, in effect, a politics of fear.

Hobbes, for example, would certainly agree with those who suggest that liberalism is established on a foundation provided by fear. However, he would disagree sharply with the suggestion that the fear that underwrote the political project of the commonwealth was a pre-political passion. While acknowledging that persons do experience a pre-political sense of fear, Hobbes noted that that aversion in and of itself was insufficient to sustain the kind of commitment to self-preservation on which the sovereign commonwealth depended. In fact, Hobbes observed, fear often gives way to other passions, such as the desire for glory and honor, thus diminishing the motivating force of self-preservation. Consequently, in order for the commonwealth to actually unite under the sovereign, fear had to be promoted as a virtue in the service of a morally legitimate concern for self-preservation, while the moral stature of virtues such as courage had to suffer a corresponding reduction. As Corey Robin puts it, "Hobbes . . . thought about the fear of death and the demand of self-preservation not as a description of an already existing reality—of how human beings actually behaved in the world—but as a project of political and cultural reconstruction, requiring the creation of a new ethos and a new man."[6]

But how, pray tell, was this new ethos to be constructed and this new person birthed? Addressing this question, Hobbes proved himself a much more astute political thinker than Machiavelli, who encouraged his prince to induce fear with the rather blunt instrument of stately violence. Hobbes realized that no prince possessed sufficient force to instill the requisite fear. Moreover, he recognized that fear alone, without a concomitant sense of investment or benefit, would not sustain obedience. In other words, what was needed was a way for citizens to participate in, and a reason for them to collaborate with, this induction of fear. For this, Hobbes turned to civil society. He thought that the leaders of civil society, particularly preachers and teachers (who had certainly shown themselves adept at inciting rebellion during the English civil war), could play a central role in the fostering of a culture of fear. Legitimating the moral elevation of self-preservation on the grounds that if one were dead, one could not pursue any goods, civic leaders could persuade the populace that it has a moral stake in perpetuating fear and moral grounds for collaborating in the establishment and maintenance of the sovereign's authority.

6. Ibid., 37–38.

Hobbes's vision provides a blueprint for the modern state erected on the negative moral foundation of fear. This fear, however, is not extra-political but rather the thoroughgoing production of political processes. Moreover, it is the product of a collaboration between the sovereign and civil society, thus calling into question the extent to which civil society is rightly understood as a space of liberty from fear.

But, alas, what does this prove? After all, Hobbes's connection with liberalism is hotly contested. As Judith Shklar pointedly observes, the mere fact that Hobbes propounds a social contract theory of the state and loathes Catholicism does not make him the father of liberalism.[7] Furthermore, is not the claim that fear is used to bolster the sovereign state a rather antiquated one, given the contemporary geo-political horizon, where, it is widely acknowledged, the sovereignty of states faces erosion by the global capitalist economic order? In other words, Hobbes's analysis may provide more heat than light simply because he was not dealing with liberal states undergoing capitalist stress. For this reason, we turn now to more contemporary analyses, beginning with Michel Foucault's account of governmentality and the modern liberal state.[8]

Governmentality, according to Foucault, is simply the art of government, the conduct of conduct. Although on the surface such a concept appeared decidedly unremarkable, as it is developed by Foucault it encompasses much more than meets the eye. Governmentality includes within its scope disciplinary power, which was paradigmatically set forth in *Discipline and Punish* and for which Foucault is widely known. Disciplinary power is that rather overt and direct power whereby the state extends its dominion and enforces its sovereignty over those whom it renders subjects. The most prominent example of this kind of power is, of course, the sword in the form of the penal power of the state, but it extends beyond blunt force to include the full range of the state's juridical reach.

Of course, at this point, Foucault has not succeeded in moving us much beyond Hobbes's analysis of the absolutist state. Indeed, Foucault acknowledges that the disciplinary power of the sovereign state is perhaps most clearly on display in the absolutist state that Hobbes theorized and, according to Foucault's genealogy, slid into crisis not long after Hobbes's death. Yet it is precisely at the moment of the passing of the absolutist state and emergence of the liberal political order that the illuminating power of Foucault's account of governmentality is most profoundly manifest.

7. Shklar, *Political Thought and Political Thinkers*, 6.
8. A more detailed treatment of governmentality in Foucault, with appropriate textual pointers, can be found in Burchell, Gordon, and Miller, *The Foucault Effect*, which includes several essays by Foucault.

According to Foucault, the absolutist state went into crisis as it was confronted by a host of forces and events—wars; rebellions, financial difficulties; demographic, commercial, and agricultural expansion—that simply exceeded the governing capacity of sovereignty and its disciplines. In response to this crisis, the art of government underwent a mutation and the liberal state was born. What is striking about the advent of the liberal state is that the link between maximal governmental effectiveness and maximal government itself is broken. Whereas sovereignty attempted to monopolize government, forging an identity between government and state apparatuses, liberalism extends or diffuses government beyond the state proper across the entire social field. Thus, notwithstanding popular rhetoric to the contrary, liberalism does not juxtapose government and freedom. Rather, liberal government is government *through* freedom. Civil society is rightly set against the state but not in the sense that civil society marks a space of liberty *simpliciter*. Rather, civil society is set apart from the state only in the sense that it embodies a different modality of government. In Foucault's language, liberal government combines macro-level disciplinary power exercised through the state with what he calls biopower—power exercised at the micro level by means of what he calls technologies of the self. Biopower is the power operative in and through the private initiatives to mold the self into a particular kind of subject that proliferate throughout society apart from, and even frequently in apparent opposition to, the state as such. In this regard it may be helpful to think of various privately led campaigns of moralization/normalization, often associated with health, education, philanthropy, or religion, that flourish in civil society. These campaigns participate in the art of government as they promote specific techniques of the self, notwithstanding their character as private initiatives. For example, by encouraging practices of saving or the acquisition of insurance or particular parenting roles or the habits of cleanliness, sobriety, fidelity, self-improvement, responsibility, and so on, such campaigns exert a biopower, essential to government, that insures an individual's freedom is exercised in a manner commensurate with the state's interests.[9]

The proliferation of various technologies of the self in civil society as a form of "private" government does not exhaust the extent to which liberal civil society is a space of government through freedom. Alongside the proliferation of techniques of the self, the expansion of liberalism's civil society was also accompanied by the decentralization of disciplinary power. The disciplinary power that under the absolutist regime was monopolized by

---

9. I owe these examples to Burchell, "Liberal Government and Techniques of the Self," 272.

the sovereign, under liberalism is now "outsourced" if you will, dispersed across society, put in "private" hands, particularly by means of the various human sciences. Hence, according to Foucault, it is no mere coincidence that with the dawn of liberalism we begin to see the state licensing what were formally independent fields like medicine, psychiatry, psychology, criminology, pedagogy, and so forth. In these ways, disciplinary techniques proliferate outside the state under the liberal governmentality.

Foucault's account of governmentality redeems Hobbes from being a mere historical curiosity, suggesting that while the absolutist state of Hobbes may differ from the liberal political order in important ways, with regard to government and fear, the difference is not as stark as is frequently supposed. Liberalism differs from Hobbes's absolutism only in the *modality* of governmental power. Liberalism is government *through* freedom, with both disciplinary and biopower dispersed across civil society. Thus, the very features that the architects of the standard account trumpet as erecting a dike against fear and terror thereby clearing a space of liberty are revealed to be quite adept instruments of fear and terror. In other words, Foucault unmasks the complex space of liberalism, revealing that in itself complex space does not preserve or protect; to the contrary, by means of the decentralized disciplines and a variety of technologies of the self, complex space can facilitate our surrender and our immersion in a culture of fear even more effectively than naked sovereign power.

There is yet another lesson to be learned regarding the contemporary culture and politics of fear from Foucault's account of liberal governmentality. "Governmentality" also sheds light on Hobbes's observation that for fear to work, people must be invested in it; they much be induced to believe in its benefits, while the counterposed virtues are marginalized. This is to say, Foucault helps us make sense of our collaboration with the production and perpetuation of a culture of fear. After all, if fear is not an extra-political intrusion but thoroughly political, and if power is not the sole possession of a sovereign but instead is always already dispersed in its various forms (disciplines, technologies of the self, etc.) across the *socius*, then it will not do to argue that the culture of fear is simply imposed from on high by an imperial sovereign upon a repressed and captive population. (No one takes those color-coded alerts that seriously). After all, as the account of governmentality suggests, there is no "on high" where power accumulates, leaving a vacuum "below." Nor, for the same reasons, will it suffice to assert a vast cabal of powerful institutions and persons. While it can hardly be denied that there are indeed powerful institutions and persons with vested interests in the perpetuation of fear, such an assertion is insufficient as an explanation in that it fails to appreciate the lesson of governmentality: fear is not merely *reflected* but is also *produced* and *reproduced* by civil society. This is to say, the security moms are not mere dupes of powerful men, but are themselves invested in fear and so reproduce it in their communities and children and so forth.

In this regard, Foucault once remarked that we have come "to desire the very thing that dominates and exploits us."[10] His account of governmentality exposes the fact that we do not live in fear because we have been beaten down. We are not simply crushed—although some are; the disciplines have not suddenly disappeared, only dispersed, like secret prisons around the globe. Rather, by means of a host of technologies of the self our desires are so shaped that we come to long for the very goods that are bound up in the perpetuation of fear. We gain by fear.

What do we gain? What goods are bound up with fear? Hobbes argued that fear was linked inextricably to the good insofar as survival was the condition of possibility for the pursuit of any and every good. John Locke held that fear was "the chief, if not only spur to human industry and action."[11] Likewise, Judith Shklar asserts that fear is the source of life's vitality,[12] while Michael Ignatieff believes that fear can nurture a new universal humanism.[13] After 9/11 a host of pundits echoed similar sentiments, proclaiming in essence that peace is dangerous and that fear alone can awaken the noblest that is within us. Nor should we forget the disconcerting insight offered by Arendt, later in her life, in the course of exposing the banality of evil. Fear presents a host of opportunities for careerists, for the ambitious.[14] Lastly, we should not overlook the possibility that fear is desired simply because it provides an adrenaline rush, pulls us out of the undertow of the terminal boredom that weighs life down in the modern technocratic West.

If Foucault's account of governmentality shows how fear can be a political product of liberal political orders and their complex space of civil society, it does not appear to address the current situation where the power of the liberal state is being steadily eroded by the global capitalist market. For a clearer picture of the relation between the nation-state, the assembly of fear, and the capitalist order we turn to Gilles Deleuze.[15]

10. Foucault, "Preface," xiii.
11. Locke, *Human Understanding*, 2.20.6. See also 2.20.10; 2.21.34.
12. Shklar, *Political Thought and Political Thinkers*, 11.
13. Ignatieff, *Warrior's Honor*, 18.
14. Arendt, *Eichmann in Jerusalem*.

15. A more detailed treatment of Deleuze in this regard, with appropriate textual pointers, can be found in Bell, *Liberation Theology after the End of History*, 12–19; 29–32. See also Deleuze and Guattari, *Anti-Oedipus*; Deleuze and Guattari, *Thousand Plateaus*, 424–73; Deleuze, "Postscript on the Societies of Control," 3–7.

Like Hobbes and Foucault, Deleuze holds that life is constituted by motion; specifically by the active power that is desire. Moreover, this desire in a "state of nature," if you will, is not reactive; it is not fearful. Rather, it is anarchic, creative, harmonic. This active, playful power that is desire only becomes reactive, fearful, or in Deleuze's terms, paranoid, as it is acted upon, as it is captured or seduced by reactive and fearful forces, which is precisely what the state-form attempts to do. The state-form assembles desire, forms and shapes it so that it is paranoid and fearful, and in so doing, the state promotes the promise of its own existence: surrender and be safe.

Deleuze's focus, however, broadens beyond the state-form to consider the contemporary political horizon as it is constituted by global capitalism. He positions his account of desire and the state-form within a universal history of capitalism. According to this genealogy, the history of capitalism's advent is the story of the state-form's slow subsumption by or becoming immanent to economy. Hobbes's absolutist state of sovereignty was able to channel all desire through the bottle-neck of the state and its mercantile economy. Yet, as Foucault noted, eventually desire exceeded the ability of the sovereign to control and contain it, and as a result the state-form mutated into the liberal state. What is novel about the liberal state is that its art of government neither requires all desire be funneled through the state (civil society is fine, as per Foucault's governmentality) nor demands that desire be subordinated to the ends of sovereignty. In this sense, liberal government is distinctly economic government; it is government that strives to further not its own ends, what an earlier political tradition called reason of state, but the ends of capitalist economy. The liberal state is immanent to the larger economic field, and its task is primarily that of minimizing intervention and interference in the workings of that field.

Yet, we might ask, have we not crossed a new threshold in recent decades as capitalism has increasingly undermined the governing authority of even the liberal, economic, state? Does not global capitalism mark a crisis of the liberal state? After all, it would appear that capital's ability to eclipse national sovereignty is approaching the point of rendering the liberal state unnecessary, a point where passports can be replaced by credit cards and citizenship replaced by membership in trade alliances and associations. According to Deleuze, we have entered a new era, but the state-form has not been rendered obsolete. Rather, it is undergoing another mutation, a shift toward a much more active or aggressive advocacy of capital. No longer is the state satisfied with merely minimizing intervention in economy; now it actively pursues the extension of economy into every fiber and cell of human life. The state has become a model of realization for capital.

More specifically, and more immediately relevant to the matter of the culture and politics of fear, the state has become a war machine. Whereas it was once the case that states appropriated war machines, today states constitute a war machine. Specifically, they are capitalism's war machine. The capitalist state is the "small state, strong state" that we see evolving all around us in response to the dictates of the global capitalist order—states long on disciplinary power and short on welfare capacity. Furthermore, the object of this machine is no longer, as it once was, war in the traditional sense of the term. Here we might recall the ways the "war on terrorism" was described at its initiation. It is a "ghost war," occurring not at the frontiers of society but, like a fog and in a manner synonymous with governmentality, permeating or blanketing society. And it is waged against a spectral enemy—be it terrorists with dirty bombs, microbes, or super predator youths[16]—by means equally spectral—stealth forces, renditions, disappearances, electronic eavesdropping, invisible break-ins, snooping librarians, truck driver informants, and so forth.

This war machine, moreover, does not simply fight *in* society, but rather it has society, peace, politics, the world order as its object. As Deleuze observes, with this latest permutation of the state-form, Clausewitz's famous formula has been inverted: War is no longer the continuation of politics; politics is now the continuation of war.[17] We are already living in the midst of the Third World War, Deleuze wrote almost thirty years ago. Politics, culture, peace, civil society are the object of this war. Thus we are submerged in a state of permanent war; permanent emergency, a permanent state of exception where the laws and civic-political associations that once offered some degree of liberty are suspended indefinitely and foreclosed.[18]

Moreover, in waging this war against peace and politics, the state-form, in a move reminiscent of Orwell's *1984*, promotes and installs a very special kind of peace: a terrifying peace, the peace of absolute terror, a culture and politics of fear. Security is now conceived as war, as organized insecurity, as distributed and programmed universal catastrophe. War is peace and freedom is preserved only by sacrificing it, and we all have a stake in this as we desire the goods that this fear makes possible.

And what goods are those? According to Deleuze, this state of permanent war, this culture of fear has as its goal the deterritorialization of desire, the separation of the productive force of desire from anything that

16. See Glassner, *Culture of Fear*, and Siegel, *False Alarm*.

17. Foucault makes a similar argument for different purposes in his *"Society Must Be Defended."*

18. Deleuze's analysis helps make sense of the claim that we are now in a "post-political" situation.

would stand between it and the capitalist market and the concomitant rendering available of this desire to this market. Thus, the culture of fear is not in service to the state *per se*, but the market. The threat of terror paves the way for capital and the goods it promises to provide. So, after 9/11 the president instructs us, not to seek out our neighbors and embrace them, but to shop, to seek out commodities and purchase them. Shortly thereafter, the US trade representative to Latin America wielded the threat of terrorism to cajole reluctant nations to fall in line with trade pacts. Likewise, homeland security and terrorism have been invoked to crush domestic labor actions, as well as popular movements against the expansion of the capitalist market. The invasion of Iraq, while falling far short of its lofty rhetoric with regard to the welfare of the Iraqi people, has gone a long way toward privatizing oil resources, abolishing unions, lowering wages, etc.—in short, furthering capital's extension in the region. Likewise, Katrina was used to repeal a host of labor and environmental laws that stood in way of the market, and the rebuilding of New Orleans has occurred in a manner that is decidedly market friendly. The list of examples of how fear and terror are used to promote the capitalist order could go on and on.

With Deleuze, we reach the end of our survey of liberalism and fear. The politics and culture of fear that envelop us is not the intrusion of an extra-political force kept at bay by the liberal political order. To the contrary, liberalism needs fear and so it produces it, and it does so not simply by the imposition of the heavy, disciplinary hand of the state and its apparatuses, but by the velvet touch (one that we even desire!) of the vast array of technologies of the self that constitute the complex space of civil society. Moreover, by means of this liberal governmentality, we come to desire our own domination and participate in a kind of political cannibalism whereby we want the very things that undercut the liberties liberalism purports to secure.

Thus, as we examine the culture of fear, we are looking as if into a mirror and glimpsing the truth of our liberal soul. Liberalism is founded on fear. As Judith Shklar has said so well, liberalism does not offer us a *summum bonum* toward which all should strive; nor does it rest upon a theory of moral pluralism as many are wont to proclaim. Rather, its foundation is much more barren. Liberalism is erected on the sheer negative, the fear of a *summum malum*. As she says, "to be alive is to be afraid."[19] But in this way the contradiction at the empty heart of liberalism is exposed: the promise of liberalism—recall Montesquieu et al.—was freedom from terror and fear; yet this it cannot and it dare not deliver, for without fear, liberalism's

---

19. Shklar, *Political Thought and Political Thinkers*, 11.

raison d'etre, even the very barren surface into which it sinks its sickly roots, erodes as if into nothing. Therefore, under liberalism, there can be no end to fear. Even death is not its terminus, but only its culmination and even its return, for death does not relieve our fears. Rather, as Hobbes insightfully discerned, face to face with death we are reminded that whatever meager goods we seek out in the midst of this vale of tears—career, family, friends, etc.—are contingent upon actually surviving to pursue them.

For an end to fear, for a politics that finally is not cannibalistic of either liberty or life and so holds forth the hope of nurturing human communion/community (the root meaning of politics), for a more generous politics beyond the (anti-)politics of color-coded insecurity and perpetual war with our neighbors, both foreign and domestic, we will have to look elsewhere. To this alternative we now turn.

II. The Gospel of Life

Even as we wander in liberalism's fields of fear, trying desperately to tend to the goods that constitute our lives—friends, families, neighbors, vocations—a word of hope, as if from on high, catches our ear: "Do not be afraid." The Christian gospel is frequently introduced in this way by both angelic messengers and Jesus. Juxtaposed to liberalism as a politics that begins by heightening fear, this gospel prelude is striking. Here we have the advent of a different and truer politics, a politics of life, and it begins with the dispersion of fear. To make sense of this gospel and its politics, we turn first to Alain Badiou's work on St. Paul.

Being For Death and Being For Life: Badiou on St. Paul

Badiou's work is about the recovery of a philosophical politics in the midst of an age disfigured by the monumental destruction of all politics. Against the ravages of the present age, Badiou posits a philosophy of the truth-event, which is nothing less than the unexpected irruption of a new way of being in the midst of the status quo characterized by what he calls imperialism, democratic totalitarianism, absolute injustice and more recently, "the disjunctive synthesis of two nihilisms," by which he means the politics of fear in both of its prominent contemporary manifestations—fascist terrorism and the western war on terrorism.[20] What attracts Badiou to St. Paul is that in Paul Badiou discerns a fellow traveler, who, under the shadow of

---

20. See Badiou, *Ethics*, lv, and Badiou, *Infinite Thought*, 118.

the Roman Empire, witnessed a similar destruction of all politics.[21] In the midst of these destructions both ancient and contemporary, Paul stands as the militant herald of a truth-event that ruptures being-for-death with the possibility of pure affirmation, being-for-life.

According to Badiou, Paul sets forth the truth-event that is Christ in terms of two subjective paths, that of the flesh and the spirit, of death and life. Actually, Christ does not present two paths. Rather, as a truth-event, Christ is a break or rupture with the surrounding site or situation, an interruption, an absolute beginning, an act of creation *ex nihilo*. Accordingly, Christ makes possible a path other than that of the surrounding situation. In other words, where there was only fear and being-for-death, with the truth-event of Christ there issues forth the possibility of life and being-for-life.

What distinguishes these two paths, these two ways of being in the world? Being-for-life is characterized by love, which is a matter of pure affirmation and universal filiation. As universal filiation it is about the extension of the self in the direction of others. As pure affirmation, it is the denial of negation. It is indifferent to death. In contrast, being-for-death is life that is centered on death, that revolves around death, that leads inextricably toward death as its orienting point, even as that life-headed-toward-death may be consumed with resisting that destiny and slowing that descent.[22] (In this regard, think of the practice of contemporary medicine, which draws its orientation not from health, but from illness and death.) Being-for-death is a labor of negation, whether it is confronting others or facing death. As such, it is either pure negation—as in nihilism—or the negation of negation—as in a dialectical vision that ineluctably tethers affirmation to negation, thereby ensuring that negation is never finally left behind but instead always lingers as the trace that is affirmation's condition of possibility. Theologically, this being-for-death takes shape in a vision of redemption that finds its center in Christ's death and the redemptive necessity of sacrifice and suffering.

If Badiou reads Paul correctly,[23] then the Christian gospel announces an interruption of the culture and politics of fear. It holds out the promise of a life that does not revolve around death and its warding off. However, it is not clear that Badiou does read Paul or the Christian vision of salvation rightly. After all, is it accurate to say that Christianity is decidedly indifferent to death, that salvation does not revolve around the redemptive significance

---

21. Badiou, *Saint Paul*, 7.

22. See, for example, Becker, *Denial of Death*.

23. 1 John 4:18. For more on Badiou's use of Paul and its problems, see chapter 2 of the present work.

of sacrifice and suffering? What, then, are we to make of the central artifact of the faith—the cross of Christ—not to mention the crosses of all those who would follow in fidelity to the truth-event that is Christ?

Perhaps Christianity is not simply a matter of affirmation, but is a vision of the negation of negation? Which returns us to the question: fear abounds, so what? Death is, after all, the enemy. Perhaps Christianity, while abjuring the crass production and manipulation of fear that currently plagues us, nevertheless does not offer a politics that is truly oppositional to the culture and politics of fear so much as it presents an alternative vision, a truer culture and politics of fear? As the Proverb states, the fear of the Lord is the beginning of wisdom (Prov 9:10).

Christ Crucified and Resurrected: The Gift of Life

In First John we are told that perfect love casts out fear[24] and Paul reminds the church at Corinth, in an almost mocking tone, that death has been swallowed up, has lost its sting (1 Cor 15). Here we have the signposts of a politics beyond fear and death, a politics of life, of pure affirmation. As Paul says, "The Son of God, Jesus Christ, whom we proclaimed among you . . . was not 'Yes and No'; but in him it is always 'Yes'" (2 Cor 1:19 NRSV). Here we behold a textual marker for a culture and politics that is finally so shockingly indifferent to death that if it is wrong, its inhabitants are of all people most to be pitied (1 Cor 15: 19) if not dealt with in a harsher manner.

Such a claim, however, runs up against the undeniable presence of the cross, sacrifice, suffering, and death at the center of the Christian narrative of salvation. As Paul says, "we proclaim Christ *crucified*" (1 Cor 1:23 NRSV). Hence, does not the cross stand in the way of any attempt to construe Christianity as pure affirmation? Is it not the paradigmatic instance of negation, and the resurrection a reciprocal act negating the negation? Consider a widely popular rendition of Christ's work of atonement on the cross. Frequently attributed by the more theologically astute to St. Anselm, but with an evident pedigree reaching back to Paul's letter to the Romans, the prevailing account of the cross goes something like this: human sin is

---

24. To be clear, this essay juxtaposes two forms of life: one oriented by fear and death, the other by life. The crux of the argument is this fundamental orientation. Given more space, an account of the place of the passion called "aversion," or what Aquinas calls "the gift of fear" could be developed that would, for example, provide a way of accounting for such well-known texts as "the fear of the LORD is the beginning of wisdom" (Prov 9:10 NRSV; Ps 111:10) and so forth without in any way undermining the force of my argument. In this regard, see Bader-Saye, "Thomas Aquinas and the Culture of Fear," 95–108.

an offense against God's honor and God, as one who must uphold justice, cannot simply forgive sin but must enforce a strict rendering of what is due. Yet sinful humanity cannot fulfill the debt, so the God-man, Christ, steps forward to pay/negate the debt through his substitutionary suffering and death on the cross.

In this commonplace reading of Christ's work, death—the sacrifice that is the loss of life, the suffering that is redemptive—is the unmistakable fulcrum of salvation. Moreover, the unspoken subtext of this account is fear—the fear of eternal damnation that is avoidable only by a death. Furthermore, the resurrection is marginalized, as evidenced by the fact that this tale could be told without any reference to the resurrection at all. At best it is given a secondary or supporting role, becoming a kind of confirmation that the substitutionary death worked, that the sacrificial suffering was redemptive, that the negation was successfully negated.

Hence, the commonplace reading is not a tale of life but of fear and death and as such it does not hold forth the promise of deliverance from the culture and politics that currently afflict us. (Thus, it is unsurprising that many theological voices see in the liberal political order the proper analog to the Gospel.) Yet, the commonplace reading is also a profound distortion of Christ's work, the product of the transposition of the gospel of life into an alien and fundamentally negative key, for Christ's work does not find its center in the death suffered on the cross but in the life of the resurrected. This is to say, Christ's work of atonement is the gift, not of death, but of resurrected life. Being-for-life. Christ's work was not that of negation—submitting to negation, and overcoming negation with an act of negation. Rather, Christ came not because he must die but so that we might live. Christ's work of atonement is a labor of sheer affirmation.

This affirmation upends the commonplace account of Christ's work. To begin with, human offense, sin, does not call forth divine negation.[25] The cross is not an instance of divine negation. As the much abused Anselm noted long ago, it is not possible that human insurrection could thwart divine creative intent[26] and as the more esteemed Augustine forces us to concede, there is finally nothing—which is after all the substance of sin, death, and rebellion—to be negated. Instead, as Anselm insisted and Scripture (including Paul) constantly affirms, the atonement proceeds according

---

25. A full treatment of this claim would necessarily consider the practice and meaning of judgment in the Christian life. For such a treatment by way of an engagement with Gilles Deleuze, see chapter 3 of the present work.

26. For a reading of Anselm against his modern detractors, see Bell, "Forgiveness and the End of Economy," 325–44; Hart, "A Gift Exceeding Every Debt," 333–49; Balthasar, *Glory of the Lord*, 2:211–59.

to the divine intentionality of/for life. In the face of human rebellion, God's honor will not let the breach stand but desires that humanity be restored to the life, to participation in the abundance of the divine life, that from the beginning God intended for humanity. Therefore, the Father sends the Son, who goes willingly to continue the labor of love that is the gift of life. Christ's labor is that of resurrecting life, not suffering death. The heart of Christ's atoning work is resurrection, the taking up of humanity into the life of charity shared by the blessed Trinity (*theosis*, deification), the effecting of ontological union with life.

But, of course, there is no evading the cross. The cross is the site of this truth-event. Yet, recall that the truth-event that is Christ is a break, a rupture, with the surrounding site. Hence, while the cross is the site of the resurrection, it is not its condition of possibility. The resurrection, in Badiou's terms, is a subtraction, not an addition, to the situation it breaks open. There is a disjunction between death and resurrection. The Gospels say as much when they testify that the response to the empty tomb is one of puzzlement and bewilderment. There is no way, beginning from death, being-for-death, that one can make sense of the resurrection. Resurrection is not the proper and expected encore to death in accord with some dialectical, rational protocol. This is the case because the resurrection does not answer death or even defeat death—both moves of dialectical negation that reify what they purport to overcome. Frankly, if the resurrection were simply the negation of death, then Lazarus, a resuscitated corpse, which, incidentally, amazed but did not bewilder, would be the icon of our hope.[27] In contrast, the Resurrected One stands starkly, blindingly alive—life's startling, naked interruption of death.

As the interruption of the site of death, the resurrected Christ does not merely defeat death or tame it or subdue it, all of which presume a relation to death, all of which entail something with which one can be in relation. Such a presumption reifies death and being-toward-death. It grants death a substance, a reality and hence a permanence that it lacks. For this reason, the Scriptures speak of death destroyed (1 Cor 15:26), of death "being no more" (Rev 21:4 NRSV). For this reason, Paul speaks of the resurrected Christ as raised into being (Rom 6:4), with the implication that death and being-toward-death are in fact not being at all; they are nothing. The offer of resurrected life unmasks death and being-toward-death as the absence of power, a void, nothing.[28] Hence, Badiou rightly observes that being-for-life is indifferent to death, because death precisely as nothing is nothing that can

---

27. Lazarus, one should note, will die again, thus proving the point that a dialectical overcoming of death always reifies that which is attempts to escape.

28. See Augustine, *Of True Religion*, §22.

be taken into account. As nothing, death cannot make a difference. Hence, death makes no difference to Christ's fidelity nor to those who would be faithful to the event of Christ and obedience even to the point of death only sounds like foolishness, only presents a stumbling block, to the unredeemed still in thrall to death, being-for-death. To the redeemed, the resurrected, death is no obstacle, no thing, nothing at all and thus no longer concerns us (see Matt 8:22) nor is it to be feared (Matt 10:28).

At this point we can see the cross for what it is, neither the satisfaction of a divine demand for death nor even a divine instrument for negating sin. Rather, the cross stands as the nadir of sin; it is the deepest depth of human rebellion. Granted the cross is a negation, or at least an attempt at such, but it is not a negation that God imposed; rather it the last futile human effort at negation. We refuse the gift of life and attempt to negate it. But alas God refuses to accept our negation. After all, since all that is is only by participation in affirmation, negation cannot be accepted because finally it does not exist. Thus, God actually refuses nothing; conversely there is nothing in our refusal for God to accept. (In fact, as the precepts of medieval theology make clear, God has never been estranged from humanity.[29]) So, Christ is faithful, obedient to the labor of life, even to the point of suffering our absurd attempts at negation. This is the work of atonement: Jesus is the gift of God's redemption, not because he endures divine negation in our stead, but because he embodies the divine refusal to negate humanity in its sin, a refusal that endures even to the point of death on a cross. And this divine refusal is nevertheless pure affirmation as the resurrected one returns to those who crucified him with the offer of life.

Similarly, just as Christ's labor of affirmation reveals death to be nothing and the cross the last futile stand of an eternally foreclosed rebellion, suffering is now seen to be neither redemptive nor necessary. Whereas the commonplace account of Christ's labor tends to privilege suffering, as in what makes Christ uniquely redemptive is that he suffered more than anyone (some responses to *The Passion of the Christ* come to mind), we now see that suffering too is nothing, that what is redemptive in Christ's labor is his fidelity to life, his refusal to depart from this divine mission by repealing the offer of life in the face of suffering. In light of the surpassing glory, the life that is ours in Christ, suffering is unmasked as nothing (Phil 3:8). Hence the supernatural calmness on display in the accounts of so many of the martyrs. In this regard, what is so remarkable about the martyrs is not their deaths, but their unflinching refusal to surrender their witness (the meaning of the Greek term, *martyr*) to life. Our perverse fascination with

---

29. See, for example, Augustine, *Homilies on the Gospel of St. John*, Tractate II §8.

the manner of their deaths notwithstanding, what distinguishes the martyrs is their eternal life, on display with particular contrastive force at the moment of their death.

Furthermore, it is clear that suffering is not necessary. The divine affirmation of life is an act of creation *ex nihilio*. It requires no preliminary or contrastive negation. Consequently, what suffering there is is revealed in the light of Christ to be the contingent effect of sin. Suffering is a contingent, historical consequence of sin and rebellion and not of the liberative and redemptive heart of God. Hence, it is only temporal, temporary, passing, and finally nothing. (In this regard, there is no such thing as radical evil whose effects persist, threatening the peaceful ontology of life.[30]) That one faces suffering and crucifixion points not to the necessity of suffering as the path of redemption but to the stubborn persistence of sin's refusal of affirmation and the brutal resilience of the culture of fear and death in producing both crosses and executioners.

Finally, as is the case with both the cross and suffering, sacrifice is transformed as it is repositioned within the theologic of affirmation or of being-for-life. Typically sacrifice is viewed as pernicious. This is to say, it is usually linked with negation. Sacrifice is understood as reductive, necessarily entailing a loss—a loss of self, a loss of dignity, a loss of identity, a loss of life. Pernicious or reductive sacrifice is always a giving up or a surrender of the lesser to the greater—the present to the future, women to men, men to the state/corporation, all to the greater good (market). Thus, morality under the sign of modernity oscillates between egoism and altruism, between self-preservation and self-sacrifice. And, perhaps unsurprisingly, modern Christian ethics has tended to embrace altruism and "self-sacrifice." In so doing, however, it rightly earns the censure of liberationists and others, for such pernicious sacrifice does not open a path to affirmation and life but only reinforces our capture by the logic of negation, loss, and death. It remains an instantiation of being-for-death.

In contrast, the truth-event of Christ initiates a non-reductive sacrifice that entails neither negation nor loss. Christ's sacrifice is one of pure affirmation. It should be clear by now that what is offered in Christ is not a death, but life. The substitutionary sacrifice Christ offered at the site of the cross is the fidelity and praise (the return of love) of the Son to the Father. Christian sacrifice is a *living* sacrifice (Rom 21:1). In this way, the Christ-event ruptures the smooth space produced by our contemporary culture and politics of fear and death, with the result that sacrifice becomes gain (Luke 9:24) and we can give ourselves in love as a gift of life to our neighbors

---

30. See Milbank, *Being Reconciled*; Badiou, *Ethics*.

without end and without loss (Matt 22:39; Mark 12:31). In Christ's sacrifice nothing is lost and everything is gained. Through his sacrifice sin, which as *privatio* is precisely nothing, is lost. Through being joined to his sacrifice, the "nothing" that we lose is the terrified, fearful self that only has the eyes to see and ears to hear the sacrifice of love as loss.

The "nothing" that is overcome is the contemporary fantasy of absolute security, the pursuit of which only entrenches us more deeply in insecurity, terror and fear and leads us (willingly!) to surrender those very goods (life, love, liberty) such security purportedly promises to preserve and protect. The "nothing" that is lost is the illusion that the politics of fear can ever deliver us from terror, conflict, and death. The "nothing" that is dispelled is the "fog of war" that deceives us into thinking that the war against terror can be anything other than a war without end—a permanent emergency, perpetual war, that offers neither peace nor hope but only grief intensified as loss is compounded by loss.

What is gained in Christ's sacrifice is abundant life, the possibility of living life as pure affirmation, as ceaseless non-reductive giving (and receiving) the gift of life. In other words, Christ's sacrifice creates the possibility of facing others without armed suspicion as well as non-reductively sacrificing oneself to and for others that life might be extended. Put concretely and too concisely, Christ's sacrifice clears a space for a politics of life, a politics of relentless affirmation, of ceaseless giving even in this midst of terror. Christ's sacrifice creates the possibility of a politics that fearlessly pursues justice not as an act of counter-terror, torture, and death but as a work of mercy whose end is the extension of communion.[31]

We have now come full circle. Christ is pure affirmation, the resurrection of life. And this gift of life is the love that casts out fear enabling us to live in peace with and service to our near and distant neighbor. Because finally no negation, loss or even death stands—they are all revealed to be nothing—in Christ we are freed from the culture of fear and politics of terror and death it underwrites and so can give our life to and for others without fear of loss, in expectation only of the gain that is filiation and communion.

The Politics of Resurrection: Augustine and the Two Cities

We might say that the Christ-event interrupts the culture and politics of fear with the advent of a politics of life, a politics of resurrection. But surely this is too glib. Merely asserting that Christian sacrifice constitutes a politics does not make it so. In fact, far from constituting a novel political intrusion, the

---

31. See Bell, "Justice and Liberation," 182–95.

refusal of negation and concomitant indifference to death that characterizes being-for-life can be and have been re-inscribed within the dominant political terrain of liberalism. Such a refusal to draw one's orientation from the fear of death is frequently dismissed in both political and theological circles as extra-political. As Shklar writes, "Self-sacrifice may stir our admiration, but it is not, by definition, a political duty, but an act . . . that falls outside the realm of politics."[32] Such a charge is of a piece with the claim, advanced by both its critics and adherents, that the gospel of life is not political but otherworldly or, to echo Badiou, about a subjective attitude. In other words, the Christian refusal of negation is extra-political because, it is claimed, the practice of such a refusal cannot sustain the life of a community, which is what politics in the last analysis is about. Indeed, such a being-for-life and its refusal of negation regularly are charged with expressing a certain contempt for physical experience, for earthly goods, and so for the things that make political life both possible and worthwhile.

Such charges against Christianity are not novel and, so for a defense of the politics of resurrection that engages these criticisms, I turn to Augustine. Long ago, he contended with similar complaints and in responding to them offered a treatment of the nature of political association and a consideration of the use of earthly goods that both exposes the failures of the politics of fear and exonerates the politics of the resurrection as holding forth the possibility of a politics that is not doomed to perpetual war but is truly a form of *living* together, as well as offering an account of earthly goods and their use that is immune to the politics of fear.

Prompted by pagans who charged Christianity with responsibility for the imminent demise of the Roman Empire, in the *City of God* Augustine offers an extended reflection on the nature of political association.[33] The argument begins with a deconstruction of Roman politics. Even according to its own philosophers' definition, Augustine argues, Rome was not a commonwealth, an authentic political community.[34] It did not achieve that to which it aspired—a common weal, a community united in a shared love.[35] Instead, Rome was a kind of republic, founded upon a lust for glory.[36] It is worth noting that Augustine reads this lust for glory as response to the fear of death.[37] As Thomas Smith says, interpreting Augustine on this point:

32. Shklar, *Political Thought and Political Thinkers*, 14.

33. Particularly helpful in reading Augustine in this regard is Williams, "Politics and the Soul," 55–72.

34. Augustine, *City of God*, 2.21; 19.21.

35. Ibid., 19.23.

36. Ibid., 19.24; 5.12.

37. Ibid., 5.14.

"Rome loved glory because of its desire to pursue a quasi-divine immortality in tangible form. Thus the Roman desire to build something glorious that will last stems from a longing for a shining divine life and a horror at death."[38] This lust for glory, born of a fear of death, actually served Rome well for a time, restraining its other vices.[39] Yet, it was not without its difficulties, for Augustine notes that the lust for glory did not in fact unite the people. Rather, it was the accomplishment of the few.[40] After all, such is the nature of glory that, unlike true goodness, it is diminished as it is shared and so prompts other vices such as murder and tyranny to thwart its dissipation.[41] Tyranny is precisely what this lust for glory led to as the people were simultaneously impoverished and held in check by fear and as the lust for glory nurtured and eventually gave way to a lust for domination exercised through war and conquest.[42]

Augustine's critique of Rome suggests that a politics built on the negative foundation of the fear of death cannot succeed in ordering human community as a way of *living* together. To the contrary, Augustine deftly reveals such a politics to be in fact an anti-politics, not a way of life but a field of battle perpetually submerged in terror and leading to death.

So where does Augustine lead us? If, as many suggest, Augustine has no positive political project, then he does not lead us very far. If, as others suggest, Augustine's political vision was but an immature or nascent liberalism, then he leads us to despair insofar as he succeeds only in prophesying the coming of the nihilistic vortex of fear and terror that is now upon us. If, on the other hand, such readings simply miss Augustine's positive political project, perhaps because they are themselves too closely wedded to modern liberalism, then perhaps a postmodern era provides an opportunity to discern and appreciate the contours of a positive political project in Augustine that were previously obscured.

This is indeed the case, for from beginning to end, *The City of God* is an argument on behalf of a true politics, a politics that is founded on a shared love that nurtures and sustains human sociality not as the agonistic struggle of war and death but as the joyous conviviality of life, a politics of resurrection. Augustine's vision is neither apolitical nor nihilistic; rather, it proclaims the politics of life and asserts that this politics is already in our midst everywhere the communion of saints is gathered. The church is constituted

---

38. Smith, "Glory and Tragedy of Politics," 193–94.
39. Augustine, *City of God*, 5.12.
40. Ibid.
41. Ibid., 15.5.
42. Ibid., 5.12.

as a counter-politics to the politics of Rome, and to all earthly cities that would rule by dominion, the lust for glory, and the fear of death. Everywhere the community of saints—the city of God on pilgrimage through this world—makes its sacrifices, whereby it is joined to Christ, taken up into the shared love that constitutes the life of the blessed Trinity, and set free to be about the work of mercy/affirmation in the world,[43] there is a truth-event and there the gospel of life interrupts the politics of fear and death.

In more concrete and contemporary terms, everywhere saints, having joined Christ's sacrifice, go forth not to shop in fear but to live and love and serve their neighbors without fear (in Karl Barth's memorable words from another menacing era, "as if nothing had happened"), there the politics of resurrection is revealed. Where Christians refuse to fear those who can (only) kill the body and relentlessly reach out to and serve others, where they speak and act against torture, against injustice and oppression, against the tyranny of terror and the war against terror, there we catch a glimpse of the politics of life.

What may make this politics both in its contemporary manifestations as well as in Augustine so difficult for many to discern is that this politics does not conform to modern parameters regarding the character of politics. As Augustine suggests, the politics of the resurrection is not Weberian; it is not a matter of fixed boundaries and armed borders. Rather, this politics, as a true politics, by which I mean an ordering of human sociality that holds forth the possibility of nurturing life and not merely delaying death, is oriented not by the fear of death but by the extension of charity. What centers this politics is not a fear but a love for God and neighbor. Thus, the very thing that establishes the Christian community as a politics—namely, love—ironically conceals the politics of the resurrection. The centrality of love to politics obscures the character of the church as a politics precisely to the extent that the communion of saints, while it has a center, Christ, does not have a fixed geographical location or armed boundaries. As Augustine says, the earthly and heavenly cities are entangled in this world;[44] the citizens of the heavenly city are properly found in the company of the citizens of the earthly cities.[45] Thus, in the contemporary situation, while there are overtly Christian efforts to push back the politics of fear and terror (think of Christian Peacemaker Teams, School of the Americas Watch, Witness for Peace, Catholic Worker houses, etc.) Christians are just as likely to be found alongside persons and a part of efforts that are not explicitly Christian. And

43. Ibid., 10.6.
44. Ibid., 1.35.
45. Ibid., 19.17; 19.26.

this is not simply because Christians have yet to figure out a way to separate and establish their own nation-state and NGOs. To the contrary, that the heavenly city is commingled with the earthly cities and that citizens of heaven work alongside citizens of this world is, as Badiou reminded us, but a reflection of the heavenly city's desire for universal filiation—the extension of human communion "to the ends of the earth."

Of course, such a claim constitutes only a partial answer to the prior objections. One might still protest that the politics of Augustine's city of God demands a turning away from all earthly goods. Is it not the case that this eschewal of the politics of fear is in fact predicated upon a renunciation of those goods that are necessary for communal life? After all, it is Augustine who said that while all desire to live without fear, "the good seek it by diverting their love from things which cannot be had without the risk of losing them,"[46] who taught that the eternal law bids us turn our love away from temporal things and instead focus on eternal things,[47] and who practiced what he preached by chastising himself for grieving the loss of a friend and henceforth declared that we should not be sorrowful at anyone's death.[48] Is it not more accurate to say that this communion of saints is not a genuine politics—a way of living together—after all, but only the byproduct of a solipsistic asceticism that escapes fear by proleptically relinquishing all earthly goods, including those things Augustine lists, such as bodily health, liberty, human relations, citizenship and so forth? In other words, it evades fear by in essence submitting to death ahead of time, as Paul says, "I die every day!" (1 Cor 15:31 NRSV).

Augustine recognized that this politics could appear problematic, for at one point he pleads, "Let no one think [this] inhuman."[49] Yet, he persists in this teaching. Why? Because it alone offered the promise of a politics that delivers us from the agony of the civil war that was unleashed by sin and continues to reap its bloody harvest as fearful humanity squares off against itself, brandishing the threat of terror and dominion. It alone ordered human relations in a manner that could resurrect politics, that could posit once again the possibility of humanity genuinely living together. In other words, this difficult teaching, far from portending the end of communion, actually guides us toward true communion. By way of explanation of this claim, I will mention two dimensions of Augustine's instruction regarding our posture toward temporal things.

---

46. Augustine, *On Free Will*, §10.
47. Ibid., §32.
48. See Augustine, *Confessions*, 4.4; Augustine, *Of True Religion*, §91.
49. Augustine, *Of True Religion*, §88.

First, behind this instruction lies the concern that we not be so caught up in temporal realities, in creatures and the creation, that we are distracted from the Creator. Thus, in a homily on 1 John, immediately after stating that we are not to love the world nor the things that are in the world, Augustine responds to the (not so) hypothetical question, "Why should I not love what God has made?" by saying, "God does not forbid you to love them, but he will not have you seek your bliss in them: the end of your esteem for them should be the love of their Maker."[50] He follows this up with another example that draws the distinction between use and enjoyment. We are to *use* the things of this world, but not *enjoy* them. In a post-Kantian world, we can hardly hear this as anything other a than call for the crass instrumentalization and manipulation of others. Yet, that is not at all what Augustine had in mind. As he clarified this distinction, by "enjoy" he means to find one's rest in something.[51] This, of course, calls to mind his well-known statement in the *Confessions* that our hearts are restless until they rest in God. So, his instruction not to love the things of this world is tantamount to saying that we should not burden the things of this world with expectations that they cannot meet. Nothing in the created order, even merely human communities, can set our restless hearts at ease.

Second, Augustine's concern is that we love truly. With regard to temporal goods, this means that we cannot love them as such. It may be helpful to note that "temporal" does not mean simply "material". Rather, it means temporary, contingent, accidental. Hence, the problem with loving temporal goods is that such love is temporal, contingent, subject to change and loss. And such a temporary love is not really love at all, or rather it is a distorted love. True love is not temporary and changing but steadfast, eternal. It is not contingent upon such accidents as geographical or biological proximity. As an example of the problematic character of temporal love, Augustine writes of someone "loving" a singer on account of some perceived advantage attendant upon such love—be it praise or glory or pleasure. When the circumstance changes and the advantage disappears, the love too disappears. Such is not the love of Christians.[52] Augustine puts it this way: "It is more inhuman to love a man because he is your son and not because he is a man, that is, not to love that in him which belongs to God, but to love that which belongs to yourself."[53] In other words, Augustine is concerned that we do not love things because we grasp, capture or possess them. (He is well aware

---

50. Augustine, "Second Homily: 1 John 2:12–17," 275. (Translation slightly altered)
51. See Augustine, *On Christian Doctrine*, 1.4.
52. See Augustine, *Of True Religion*, §89.
53. Ibid., §88.

that those things we attempt to possess have the uncanny ability to turn the tables and possess or capture us.) Rather, those things that we love, we should love as gifts received from the Creator.[54] Here there is overlap with the preceding point: we rightly love things only when we love God in them, or, when we love them in God.[55] In this way, our love of temporal things is not temporary, or perhaps more accurately, what we love in things is not what is temporary or contingent, but that which is eternal. Thus, Augustine writes of loving our enemies: "Let your desire for him be that together with you he may have eternal life: let your desire for him be that he may be your brother ... You love in him, not what he is [i.e., temporally, an enemy], but what you would have him be [i.e., eternally, a brother]."[56]

Here again, as with the preceding point, Augustine reveals the politics of the resurrection not to be antithetical to human community but rather foundational to genuine human community. In not loving *temporal* things, the point is not to effect dispassionate detachment but rather to love things truly, eternally, without regard for or limitation by accident or advantage. In such a love alone is there hope for a communion that can withstand the vicissitudes of temporal existence that tempt us to civil war.

The preceding paves the way for appreciating Augustine's comments on not grieving the dead. While we might quibble with a rigor that fails to recognize the appropriateness of grief to this time between the times when we await the fullness of the resurrection in which we already participate,[57] there is a salutary point in Augustine's claim. To put it bluntly, one does not grieve because finally anyone who is loved truly is not lost in death. As Augustine says, "He is not made sorrowful by the death of anyone, for he who loves God ... knows that nothing can perish for him unless it perish also in the sight of God."[58] The unspoken premise of this startling claim is the resurrection. We need not fear death, not because we have already surrendered to it, but because it has no sting. After all, the Resurrected One has revealed it to be no loss, nothing. Accordingly, it cannot rupture human community. This is the lesson Augustine wants us to learn from the discussion of his friend's death in the *Confessions*, not that we should disavow human bonds. Thus he writes that friends are bound together when they love God, or as Gerald Schlabach says, "mutual clinging to God joins

---

54. For more on grasping and receiving in Augustine, see Schlabach, "Love Is the Hand of the Soul," 59–91.

55. See Augustine, *Confessions*, 4.12.

56. Augustine, "Eighth Homily: 1 John 4:12–16," 323–24.

57. In this regard, it is interesting that whereas Augustine permits no eschatological leeway with regard to grieving, he is permissive with regard to coercion.

58. Augustine, *Of True Religion*, §91. See also Augustine, *Confessions*, 4.9.

believers together in mutual clinging to one another."⁵⁹ In other words, the resurrection makes possible a way of life, a communion, a politics that cannot be rent by death.

Augustine's apparent otherworldliness that would seem to undervalue or neglect the earthly goods necessary to sustain human community turns out to disclose that the politics of the city of God is not only without fixed geographical boundaries but is without temporal boundaries as well. It is indeed the politics of resurrection, of heaven, a politics that extends the communion of life beyond the grave. So Hobbes and liberalism are wrong and the veil of terror that has descended upon us in these latter days is rent. The goods worth pursuing in this life are not threatened by death; they are not capable of finally being lost at the hands of those things and persons we are incessantly instructed and formed (recall Foucault's account of governmentality) to fear.

Thus, what appears as an otherworldliness that severs the nerve of any positive politics in Augustine and so eviscerates the city of God as a fully political presence and possibility actually sets us free. Whereas the politics of fear inevitably curtails our liberty; the politics of resurrection extends freedom. Moreover, it sets us free not in a postmodern and post-political sense of license from responsibility for renewing and extending community, but in the sense that we are freed for politics. We are freed from the fear that would inhibit our living and loving and serving and giving (and receiving), precisely those things that constitute the heart of a true politics. Secure in the hope of the resurrection, we are set free to live and love and serve others, confident in the knowledge that although we and those we love and serve may die, we will not perish. Death has lost its sting; it cannot break the bonds of communion.

～

Gripped by fear of those threatening to overrun their fortified borders and extinguish Rome's dominion, pagans charged Christianity with undercutting the politics of fear and dominion. Augustine's defense of Christianity amounted to a concession that the pagans were right. The city of God establishes another politics, one not oriented by the fear of death and sustained by violent dominion. Instead, the city of God is animated by a politics of resurrection, a politics of love that exceeds the boundaries of both time and space in its effort to share the *summum bonum*, the extension of universal filiation, the communion of all in love.

---

59. Schlabach, "Love Is the Hand of the Soul," 84.

Writing a community at the very heart of the anti-politics that dominated his age, a community that no doubt felt the pressures of the surrounding culture and politics of fear and death, Paul assures them that nothing is able to separate them from the love of God that is theirs in Christ (Rom 8:39)—neither imperial rulers nor terrorist powers, neither vague threats in the present nor speculative threats of things to come, neither microbes nor mad cows, neither hurricanes nor hate. In Christ, sharing in his resurrection, they have received the gift of life.

And, of course, this is no gift of sentimental solitude (more accurately, "resignation") nor an otherworldly consolation. This is the love that has always moved saints and martyrs—like the Christian Peacemaker Teams—to risk all (in the fear of finally losing nothing) for the sake of breaking down the dividing walls of hostility and in the midst of terrified and fearful individuals, creating communion, community.

This gift of love, this gift of life, this resurrected life, is our political hope. In the midst of a world that purports to have attained its end in political liberalism,[60] which is a world of war without end, a world where we discover no end either to fear or death, into this world Christ enters, a truth-event that ruptures the culture of fear and the politics of death with the gospel of life. And where the gospel of life inflames saints to make true sacrifices, which are works of mercy that relieve distress and spread the joy of communion, there we are set free from fear and death and being-for-life is made possible. There, in the midst of the smoldering rubble of a terrified and terrifying post-political age, politics—the possibility of genuine human community—is being born again.[61]

---

60. See the well-known thesis of Fukuyama, "The End of History?" and *The End of History and the Last Man*.

61. I am grateful to Jeffrey Robbins and Peyman Vahabzadeh for their helpful comments on a draft of this essay.

CHAPTER 2

The Politics of Indifference and the Overcoming of Capital

Exceeding the threadbare debates of an earlier age, in recent years cultural theory has raided religion and so produced a host of new social and political paradigms. While many religionists might take heart in their new-found relevance, some of these raiders have been driven by less than charitable motives. Thus, in a wonderfully honest moment, Slavoj Žižek remarks that one of the most deplorable aspects of the postmodern era is the return of the religious, and he considers how a fighting materialist is to counter this massive onslaught of obscurantism. He suggests that instead of adopting a defensive stance that ferociously attacks this trend, one should follow Alain Badiou in his path-breaking book on Saint Paul and endorse the Christian legacy, for it is "much too precious to be left to the fundamentalist freaks."[1] Žižek's raiding is clearly hostile, an indirect attack that hopes to route the enemy by means of cooptation. While it says much about Žižek's own work, his confession of intent is less than helpful, if not downright misleading, when it comes to assessing Badiou's engagement with Saint Paul. For Badiou is forthright in acknowledging that his interest in Paul is not a reactionary one, born of the moment—even a deplorable postmodern moment populated by fundamentalist freaks—but rather is enduring.[2] For this reason, Badiou's resurrection of Saint Paul is among the more compelling of postmodern engagements with the Apostle to the Gentiles.

How has Saint Paul captured Badiou's imagination? Whereas it has long been held in the academic religious disciplines that Paul, caught up in eschatological expectations of another age, had little to offer movements of

---

1. Žižek, *Fragile Absolute*, 1–2.
2. Badiou, *Saint Paul*, 1. In this regard, he can be situated in a long line of philosophical interest in Paul.

social and political change in this age, Badiou deftly argues that Saint Paul presents the possibility of a universal politics of truth.

He advances this claim beginning with the startling proposition that Paul is our contemporary.[3] Paul is our contemporary by virtue of a "philosophical proximity" identified as the possibility of a universal teaching.[4] This is to say, Paul offers the possibility of a true universalism for those who currently struggle under the regime of an empty or false universalism named capitalism.

According to Badiou, capitalism is an abstract universality that extends itself by configuring the world as a market. The world-market, in turn, is an abstract universality insofar as it operates according to the count, that is, by means of monetary homogenization. All of this is to say that capitalism is universal precisely in its ability, effected by means of monetary homogenization, to set everything free, to foster the free circulation of everything by means of the count. Yet, Badiou asserts, this a false or empty universalism. Why? Because while the count enables everything to circulate freely, only that which permits itself to be counted may circulate freely. Thus Badiou exposes a paradox that lies at the heart of capitalist universalism. At the very moment when the capitalist market's extension is veritably unlimited, laws and regulations prohibiting the circulation of persons are everywhere being multiplied. He captures the paradox so: "Free circulation of that which lets itself be counted, yes . . . Free circulation of that uncountable infinity constituted by a singular human life, never!"[5] This leads to his rather enigmatic conclusion, "capitalist monetary abstraction is certainly a singularity, but a singularity that has no consideration for any singularity whatsoever: singularity as indifferent to the persistent infinity of existence as it is to the evental becoming of truths."[6]

Enter Saint Paul; although he does not arrive on a scene devoid of efforts to resist capital. On the contrary, the contemporary situation is awash with a host of ethics—a kaleidoscope of communitarianisms, identitarian and minoritarian logics as well as ethics of difference/the Other, of human rights and so forth—convinced that their particularity will be able

---

3. Ibid., 4–15.
4. Ibid., 5.
5. Ibid., 10.
6. Ibid., 10. Original italicized. He elaborates on this, saying, "[E]very truth procedure breaks with the axiomatic principle that governs the situation and organizes its repetitive series. A truth procedure interrupts repetition and can therefore not be supported by the abstract permanence proper to the unity of the count. A truth is always, according to the dominant law of the count, subtracted from the count. Consequently, no truth can be sustained thorough capital's homogeneous expansion" (*Saint Paul*, 11).

The Politics of Indifference and the Overcoming of Capital 31

successfully to elude capitalism's universalizing gaze. The problem, Badiou asserts, is that in the final analysis these ethics perfectly intertwine with capital. There is nothing more captive, more amenable to capitalist homogenization than the proliferation of new communities, new subjective and territorial identities. Indeed, capital demands such endless permutations; they stimulate its universalizing processes even as they provide the fodder for new product lines.[7] Likewise, the ethics of difference and so forth unwittingly capitulate to capital as they finally accept necessity (which under the sign of modernity is but another name for economics, specifically capitalist economics) as the objective basis for all judgments of value, thereby foreclosing the positive prescription of possibilities, the emergence of hitherto unknown emancipatory paths and projects.[8]

Onto this political-ethical scene, characterized by Badiou as nihilistic for its resignation to capital,[9] strides Saint Paul. The absolute sovereignty of capital's empty universality has as its only genuine opponent another universal project.[10] And this is what Paul proclaims, another universalism, which Badiou explicates in terms of an ethic of truths.

∼

This lengthy introduction to Badiou's treatment of Paul is necessary to situate properly the critique that follows, for surely the immediate temptation confronting a professional obscurantist (read: theologian) is that of the purely defensive reflex. Upon reading a pagan appropriation of Paul, the religious instinct may issue in what is arguably the easiest and most superficial if not pointless critique of Badiou, namely, that which in the name of preserving and protecting "the authentic Paul," challenges his

7. Ibid., 10–11.
8. Badiou, *Ethics*, 30–32. The details of his argument can be summarized as follows. With regard to human rights, he argues that such ethics are grounded in consensus, which curtails positive action, and are oriented toward death, which inhibits action indifferent to death, thereby compelling one to attend to necessity, which is capitalist economy. With regard to the ethics of difference and "concern for the other," his objection is first that the concern is thinner than its proponents perceive—the Other who is the object of concern is inevitably the Other whose difference is acceptable and good, which means the same (see *Ethics*, 24). In other words, it offers no protection for the vigorously sustained different one. Furthermore, the ethic of difference appeals to law (and frequently human rights) to regulate the situation that threatens the Other. In this way it too is rooted in an ethically stagnant consensus that curtails positive action as well as sharing an orientation toward death that delivers to (capitalist) necessity (see *Ethics*, 10–16).
9. Ibid., 30.
10. Badiou, *Saint Paul*, 7.

exegetical moves, argues he does not get Paul right on historical or textual grounds—basically, taking issue with Badiou's reading in the name of defending an authentic or canonical Paul. In what follows, I will indeed take issue with Badiou's reading and use of Saint Paul, but *not for the sake of defending Paul*. This is due in part to the fact that Badiou is quite forthcoming that his engagement with Paul is "subjective through and through," that he is unconcerned about whether or not his reading measures up to some canonical rule of the genuine or authentic Paul.[11] Instead, I will take issue with his use of Paul for the sake of something that does matter to Badiou, namely, the overcoming of capital.

In other words, in what follows I both affirm and exceed Badiou's hopes. I will affirm his desire to overcome capital and to do so by means of a political recovery of Paul; I will exceed his vision by suggesting that the ways Badiou fails to get Paul right are indicative of deficiencies in his thought with regard to its articulation of the possibilities for generating and sustaining resistance to capitalism. Put differently, my claim is that Badiou retreats from the full radicality of Paul's gospel, mimicking others whom he names in the course of his study (Peter, the Jerusalem conference, possibly the early church in its dealings with Marcion, Pascal[12]) and that as a consequence, his thought does not foreshadow liberty and liberation from capital. Instead, Badiou's vision can offer nothing more than a politics of indifference that is incapable of differentiating itself from capital. The implication of all this is that Paul's gospel, or better yet, the truth-event which gave birth to Paul and to which he was faithful, founds the universalism that alone nurtures the hope of liberation from the depredations of capital. Only a Pauline concrete universalism is capable of generating and sustaining the faith, hope, and love that may live up to the promise of delivering us from the evil that is capital.

My argument proceeds in three steps. First, I offer a brief overview of Badiou's use of Paul to articulate the formal conditions of the truth procedure. Second, I consider the ways in which his faith, hope, and love do not bear the promise of resistance and liberation. Finally, I offer a theological reading of Paul that turns, not around the universal singular, but around the concrete universal, wherein lies the hope of deliverance from capital.

---

11. Ibid., 2. Of course, this raises the question as to why Badiou felt compelled strictly to limit his engagement to those texts of Paul that have been authenticated by contemporary scholarship. This suggests at least the trace of more than a subjective concern.

12. See Ibid., 22, 35, 47.

I. Badiou's Paul

In the face of the dilemma posed by the current situation (marked both by capitalism's false universality and the futile resistances of the particularity of interests associated with various groupings), Badiou turns to Paul because his gospel is, in Badiou's words, "a case of mobilizing a universal singularity both against the prevailing abstractions (legal then, economic now), and against communitarian or particularist protest."[13] Badiou begins his treatment of Paul with the question, "Who is Paul?" Badiou's Paul is not a religious figure. He is neither an apostle nor a saint. Indeed, Badiou admits, he is not at all interested in Paul as a religious figure—no transcendence, nothing sacred, the perfect equality of Paul's work with every other.[14] Badiou cares nothing either for the Good News Paul preaches nor for the cult dedicated to him. Thus, Christianity is deemed a "virulent fable" and in Paul's case this virulence is all the more virulent for his having reduced Christianity to a single statement: Jesus is resurrected.[15]

Thus, Christianity is not regarded by Badiou as a genuine truth-event, and the universalism it portends is not in fact a real universalism.[16] Instead, Paul is acclaimed as the *theoretician* of the *formal conditions* of the truth procedure.[17] What are the formal conditions of a truth-event? Paul illuminates the realities of subtraction, subjectivation, fidelity, and laicized grace.

The Subtraction of a Saint

With regard to subtraction, Badiou's Paul exemplifies the way in which truth is evental, that is, truth is a matter of a singular break or rupture with the opinions and instituted knowledges that constitute the situation out of which truth arises. Actually, talk of truth "arising" out of a situation is not quite right, for Badiou insists that the event of a truth's emergence is a matter of a *subtraction* from a situation. A truth is not built upon or an addition to received opinion and knowledge but is a rupture or delinking with the situation that constitutes a real break—nothing less than an absolute beginning, a creation *ex nihilo*, the emergence of a naked singularity.[18] If

---

13. Ibid., 14.
14. Ibid., 1.
15. Ibid., 81, 5.
16. Ibid., 107–8. See Badiou, *Ethics*, 124, where he notes that Paul and Christianity provide only "parallels" to truth events.
17. Žižek, *Ticklish Subject*, 146.
18. Badiou, *Deleuze*, 91.

the received knowledges and opinions establish the "sense" (meaning) of a given situation, then the truth-event is subtractive in the sense that it is effectively the irruption of "non-sense."[19] The event names the void or the not-known of a situation, a notion that is illumined by the four figures of the subtractive that Badiou offers: the undecidable, the indiscernible, the generic and the unnamable.[20]

Paul's gospel and Paul's life manifest the subtractive nature of the truth-event. First, Paul's gospel—that Jesus was resurrected—is an "unprecedented gesture" that subtracts truth from its situation; it is a pure event, pure beginning.[21] As Badiou describes it, Paul's gospel is a break with all available generalities, be they statist or ideological. It breaks with the statist generalities of Roman legality, for instance defying the boundaries between free and slave, male and female, and so forth; it breaks with the ideological generalities of both Greek philosophy and Jewish moral law (about which I will say more shortly). Badiou even suggests that Paul is the herald extraordinaire of the event because he makes the clean break that even the gospels and early Christianity were reluctant to make. Thus he asserts that with Paul a powerful break occurs that "is still illegible in the teaching of Jesus."[22] Put simply, by reducing Christianity to a single point—Jesus died on the cross and was resurrected (jettisoning even Jesus' life, his teachings and miracles!)—he subtracts truth from every situational support.

Paul's life, likewise, is an exemplification of the evental character of truth; for his life is marked by the break that occurs on the road to Damascus, the encounter with the resurrected Jesus. As a consequence of this event, Saul's life is ruptured; the ties—communal, moral, philosophical—that situated and made sense of his identity are broken and Paul, no longer the Hebrew among Hebrews but the apostle to the Gentiles, emerges.

Indeed, it would not be too much to say that the event literally makes Paul's life as it produces the subject that is Paul. Thus, Paul is for Badiou exemplary of that dimension of the truth process called subjectivation. The subject is not the source of truth; rather the truth-event is the source of the subject. The truth-event convokes a subject. "The subject," writes Badiou, "in no way pre-exists the process. He is absolutely non-existent in the situation 'before' the event. We might say that the process of truth *induces* a subject."[23] In a move that is clearly well suited to Paul's proclamation of

19. Badiou, *Ethics*, 43.
20. Ibid., 69; Badiou, *Manifesto for Philosophy*, 143.
21. Badiou, *Saint Paul*, 48–49.
22. Ibid., 107.
23. Badiou, *Ethics*, 43.

the resurrection, Badiou conceptualizes this subject that is induced by the event as the appearance of the immortal, the appearance of one who has shed the orientation to death that tempts humanity, and that in capitulating to we reveal ourselves to be mere animals (and not particularly charming ones at that[24]) and this characterizes as well the various ethics previously mentioned, which, governed by necessity, curtail genuinely human action in favor of an animal's concern for mere survival and warding off death.

This notion of the immortal leads nicely to Badiou's use of Paul as the exemplification of fidelity. An event interrupts a situation with a heretofore indiscernible truth that in turn convokes a subject, who is no longer being-for-death. The immortal is being-for-truth and this being-for-truth is a matter of continuing the break that was inaugurated by the truth-event. This commitment to the event, which is necessarily public and militant (i.e., declared), is given the name "fidelity." Fidelity, quite simply, is the conviction that sustains the truth process initiated by the event. It is the subjective conviction to "keep going" in the face of all that would oppose or block the eventual becoming of a truth. As such it is correlative to the consistency (defined as fidelity to a fidelity) and courage that persevere, even (or we might say "especially") indifferent to the interests and perpetuation of the animal that tempt humanity to be merely mortal.[25] This fidelity is vividly on display in the life and proclamation of Paul, who in fidelity to the event of the resurrected Jesus, courageously declared that event in defiance of the Jews, the Jewish Christians and Rome, all the while indifferent to that proclamation's consequences for his mortal survival.

This description of fidelity only begins to approach the heart of Badiou's use of Paul in this regard, and so we will return to it momentarily. Before doing so, however, a question imposes itself, a question that Badiou puts this way, "From what source will man draw the strength to be the immortal that he is?"[26] Stated a little differently, what accounts for the irruption of the event and subsequent subjectivation? From the foregoing discussion, it is clear that the nature of the event as a subtraction means that the situation, the established opinions and knowledges, cannot account for or give impetus to the event. Likewise, Badiou's dismissal of the divine as a fable, his militant atheism, precludes any appeal to transcendence. Here it is worthwhile to note that Badiou's rejection of any substantive foundation for the event extends even to the "vitalism" of Gilles Deleuze, which he argues, functions as a kind of "inverted transcendence" just to the extent

24. Ibid., 11–12.
25. Ibid., 46–48.
26. Ibid., 14.

that it attributes the possibility of an event to a power intrinsic to univocal being, such that the novel is but an unfolding of what is always already (virtually) present and available.[27] In place of this vitalism, Badiou articulates a mathematical ontology that rejects any substantive foundation and posits instead a neutral, non-predicated, empty being that is conceptualized as the void.[28] Thus he can assert that truth is not the unfolding of being, but what comes to being.[29]

Yet how then are we to account for this truth-event, this singularity, that comes to being *ex nihilo*? Badiou is clear. There is no accounting for it; it is an act of grace. That as a sheer break or interruption *ex nihilo*, the event as well as the subject to which it gives rise cannot be accounted for in thought is designated "grace," albeit Badiou is quick to point out that this is a wholly secularized or laicized grace.[30] As such this grace is akin to the dice-throw or chance, understood in the Mallarémean sense of a chance that is ontologically discrete and therefore not subject to calculation, probability or prediction.[31]

This brief excursus on grace enables a more thorough appreciation of Badiou's understanding of fidelity. Not only is fidelity a matter of a commitment to the truth-event in the face of possible opposition, but it is a *groundless* persistence. As suggested earlier, it is a continuation of the event and it is so precisely to the extent that, like the event that inaugurates it, fidelity can appeal to nothing to vindicate itself. Recall, that the event itself is precisely an eruption of nothing, the indiscernible and unnamable of a situation. In

---

27. See Badiou, *Deleuze*, 46; Badiou, "Gilles Deleuze, 'The Fold: Leibniz and the Baroque'"; Hallward, *Badiou*, 175. On Deleuze's concept of the "virtual," which Badiou finds terribly problematic, see Badiou, *Deleuze*, 43–53.

28. Badiou, *Ethics*, 73, 127, 129. See Hallward, *Badiou*, 174–77. A note on Badiou's mathematical ontology. He draws from the "transfinite" set theory of the German mathematician George Cantor (1845–1918) as well as that theory's development by Gödel and Cohen. Set theory enables Badiou to think the immanent multiplication of the multiple, the immanent excess of parts of elements, that neither has need of cosmic or chaotic vitalism nor is finally containable within a universal set, the One-All. See Hallward, *Badiou*, 66–71, 103, 89, 323.

29. Badiou, quoted in Hallward, *Badiou*, 114.

30. Badiou, *Saint Paul*, 66; Badiou, *Ethics*, 122–23.

31. According to Badiou, the chance of every event is absolutely distinct, meaning that every chance is ontologically distinct from every other chance and thus incapable of being composed into a series or totality of the count that would render it susceptible to calculations of probability. Every event is the chance occurrence of a chance. This is in contrast with Deleuze, for whom chance is the play of the One-All, the vitality of univocal being, such that chance is expected and hence open to calculations of probability, etc. On the concept of chance, see Badiou, *Deleuze*, 67–77.

other words, fidelity is a pure subjective commitment to keep going in the absence of any proof.

Badiou explicates Paul's fidelity in this regard by contrasting his faith with that of Pascal. Badiou manifests a certain affinity for Pascal, acknowledging his valiant effort to articulate the Christian subject.[32] Yet, finally, Pascal falls short of Pauline radicalism because he cannot bear to sustain fidelity as sheer subjective conviction, instead resorting to proofs from prophecy and philosophical wagers.[33] In contrast, for Paul it is precisely the absence of any knowledge, any proof—be it in the form of prophecy, miracle, or wisdom—that characterizes faith: "For Paul, the event has not come to prove something; it is pure beginning. Christ's resurrection is neither an argument nor an accomplishment. There is no proof of the event; nor is the event a proof. Knowledge comes for Pascal where, for Paul, there is only faith."[34]

Having considered Badiou's use of Paul as the formal exemplification of faith as the subjective conviction that continues the subtractive break that creates the saint, we are now in a position to consider the heart of Paul's appeal for Badiou, namely, how Paul founds universalism.

The Politics of Indifference

The way Paul displays the formal conditions of a truth-event and the subject it evokes is just a precursor to what is really of interest to Badiou, namely, the linking of fidelity to universalism, which he calls Paul's "unprecedented gesture" and for which he "must be given exclusive credit for establishing."[35] Recall that Badiou's project is driven by the quest for a universalism that might oppose capitalism's false universalism. Such a universalism, asserts Badiou, is that of the "universal singular." What is this universalism and how does Paul theorize the universal singular?

In an important caveat to his account of the event, Badiou warns that not every novelty constitutes a genuine truth-event.[36] Although every truth-event is a novelty, not every novelty constitutes a genuine truth-event. Some novelties merely mimic an event and in fact simply absolutize a particular. Think, for example, of the Nazis or perhaps the way 9/11 might be used cynically to secure a nation's hegemony.

32. See Hallward, *Badiou*, 109.
33. Badiou, *Saint Paul*, 49–51.
34. Ibid., 49.
35. Ibid., 49.
36. Badiou, *Ethics*, 72.

What distinguishes a genuine truth-event from its simulacrum is whether the event involves universalism, a genuine break from a particular situation, or merely intensifies, fulfills, or absolutizes a particular situation. The problem with an absolutized particular is that is cannot be for everyone; it is not available to all. On the contrary, it is by definition a closed set, open only to a particular, limited set of persons.

Over against any and every absolutizing of the particular stands Paul, who proclaims a fidelity that is universal precisely in its "subtracting truth from the communitarian grasp, be it that of a people, a city, an empire, a territory, or a social class."[37] For Paul, fidelity to an event "exists only through the termination of communitarian particularisms and the determination of a subject-of-truth who indistinguishes the One and the 'for all.'"[38] The nature of this universalism and how it is an expression of the universal singular can be explicated in a variety of ways. Consider Paul's monotheism, his account of Jesus, and his teaching regarding worldly differences.

In Romans 3, Paul unpacks the import of God's being one.[39] He argues that because God is one, God is not the God only of the Jews but also of Gentiles. Badiou insightfully observes that here monotheism is not engaged philosophically as speculation concerning a supreme being but rather is the expression of a genuinely revolutionary conviction that the sign of the One is the "for all," or "without exception." The One is a trope for the universal and it is universal only insofar as it inscribes no difference in the subjects to which it addresses itself. Hence the maxim of universality is "The One is only insofar as it is for all."[40] This is what Badiou means by egalitarianism, which is one of the central principles of his politics. A process is universal/egalitarian to the extent that any subject (no particular subject, no particular multiple/grouping) may take part in it.

With regard to Paul's engagement with Jesus, we have already indicated how Paul essentially ignores the details of Jesus' life and teaching and instead concentrates his gospel on a single point: Jesus was resurrected. Here we see Paul shedding the particular in order to focus on the singular that is of universal import. Badiou writes of this at length:

> For Paul, the event is certainly not the biography, teachings, recounting of miracles, aphorisms with a double meaning, of a particular individual: to wit, Jesus . . . He simply reminds us, even if only by deliberately neglecting to mention these

---

37. Badiou, *Saint Paul*, 5.
38. Ibid., 5, 108.
39. Verses 27–30. See Badiou, *Saint Paul*, 75–76.
40. Badiou, *Saint Paul*, 76.

extraneous virtuosities, that none of this is enough to found a new era of Truth. What the particular individual named Jesus said and did is only the contingent material seized upon by the event in view of an entirely different destiny. In this sense, Jesus is neither a master nor an example. He is the name for what happens to us universally.[41]

What is of universal significance about Jesus for Paul is his embodiment or enactment of the form of the event. For Paul the Christ event establishes the authority of a new subjective path, open to all, that is the destiny designated "new creature." Hence, writes Badiou, "that is why we need retain of Christ only what ordains this destiny, which is indifferent to the particularities of the living person: Jesus is resurrected; nothing else matters, so that Jesus becomes like an anonymous variable, a 'someone' devoid of predicative traits, entirely absorbed by his resurrection."[42]

What should be carefully noted here, and what may be lost in the shadow of reference to "anonymous variables," is that Badiou is not suggesting that Jesus as someone is lost or sacrificed in the event of the resurrection. To the contrary, it is the eventual character of the resurrection that establishes Jesus as "someone," that is, as a someone devoid of predicates, of communal ties and particular identities that inhibit being for everyone or for all, which means that it is the resurrection that marks the emergence of the generic, singular being that precisely for being generic is not closed off in a particular identity or community, but is universal, accessible to all. This is the force behind Badiou's startling claim that "the whole ethical predication based upon recognition of the other should be purely and simply abandoned. For the real question—and it is an extraordinarily difficult one—is much more that of *recognizing the Same*."[43] The universal is a matter of the collapsing of differences and the recognition of the same. The ethical issue is not preserving difference, but recognizing the Same.

This, argues Badiou, is the core of Paul's universal teaching, expressed so well in passages such as Galatians 3:28 or Romans 10:12. The Christian subject, according to Paul's gospel, is required to be neither Jewish nor Greek, nor is the Christian subject required to be from this or that social group or belong to this or that sex.[44] Christianity's universality (in its Pau-

41. Ibid., 60.

42. Ibid., 63. Note the affinity with the Christology of Paul Tillich in the second volume of his *Systematic Theology*, 107, 98. No doubt this influence can be traced via Bultmann who taught Bornkamm, whose work on Paul served as a foundation for Badiou's work on Paul.

43. Badiou, *Ethics*, 25.

44. Badiou, *Saint Paul*, 14.

line vein) refuses such distinctions. The Other is subsumed by the Same.[45] Paul's proclamation of the truth as universal singularity is the proclamation that terminates the predicative particularity of cultural subjects, that declares the nondifference between Jew and Greek.[46] As Badiou says, "Paul demonstrates in detail how a universal thought, proceeding on the basis of the worldly proliferation of alterities (the Jew, the Greek, women, men, slaves, free men, and so on), *produces* a Sameness and an Equality (there is no longer either Jew, or Greek, and so on). The production of equality and the casting off, in thought, of differences are the material signs of the universal."[47]

The caveat in the last sentence is important, and easy to pass over. The universal is a matter of the casting off, *in thought*, of differences. The annunciation of the universal, according to Badiou, is not rightly understood as a destruction of difference, of the particular. The particular is not simply negated or destroyed. (In this regard, Badiou is avowedly anti-dialectical.) "Paul," he insists, "is not a dialectician. The universal is not the negation of the particular."[48] Indeed, one might even argue that the particular retains a certain value for Badiou as the bearer or carrier of the universal. "What matters, man or woman, Jew or Greek, slave or free man," he writes, "is that differences carry the universal that happens to them like a grace."[49] Differences are the site, the situation, from which the truth-event erupts. This is captured in Badiou's rendition of the Pauline theme of the conflict between the spirit and flesh, the divided self. The subject that is the product of the event is characterized by a "not . . . but" (see Rom 6:4), with the "not" referring to the dissolution of closed particularities that constitute the site or situation of the event and the "but" signifying the task of fidelity assigned to the subject convoked by the event, a task that is distinctly universal or egalitarian insofar as it is a labor for all.[50] In other words, the universal, divided subject is subtracted from the undivided subject of various communitarian, particular identities, so that the differences dividing those particular identities might be suspended in the emergence of the generic same.[51] "This," writes Badiou, "is the reason why Paul, apostle of the nations,

---

45. Ibid., 109.
46. Ibid., 59.
47. Ibid., 109.
48. Ibid., 110.
49. Ibid., 106. Italics omitted. See also Badiou, *Ethics*, 68–69 where he speaks of the void that marks the event as being a "situated void."
50. Ibid., 63–64.
51. Ibid., 55–64.

not only refuses to stigmatize differences and customs, but also undertakes to accommodate them so that the process of their subjective disqualification might pass through them, within them."[52]

What this amounts to is a universalism that is indifferent to differences,[53] that recognizes that differences have no signification, whether positive or negative.[54] Perhaps the most profound example of this is found in Paul's relation to Judaism. About that relationship, in a reflection on Paul's role in the proceedings of the Jerusalem conference (Acts 15), Badiou argues at length:

> In [Paul's] eyes, the event renders prior markings obsolete, and the new universality bears no privileged relation to the Jewish community. Certainly, the components of the event, its location, everything it mobilizes, have this community as their site. Paul himself is entirely of Jewish culture and cites the Old Testament far more frequently than the putative words of the living Christ. But although the event depends on its site *in its being*, it must be independent of it *in its truth effects*. Thus, it is not that communitarian marking (circumcision, rites, the meticulous observance of the Law) is indefensible or erroneous. It is that the postevental imperative of truth renders the latter *indifferent* (which is worse). It has no signification, whether positive or negative.[55]

The event does not abolish differences, and certainly it does not destroy the different. Even as Badiou is critical of ethics of difference and asserts that the true ethical challenge is that of the same, he does not seek the elimination of differences. Indeed, his "Platonism of the multiple"[56] begins with the confession that infinite alterity is quite simply *what there is* and that any experience at all is the infinite deployment of infinite differences.[57]

52. Ibid., 99.
53. See Badiou, *Ethics*, 27.
54. Badiou, *Saint Paul*, 23.
55. Ibid.
56. Badiou, *Manifesto for Philosophy*, 103.
57. Badiou, *Ethics*, 25. Badiou writes of the experience of difference: "Even the apparently reflexive experience of myself is by no means the intuition of a unity but a labyrinth of differentiations ... There are as many differences, say, between a Chinese peasant and a young Norwegian professional as between myself and anybody at all, including myself" (*Ethics*, 25–26). Such a claim is enabled by his mathematical ontology, rooted as it is in set theory, which holds that the number of possible ways of grouping the elements of a set exceeds the number of members of a set. See Badiou, *Deleuze* for a sustained argument on behalf of multiplicity in the face of what Badiou believes is Deleuze's containment of multiplicity under the regime of the One. Note especially

Moreover, rightly interpreted, his advocacy of this universalism that is indifferent to differences should be seen as an effort to protect and preserve alterity—the infinite multitude of singularities, the multiple of multiples—which it does by insisting that differences do not matter and hence are neither a requirement nor a bar to participation in truth processes. This is his egalitarian politics, the politics of indifference.

The Withering of the Jews

Badiou's reading of Paul's universalism, particularly in relation to the Jerusalem conference, provides a natural transition to his treatment of Paul's polemic concerning the Jewish law, which in turn prompts one more consideration of the question of the place of differences in this universalism as Badiou takes up the charge of anti-Semitism leveled against Paul. We begin with the law.

Paul's radical critique of the Jewish law as obsolete and harmful, according to Badiou, is of a piece with the entirely subtractive-subjective character of the truth-event that he proclaims. It is necessary to reject the law (and, incidentally, all law) as being on the side of death because it blocks the subjectivation of grace's universal address as pure conviction or faith.[58] The manner in which it blocks an event's universal address is two-fold.[59] First, the Jewish law is inescapably particular. It is not "for everyone" but only for those who acknowledge and practice its injunctions. Second, the law is unfailingly "statist" in the sense that it is part of the constitution of a situation, which, we recall, is what an event pierces. The law fixes desire; it fixes desire in an automatism of repetition, a cycle of transgression and death.[60]

In contrast with the law, the truth-event is an instance of grace. As such, the truth is translegal. As a matter of subtraction, it occurs without assignable reason as an unmerited, unexpected break, and as a matter of fidelity, it continues that break by refusing any external law. This is to say, it defies the legal logic of what is due in its emergence even as it defies all legal fixity in its aftermath. Hence, for Paul the Christ-event is the abolition of the law and subjective fidelity to the Christ-event entails freedom from the

---

that he declares the central problem of philosophy today to be that of the immanent conceptualization of the multiple (Badiou, *Deleuze*, 4).

58. Badiou, *Saint Paul*, 75.

59. What follows is drawn from Badiou, *Saint Paul*, 75–85.

60. This is the logic of Paul's argument in Romans 5:20–21, regarding the law's increasing trespass and the reign of death. See also Badiou, *Saint Paul*, 78–79.

law.[61] So we find him resisting demands in favor of prohibitions, customs, and observances; refusing moral judgment; and declaring that everything is permitted within the order of particularity.[62] Truth as fidelity to the event is the capacity to exceed its own limit, whose cipher is the commandment of the law; truth is a random course or kind of escapade.[63]

Such a truth, however, cannot stand simply as an overturning of the law. After all, as previously stated, the truth procedure does not simply negate or destroy the particular. Likewise, even as Paul rejects the law, he affirms Christ as the end of the law and love as the fulfilling of the law. To resolve this apparent dilemma, Badiou speaks of a transliteral law. A transliteral law is a law beyond law; it is the law of love.[64] In terms of the truth procedure, if fidelity is the militant's conviction, love is the militant's power to declare the event and the transliteral law of love is the consistency of that declaration and its effect. "Love," writes Badiou, "underwrites the return of a law that, although nonliteral, nonetheless functions as a principle and consistency for the subjective energy initiated by the declaration of faith."[65] This nonliteral law of love, which is the consistency of the truth effect, is a law of life. It is the law of the immortal, the subject-of-truth who has broken with being-for-death, which the old law fixed. It is the law of pure affirmation, enveloping no prohibition; here it recollects the content of the old law of sin and death, "love your neighbor as yourself." The new law is a matter of deploying the power of self-love in the direction of others, addressing it to everyone (it is universal) in a way made possible by subjectivation (conviction).[66]

It is unsurprising that Paul's polemic against the Jewish law has elicited charges of anti-Semitism and Badiou is vigorous in his defense of Paul against such charges. The charges stem from the way in which the Christ-event that Paul proclaims is a break from its surrounding Jewish situation, a break that, given the ground we have already covered, can be summarized in a few broad strokes. Jesus is shorn of every connection to Judaism, save the title "Messiah," which does little work in terms of the truth procedure.[67] Paul's universal gospel bears no privileged relation to the Jewish community. Indeed, the truth is not tied to any particular observances and signs.

61. Badiou, *Saint Paul*, 86, 48.
62. Ibid., 101.
63. Badiou, *Deleuze*, 78, 58.
64. Badiou, *Saint Paul*, 87.
65. Ibid., 89. What follows is drawn from here.
66. Ibid., 90.
67. Ibid., 20.

Likewise, the law is rejected and Jewish discourse is discredited (as is Greek discourse) as one of mastery precluding universality.[68]

Yet, argues Badiou, the charge of anti-Semitism is misplaced; Paul's relation to Jewish particularity is essentially positive.[69] Indeed, Paul attributes to the Jews a certain pride of place insofar as theirs is the first difference to be traversed so that the universal can be constructed. Moreover, even as he proclaims the collapse of customary and communitarian differences, Paul never wavers in his conviction that the Jews will be saved. Therefore, asserts Badiou, the rupture that Paul stresses with regard to Judaism is militant and not ontological.[70] In other words, the break is the break that truth effects for the sake of the recognition of the universal genericity, the sameness that transcends mere particular differences. For an ontological separation that diverts Christianity from its universal teaching by positing exceptions and exclusions, one has to look elsewhere, to the Gospels and especially John. Paul's task is not that of abolishing Jewish particularity but of resubjectivating it. His philo-Judaism is a subtle strategy meant to effect just such a reanimation (not destruction or exclusion) of Judaism according to the novel event of Jesus' resurrection. Said differently, to strip Judaism of its exclusivistic privilege is not to consign Judaism to the furnace (Christian anti-Semites and Nazis will find no consolation here) but to render it amenable to the Same, the universal. And this is in complete accord with the good news of the universalism that is indifferent to difference.

Such is the basic form of Badiou's Paul, the theoretician of the formal conditions of the truth procedure that gives rise to universal singulars. How does it stand up to the challenge of capital? To this we now turn.

---

68. See ibid., 40–44. Judaism's mastery is prophetic; it entails not the mastery of the cosmic whole as Greek wisdom does, but of a literal tradition and the deciphering of signs (ritualism and prophetism). Moreover, it precludes universality because, according to Paul, the Jewish exception—the sign of the "minus one"—requires the other, the totality, that is the Greek for its coherence. It is worth noting that here Badiou comes close to repeating the Marcionite heresy he described and from which he distanced Paul. Specifically, Badiou notes that Marcion distinguished two Gods (*Saint Paul*, 35). Yet in his treatment of Jewish and Christian discourses, he associates Jewish discourse with the Father (a figure of mastery) and Christian discourse with the Son (a figure of weakness, associated for Badiou with the sheer subjective conviction that is fidelity). What renders this suspect is Badiou's claim that Paul was not trinitarian and that he did not think Jesus divine (*Saint Paul*, 73, 102).

69. What follows is drawn from Badiou, *Saint Paul*, 101–3.

70. Ibid., 35.

II. Badiou's Vices: The Betrayal of Faith, Hope, and Love

Over against the empty or false universalism of capital, a universalism that is false and empty precisely because it does not accommodate but instead disciplines by means of the count—monetary homogenization—the aleatory and infinite becoming of multiple being, Badiou posits an ethic of truths that promotes the eventual emergence of universal singulars—universal in that they are open to all and singular in that they are bound by none. But does it liberate? Is Badiou's Paul an immortal declaring life or an angel of death? In what follows, I will suggest that Badiou's thought fails *on its own terms* to articulate a universalism capable of sustaining resistance to capital. I do this by challenging his faith, hope, and love. I begin by questioning his faith.

Bad Fideism

Žižek suggests that Badiou might be positioned as the last of the great French Catholic dogmatists.[71] This is to say, he charges Badiou with being religious. After all, Žižek points out, the paradigmatic example of the truth-event is religion and more specifically, Christianity. It would appear that (Christian) religion is the unnamed dimension of truth, alongside love, art, science, and politics.[72] Answering Žižek, Peter Hallward denies the accuracy of the charge by, among other things, noting that Žižek virtually ignores the way Badiou's thought is grounded in post-Cantorian mathematics and not religious faith.[73] Thus, Hallward declares, Badiou is rigorously atheist and not religious.

---

71. Žižek, *Ticklish Subject*, 142.

72. For the four conditions of truth, see Badiou, *Ethics*, 28 and Badiou, *Manifesto for Philosophy*, 79.

73. Hallward, *Badiou*, 149. Incidentally, I am persuaded that Hallward is absolutely correct. Badiou's thought is generally recognized as religious, along the lines of Žižek's critique, in spite of Badiou's militant claims to atheism. The evidence for this is precisely his use of Paul, et al.; his invocation of faith, hope, love, and grace and so forth. And so, one criticism goes, Badiou cannot account for his faith, hope, and love and therefore he ought to go ahead and own up to his religion, Christianity. This critique is misguided. Badiou's thought is not "religious" in any sense that should appeal to adherents of orthodox Christianity. Rather, it is mathematical and distinctly modern. (Neither of these are surprising claims. Badiou is forthright about both.) What he does with religious terms is "resubjectivate" them in a thoroughly mathematical and modern idiom. Hence, the issue is not that Badiou cannot account for his faith, hope, love, grace, etc. On the contrary, his mathematical ontology goes a long way toward that accounting (if it still is

It is at this juncture that I raise the specter of a bad fideism on Badiou's part, one that threatens to undermine the universality of his thought on its own terms, rendering it a closed set of the particular. Badiou conceptualizes fideism as sheer subjective conviction. And this is precisely what Badiou displays with regard to atheism. To be fair, Badiou also associates fideism with commitment to a truth-event, and no doubt he would argue that his dismissal of the theological dimension of Paul, his pronouncing the resurrection a fable, is simply a matter of fidelity to the truth of science, and more specifically of post-Cantorian mathematics along the line of Žižek's observation that "although the Truth-Event does designate the occurrence of something which, from the horizon of the predominate order of Knowledge, appears impossible . . . today, any location of the Truth-Event at the level of supernatural miracles necessarily entails regression into obscurantism, since the event of Science is irreducible and cannot be undone."[74] Such a response, however, is insufficient, for neither science nor math requires atheism. Indeed, as Hallward notes, Cantor himself, and no doubt many other post-Cantorian mathematicians, understand such a mathematical ontology as amenable to transcendence.[75] While positivist strands of science may incline toward atheism, both science and mathematics can be construed in a more Thomistic vein and so not only be open to but require Paul's theological sensibilities.

There is, however, another way to approach Badiou's fidelity. He openly acknowledges his commitment to modernity—at least its thought, if not its politics, ethics, and economy.[76] (Although his commitment to the last three is the question before us.) This is the ground of his fidelity. He is committed to the knowledge and opinion of modernity, and in this sense his ethic of truths is not itself eventual but thoroughly situated. Accordingly,

---

not entirely satisfactory). Each of his concepts has a mathematical axiom behind them. Rather, the issue with Badiou, which is what I am suggesting in this section, is that once we recognize how these terms have been resubjectivated mathematically and in accord with modern judgments and opinions, they are in fact not worth accounting for.

74. Žižek, *Ticklish Subject*, 142.

75. Hallward, *Badiou*, 92. Note that this is not an argument for the "God of the gaps." Such an argument hinges on determining where God is necessary. Yet God's involvement in creation is not a matter of necessity; it was and remains a free gift. Instead, this is a challenge to the univocal causal nexus that Badiou presumes along with much contemporary science. In other words, I am suggesting that something still recognizable as modern science would be possible with an analogical understanding of being that also recognized the lordship of Christ. Indeed, I take it that this is what undergirds—whether they could verbalize it or not, although no doubt there are some good Thomists who are scientists today, perhaps among the Jesuits—the practice of many faithful scientists.

76. See Badiou, *Manifesto for Philosophy*, 43.

Badiou insists that what is needed today is *not* a veering toward the limit of modernity, but an additional step in the modern.[77] Badiou has sutured the conditions of truth to the modern construal of those conditions, which precludes transcendence. Hence, Badiou's thought reflects not the fidelity that is consistent with a truth-event, but the opinions and judgments of modernity. Here we have perhaps the purest fideism, one unconnected to a truth-event: pure subjective conviction, pure assertion of the will—the will not to believe. There is nothing in the formal conditions of his ethic of truths that necessarily precludes divinity. In the end, it is only modern prejudice that declares "a subject exists only in the strict order of one of the four types of genericity. Every subject is artistic, scientific, political, or amorous . . . for out of these registers, there is only existence, or individuality, but no subject."[78] Indeed, Badiou's thought approaches the level of the dogmatically modern when it simply begins with the supposition that the theological has been finished off once for all, and debars Paul the theologian, treating him as if he did not exist.[79]

Having said this, I have no desire to advocate for an opening of Badiou's thought to divinity, nor for the offspring conceived by divinity joined to his Platonism of the multiple. My point is only that Badiou's thought is not universal on his own terms. His dogmatic atheism appears as but another communitarianism that depends for its viability on the positing of an enemy. And on his own terms, does this not undermine its universality as much as any commitment to blood, soil, or race? More charitably, if Badiou's thought constitutes a universalism, it is not clear how it is any more accommodating "to all" than capital. Just as capital excludes singularities that resist the count, so Badiou's ethic of truths excludes those who resist his axiomatic atheism. Hence, one can ask if Badiou actually succeeds in articulating a universalism that counters capital, a question to which we will return momentarily.

Hopelessness

Hope is a second problematic dimension of Badiou's thought. The question of hope can be posed in terms of the power of the truth-event. What power unleashes the event and maintains it so that the truth process does not degenerate into the evils of terror, betrayal, and disaster?[80] Critics have

77. Badiou, "Finally Objectless Subject," 24.
78. Badiou, *Manifesto for Philosophy*, 108.
79. See ibid., 132–33, where Badiou is critical of philosophers treating sophists in such a dismissive way. See also 122, 134 for his critique of Plato on similar grounds.
80. See Badiou, *Ethics*, 71.

suggested that Badiou appeals to a "problematic ethical power somehow above or beyond that of the truth itself" in order to explain the irruption of a truth-event and its avoiding evil.[81]

Yet, as we have seen, Badiou does answer this charge; his answer comes in the form of a secular or laicized grace. At first glance, this answer may appear a disingenuous move akin to an appeal to magic—precisely the sort of supernaturalism his critics suspect him of and that Badiou has ruled out of bounds. Such a characterization of his appeal to grace, however, misses the mark insofar as it fails to appreciate the importance of Badiou's mathematical ontology at this point, for Badiou's grace is not magical, it is mathematical. Set theory provides the explanation of the possibility of the irruption of the truth-event and its subsequent faithful subjectivation insofar as it theorizes the aleatory extension of the supplement. Thus, the question of hope with regard to the power of the event is not that of a magical lacuna in Badiou's thought so much as it is the question of whether matter's behavior conforms to the axioms of post-Cantorian mathematics.[82]

One might pursue this question down several avenues. For example, one might argue that explaining the (real) theoretical possibility of a truth-event does not account for an event's actuality, or one might question whether mathematics cogently explicates the relation of the finite and the infinite.[83] However, one might grant Badiou his mathematical grace and still be skeptical of his hope. One might ask, not "*can* we hope and if so on what grounds?" but "for *what* can we hope?" When the question of hope is posed in this way, one is struck by the profound modesty of Badiou's hope. Turning to Paul, he all but eliminates the apocalyptic dimension of the apostle's thought.[84] Paul, he argues, did not hold hope in an objective victory; instead, Paul understood hope as the product of a subjective victory. This is to say, hope does not find its orientation in the future, looking forward, but in the past, looking backwards. Hope is the product of considering the event and the fidelity that spans the gap between the event and the present. Badiou writes:

> The subjective dimension named "hope" is the ordeal that has been overcome, not in the name of which it has been overcome. Hope is "enduring fidelity," tenacity of love through the ordeal, and in no way vision of a reward or punishment. Hope is the

---

81. Hallward, *Badiou*, 180.
82. See ibid., 277.
83. Hallward (*Badiou*, 170) and Milbank ("Materialism and Transcendence," 405, 407, 409) both raise this question.
84. Badiou, *Saint Paul*, 95.

subjectivity of a victorious fidelity, fidelity to fidelity, and not the representation of its future outcome.[85]

As such, hope has nothing to do with the future; it is the confidence of the militant that is born by considering the militant's own fidelity. Hope is the product of fidelity thus far. There is, in a sense, no hope for the future.

This redrawing of hope, without any orientation toward the future, returns us to Badiou's mathematical grace. If his mathematized grace articulates the possibility of the event's irruption, it does so only on the order of pure chance. Recall the earlier discussion of grace as a dice-throw, as chance in the Mallaremean sense of the chance of chance. One cannot hope for the future because whether or not truths will blossom in the future is a matter of pure chance. The truth process is sheer risk, with no guarantees, all the way through. Indeed, because this chance, as the chance of chance, is not susceptible to calculations of probability one cannot even say that victory is as likely as defeat. One simply cannot say. Instead, one can only take confidence in one's own fidelity thus far.

Badiou's comments on the Good further illumine the character of his hope. One of the central points of his critique of contemporary ethics is that the development of an ethic around a consensus of what evil is inevitably cuts the nerve of the effort to imagine and work toward unknown possibilities of the Good.[86] Yet, Badiou himself is careful to reign in expectations with regard to the extent to which the Good might actually be accomplished. Thus, he writes, "There is no world that might be captive to the coherence of the Good. The world is, and will remain, beneath Good and Evil. The Good is Good only to the extent that it does not aspire to render the world good . . . So it must be that the power of truth is a kind of powerlessness."[87] The Good cannot prevail; indeed, it must not prevail. It must not even *aspire* to prevail. Such a victory, or even the aspiration to victory, would ironically be the triumph of evil. "Every absolutization of the power of the truth organizes an evil."[88] The world must remain beneath Good and Evil because the victory of the good can only mean the ruin of its very foundation—the animal interest that divides every subject, the mortal who is overcome without being left behind by the immortal.[89] In other words, there is no expectation of

---

85. Ibid., 95.
86. Badiou, *Ethics*, 13–14.
87. Ibid., 85.
88. Ibid.
89. Ibid., 84. Badiou explains this necessary conflict accordingly: "The place of ethics is indicated by the chronic conflict between two functions of the multiple material that makes up the whole being of a 'some-one': on the one hand, its simple deployment,

peace, of the cessation of struggle. Hope is the singular, aleatory victory; the permanent revolution (although who can really say what its duration might be, since prophetic utterance is banished) born of the immortal's ability to sustain indifference to its death.

This is not a robust hope. In this regard, it mirrors the turn in Badiou's politics in recent years, which, Hallward notes, has been marked by a relinquishing of the historical realization of communist ideals in favor of subjective commitment.[90] It is also reminiscent of the motto of the East Timorese resistance: "to resist is to win," which is admirable and perhaps sustainable for a time between the times, but is not likely to be maintained indefinitely. Indeed, we are left asking, is it worth struggling, Sisyphus-like, in a world of perpetual struggle? And is such a modest hope really all that different from the hope that capital offers? To this we will return as we turn to the question of love.

Strange Love

Love is the deployment of the power of self-love in the direction of all others. Love, according to Badiou, is the effectiveness of the truth-event; it is the labor of truth. Does it offer the promise of liberty from the depredations of capital? We begin with the politics of indifference, the way the ethic of truths is indifferent to difference. Why begin here? Because love as the power of self-love is the power of the subject to affirm its generic singularity, an affirmation which, precisely because its object[91] is generic singularity, is an affirmation of everyone, indifferent to their differences. Love is the power of indifference to difference.

Underwriting the politics of indifference is the assertion that difference is not the ethical issue, that the ethical question is the question of the same. Yet does not his politics of indifference belie this? Is it not the case that the ethic of truths effaces differences, that it is truly indifferent only to those who carry their differences indifferently? Granted, one no longer seeks to eliminate particulars; one simply disregards them as insignificant and

---

his belonging to the situation, or what we might call the principle of interest; on the other, consistency, the linking of the known by the not-known, or what we might call the subjective principle" (*Ethics*, 48).

90. Hallward, *Badiou*, 44, 241.

91. It should be noted that Badiou desires a subject without an object, a desire he traces to Descartes. My use of "object" here does not imply that generic being is an object. On the contrary, generic being as generic can only be an objectless subject. See Badiou, *Manifesto for Philosophy*, 93, 45, 79, 82. For a contrary reading of Descartes, see Balibar, "Citizen Subject," 33–57.

worthless in light of the surpassing value of the generic "same" that traverses all difference. Think of Badiou's subject. The militant subject, the some-one convoked by a truth is impersonal in the sense that it is a singular deposed of all particular identity insofar as it never identifies itself except on the basis of the universal. Thus, Badiou's subject is always a generic (nondescript, nameless) some-one, which is but another nomination of "anyone," which is a necessary implication of his universalism as "universal singularity."[92] This erasure of differences is not the same as a call for the physical destruction of differences; nevertheless, such indifference is its own form of destruction. Consider his treatment of the Jews.

What is left of the Jews by the time Badiou's indifference has passed over their particularity, their difference? Everything and nothing. Everything is left insofar as Jewish particularity is affirmed in the abstract. Time and again, Badiou has Paul affirm that he will not quibble over customs and rites and obligations, that his gospel does not entail the destruction of the particular. Indeed, Paul even grants to the Jews a certain pride of place. But what hides in the shadow of such affirmations? A mere shell of Judaism, a withered Judaism. What remains when Judaism's law has been discredited, its discourse rejected, and its prophecy dismissed? When Paul's subtle strategy of philo-Judaism has had its way? What remains is a "resubjectivated" Judaism that can only be a nominal Judaism whose adherents "go through the motions" of maintaining their distinctive particularity, all the while aware that such distinctives are of no real import, that they are really the same as everyone else. What remains is a Judaism whose law is love, where everything is permitted, and subjective commitment is the cornerstone of the gospel. In other words, what remains is modern Protestantism,[93] and the hope that real Jews will come to their senses and realize that they are just like everyone else.

In the end, Badiou's Paul and Badiou's universalism are anti-Jewish, Badiou's protestations notwithstanding. Yes, Jews remain; but they are

---

92. In this regard, one might argue that the difficulty with Badiou's thought is not that it is too abstract, disconnected from the real world (*pace* Hallward, *Badiou*, 106), but that his thought casts the real materially existent world as too ephemeral (Hallward, *Badiou*, 180). The differences that Badiou suggests are the baseline of reality all but disappear in this thought, overshadowed by the reality of generic multiple being, of which in a sense they become the shadow. Hence, the charge that Badiou's thought is disconnected from the real world and too abstract gets it backwards. The really real world of generic multiple being only appears abstract to those trapped in the illusions of insignificant particularity and the veneer of difference.

93. Žižek's account is consistent with Badiou on this point. There is a transubstantiation of the chosen people. The Jews are now the Christians, and those formerly known as Jews are just one more ethnic group. See Žižek, *Puppet and Dwarf*, 130.

deracinated. They are Jews like a food-court taco is a taco. Ironically, Badiou's claim that this universalism is not anti-Semitic (in itself a misstatement of the issue) proves the point. His argument that Paul's universalism only entails a militant and not ontological break with Judaism (which he erroneously attributes to the Gospels) is disingenuous. After all, in Badiou's vision Judaism as a particular material formation only persists at the level of "militancy" and not ontologically, where we are all the same by virtue of the neutral, univocal being of the void. Thus, Badiou's defense in effect asserts that Paul does not break with particular subjects as subjects, only with those subjects as Jews.

Accordingly, Badiou's love is a strange form of love, but how does this revelation shed light on the issue of resisting capital? To begin with, it suggests that Badiou's universalism, effacing as it does differences and particularity even as it indifferently affirms them, actually mirrors capitalism's abstract homogenization of differences and particularities. Indeed, it is not immediately clear what distinguishes the truth procedure that traverses differences and the generic subject that results from the commodities produced by capitalist monetary homogenization.

Such a claim, however, is neither surprising nor troubling for Badiou. On the contrary, he affirms the similarity, admitting that he runs the risk of being an unconscious agent of capital.[94] And at one point at least, he embraces capitalism. The similarity lies in the way his ethic of truths and capitalism both treat particular differences. Indeed, he states that one of the challenges that lay before any genuinely emancipatory politics is that it must be at least equal to the challenge of capital. By this he means that emancipatory politics must move beyond the "reactionary nostalgia" that pines for lost territoriality and embrace capitalism's deterritorializing force.[95] There is no going back on capitalism's deterritorializing of the particular, its severing of traditional bonds (between man and nature, men, groups, and the *polis*, moral and eternal life, etc.) and subsequent unleashing of a generalized atomism.[96] This atomizing is declared an ontological virtue in spite of the fact that "this destitution operates in the most complete barbarity" on the grounds that it is a clear indicator of the reign of Being as multiple. Moreover, it is time, he suggests, that we recognize that Capital has been the historic medium of the advent of a subtractive ontology, which leads him to pose the question, "What has happened to philosophy for it to refuse with a shudder the liberty and strength a desacralizing [read: capitalist] epoch

---

94. Badiou, *Ethics*, 113.
95. Badiou, *Manifesto for Philosophy*, 53, 58; Badiou, *Ethics*, 113.
96. Badiou, *Manifesto for Philosophy*, 55–56.

offered it?"[97] Badiou's embrace of capitalism's deterritorializing power leads him to acknowledge that on this point he is better understood as a rival rather than an opponent of capitalism.[98]

In the face of this affirmation of capital's abstract universalism, we are prompted to wonder, what then distinguishes the two universalisms? Badiou responds that his is a vision of differences that are traversed, conserved and deposed according to a logic other than selfish calculation.[99] This other logic is the "law of love" he extracted from Paul. What distinguishes this love from capitalism? What makes it something other than selfish calculation? Here it is helpful to recall Badiou's critique of capital on the grounds that it has no consideration for any singularity whatsoever. Capitalist universalism is faulty because, Badiou argues, it does not affirm generic singularity. Instead, even as it rightly severs all bonds to the particular (thereby gesturing to the truth of multiple being; which is capital's ontological virtue), it immediately reifies or reterritorializes multiple being according to a brutal logic—animal, mortal interests, survival, being-for-death. According to Badiou's own account, capital recognizes generic singularity in its deterritorializing; the problem is that once liberated, those generic singularities are then circulated according to a selfish calculation, that is, according to non-universal or particular interest. What Badiou desires is a circulation according to universal subjective principle, which is the freedom of (inconsistent) multiple-being, "the reign of liberty in infinite situations."[100]

The question is can Badiou's thought sustain this critique? Does his ontology admit this critique, or do we detect the faint hint of incense, a (Derridian?) trace of a mystical revelation from outside his thought?[101] Here we raise the issue of relationality in Badiou's thought.

Already we have seen Badiou's praise for the breaking of bonds in his affirmation of capital's deterritorializing. The renunciation of relations characterizes his thought as a whole. He says of the break effected by the event that it is asocial, and he goes on to characterize the militant subject of truth as isolated and solitary and he denounces every invocation of community as antithetical to truths.[102] Fundamental to his vision is the critique of any communal notion of relation or "being together." Such being together

---

97. Ibid., 58–59.
98. Badiou, *Ethics*, 113.
99. Ibid.
100. Badiou quoted in Hallward, *Badiou*, 241. On consistency, and its being the presentation of the inconsistency of multiple being, see Badiou, *Manifesto for Philosophy*, 103–9.
101. See Badiou, *Saint Paul*, 51–52.
102. Badiou, *Ethics*, 54, 76. What follows draws from Hallward, *Badiou*, 26.

is but the product of the assemblage of particular, animal interests, which is contrasted with the solitary immortal singularity sustained by the sheer subjective conviction that is fidelity to the truth-event. Likewise, the goal of truth is a self-sufficient purity where truth is no longer retained in any relation.[103]

This is the concomitant of his mathematical ontology that has as one of its founding axioms the assertion that a set is defined in terms of it elements alone, irrespective of their relations.[104] It also comports well with his embrace of the univocity of being, whereby multiple being is generic, fungible, specifically indistinguishable and mutually substitutable.[105]

Recently Badiou has acknowledged that he needs to address relations and he is in the process of developing a mathematized logic that conceptualizes relations in terms of a localization and "being-there" that is distinct from his ontological engagement with Being.[106] While his work in the area is neither fully developed nor widely available, what is available does not suggest a fundamental shift in his thought. The turn to relation is the supplementation of ontology with logic.[107] Relations, the subject of a logic, remain derivative and without ontological purchase. As such, they are connections of will, of sheer enthusiasm or subjective commitment, that make no difference, that play no constitutive role in shaping the individuals that they connect or divide.[108]

Yet, if this vision of universal singularity is as indifferent to relations as it claims, if it is as hostile to the suggestion that relations matter as it appears, then we are compelled to ask, why the concern with capitalist relations? If singularities are not identified by their particular relations any more than they are by their particular differences (even as singularities do not simply escape or shed their particularities, differences, and relations) then why is a universalism that purports to be indifferent to differences not indifferent to this particular relation and the host of particular, mortal interests that propel it?

This matter of relations, and Badiou's concern for capitalist relations in particular, raises a further question. One of the objections that Badiou has to the investment of particularity with significance is that fidelity to

---

103. Badiou, cited in Hallward, *Badiou*, 273.

104. See Hallward, *Badiou*, 275.

105. This, too, follows from an axiom of set theory. See Hallward, *Badiou*, 275.

106. See Badiou, *Ethics*, lvi–iii; 136–37. See also Hallward, *Badiou*, 293. What follows draws from this.

107. Ibid., lvii.

108. Hallward, *Badiou*, 314.

particularity takes the form of terror and has as its content war and massacre.[109] This is the case because, according to Badiou, establishing and maintaining such an investment in particularity necessarily entails voiding what is around it, a voiding that is "obtained by cutting into the flesh itself," and that rests on the presumption that the ones so voided are nothing more than strictly particular existences as human animals.[110] Against such a possibility, Badiou asserts that the one thing that distinguishes humanity from the predatory animal that it also is is its capacity to enter into truth procedures that convoke the generic subject.[111] Yet we are compelled to ask, from what source springs Badiou's hope? On what grounds can he claim that univocal being, particularly construed as it is in terms of an absolutely neutral multiple being of nothing, wards off conflict?

Already, in considering his account of hope, we have seen how conflict is endemic to his thought. Struggle is perpetual as hope is reduced and we are told the good cannot, indeed must not, prevail. Likewise, the pervasiveness of struggle and conflict is confirmed by his account of particularity. Not only are "differences what there is" but they are essentially in conflict. That is, after all, what makes the recognition of the same so difficult. Valuing particularity necessarily leads to cutting of the flesh and construing others as mere animals. Indeed, it is the investment in particularity, difference, that marks us a predatory animals and it is only the becoming indifferent to difference, renouncing the significance of the particular, that marks our becoming human. Clearly, then, in Badiou's thought, particularity lends itself to a Hobbesian world where war and dominion are the norm.

Whence cometh peace? As we have seen, Badiou's mathematized grace can actually promise nothing in the way of deliverance. Badiou renounces all prophetic utterance regarding the future. As the chance of chance, there is no promise that it will appear. And if it does appear, its intrinsic weakness cannot carry the day. As such, peace can only be an interruption of an eternal struggle and conflict. But the problem runs deeper than the aleatory character of Badiou's grace. What is the source of the real possibility of the advent of the peaceful same? What is the source of his optimism that the unleashing of inconsistent multiple being will result in liberty and not the war of all against all? Here we might even ponder whether he is able to deliver even the modicum of hope that capital proffers, insofar as there is some truth to the claim that capital wards off the total war of more bellicose passions by means of fostering commercial ones. Perhaps the source

109. Badiou, *Ethics*, 74.
110. Ibid., 76.
111. Ibid., 90.

of Badiou's optimism is the void of neutral being. If this neutrality were a *positive* attribute then it could conceivably be construed as a positive indifference that amounted to a drive toward solitude.[112] However, Badiou rejects all such vitalist/organicist accounts of being in favor of the being of nothing, the absolutely neutral void. Furthermore, were it the case that neutrality was a positive attribute, one would still have to account for the distance between a peaceful ontology of singularities and the Hobbesian existence of particulars.[113]

What has this to do with resisting capital? Badiou celebrates the ontological virtue of capitalism, its grounding in a univocal being that defies the bonds of relation, even as he decries the barbarity with which it severs those bonds; he clearly prefers the subtlety of what he deems Paul's strategic philo-Judaism. But Badiou has not succeeded in establishing that capitalism's agony is an ontological deviation. The ethic of truths' indifference to relations, the modesty of its hope, the agony of its particulars, the neutrality of its being, all fail to provide any grounds for calling into question capitalist relations. In other words, the (minimal) distance Badiou asserts exists between capitalism's universality and his own universalism of love has failed to materialize as anything more than a mere wish.

Badiou is certainly right when he argues that only another, albeit very different, universalism stands a chance of resisting capitalism. His ethic of truths, sowing universal singulars, however, fails to prove itself up to the challenge. At best, it may be counted a rival. For a genuine alternative and more robust hope of deliverance from the agony of capital, we must look elsewhere. We must look for a universality funded not by the aleatory production of universal singulars but by the concrete universal whom Paul announces, the Jewish Messiah. To this we now turn.

III. Paul's Gospel

Although his vision of the universal singular is not capable of sustaining resistance to capital, there is much that is helpful and promising in Badiou's use of Paul. He is right that resisting capital is a matter of the advent of another

---

112. Although this is not very positive. Think of C. S. Lewis's vision of hell in *The Great Divorce*.

113. In this regard, it is interesting to note Hallward's discussion of the "absolutist" dimension of Badiou's thought, focusing on its general logic of actively nonrelational singularity. Although Hallward quickly dismisses any suggestion that Badiou's position is authoritarian or despotic, the similarities are provocative, particularly if my reading is correct and Badiou cannot account for how his thought does not underwrite despotism. See Hallward, *Badiou*, 285–86.

universalism, that Paul's gospel is the annunciation of this other universalism, that this universalism is a labor of love advancing only eventually, involving grace and fidelity and hope and so forth. Tapping the promise of Badiou's thought, however, requires resubjectivating it. It is necessary to transpose his account of the truth-event and fidelity and universalism and law from the alien, univocal key into its proper, analogical key. And St. Paul the obscurantist, the theologian, points the way, a way that begins with the Jews.

Subtraction: The Election of the Jews

I begin with the Jews, and more specifically, with the election of the Jews. Recall that Badiou characterized Paul's relation to the Jews in terms of an eventual break—he rejects the law and refuses to attribute significance to any particularity or community—but he did not thereby simply negate that particularity or law; rather, he resubjectivated it in terms of universality and a transliteral law of love. Finally, Badiou defended Paul from the charge of anti-Semitism by highlighting instances of philo-Judaism in his writings, which was Paul's strategy, motived by the hope for their redemption expressed in Romans 9–11, for winning them over to this resubjectivated Judaism, which bears a striking resemblance to modern Protestantism.

The difficulties with this rendition of Paul are legion, and need not detain us since they are addressed thoroughly elsewhere by scholars such as W. D. Davies, E. P. Sanders, Douglas Harink, John Howard Yoder, and Scott Bader-Saye. Instead, I will focus on two points only: the replacement of Judaism by Pauline Christianity, and the character of the resubjectivation implied in Paul's appeal to Abraham.

First, regarding the break between Judaism and Pauline Christianity, Badiou's reading is anachronistic. Granted, Badiou glosses over the break to a certain extent by acknowledging, although significantly understating and distorting, Paul's philo-Judaism; nevertheless, he attributes to Paul a subjective break, bearing consequences for understanding both cult and law, that is more accurately located long after Paul, no earlier than the mid second century—indeed, one could argue, no earlier than the Reformation or even Bultmann.[114] From the "Christian" side, Justin Martyr (c. 135 CE) is the first to give voice to themes that we hear in Badiou, although he is by no means indicative of the dominant attitude of Christians toward Jews at that time.[115]

---

114. Rudolph Bultmann being the teacher of Günther Bornkamm, whose book, *Paul*, Badiou recommends. For an overview of the genealogy of what is the standard modern Protestant reading of Paul, see Sanders, *Paul and Palestinian Judaism*, 2–59.

115. Listen to Yoder's synopsis of Justin Martyr's view. The themes that will

Indeed, even much later, Origen and Chrysostom continued to preach to Christians on Sunday who had attended synagogue on Saturday.[116] Likewise, on the "Jewish" side, there are no grounds for locating the break prior to what we might call the rabbinic achievement of a normative Judaism in the aftermath of the dispersal associated with the defeat of Bar-Kochba in 135 CE, and the division is more compellingly associated with the rabbinic compilation of the *Mishna* (early third century), which clearly prohibits intervisitation between messianic and non-messianic Jews.[117] Prior to these second-century developments, Christianity did not designate a break from Judaism; rather, it was one more grouping—at times engaged in bitter, if typical, internecine polemics[118]—within a dynamic Judaism.[119]

Moreover, Paul's theological argument is not that the Jews are displaced by (Protestant) Christians and his hope is not simply that the Jews will come around and allow themselves to be traversed by the universal that evacuates their particularity of significance. Rather, his assurance is that all Israel will be saved, and it will be saved as Israel, because they are Jews and not in spite of it. Everything hinges for Paul on sustaining the elective significance of Jewish particularity; it is because the Jews, in particular, are elect and that election is irrevocable, that all may have hope. This is the argument of Romans as a whole, and it is the argument of Romans 9–11 in particular. His use of the metaphor of the olive tree (Rom 11) is instructive in this regard. The pruning of the olive tree that is effected by some Jews' unbelief in the Messiah is but a temporary act by God (see Rom 9). It is temporary; it will be mended. Pruning is not an uprooting; it is a stumbling and not a falling (here the metaphorical image of pruning tempts post-schism readers to infer too much). No axe is laid to this tree; the tree onto which the Gentiles are grafted remains Jewish, and the Gentile grafts remain wild additions,

---

reverberate in Badiou are clear. Justin Martyr "reconceived the Christian message so as to make it 'credible' to non-Jewish culture . . . detached the message of Jesus from its Jewish matrix and thereby transposed it into an a-historical moral monotheism with no particular peoplehood and no defenses against acculturation." Yoder, *Jewish-Christian Schism Revisited*, 152.

116. Ibid., 119.

117. Ibid., 57, 106, 153. It is worth noting that the Jewish scholar, Peter Ochs, confirms Yoder's claims in his interspersed commentary. For Yoder's treatment of the standard arguments on behalf of an earlier dating of the split from the rabbinic side—arguments that appeal to anathemas, messianic claims, the refusal to support Jewish revolts of 70 CE or 130 CE—see 49–57.

118. Ochs, "Commentary," 67.

119. Yoder, *Jewish-Christian Schism*, 31–32, 47–48, 58; affirmed by Ochs, "Commentary," 67, 39; Sanders, *Paul and Palestinian Judaism*, 423; Davies, *Jewish and Pauline Studies*, 97, 135.

even when the natural branches retake their place attached to the Jewish root. In other words, this is not the tale of the eclipse of the redemptive significance of Jewish particularity in favor of Protestant Christian universalism, to which the Jews may one day submit. The metaphor is not about the replacement of Israel, but about the hope that is born of Jewish election, as that election is played out in both stumbling/pruning (which calls for attention to the witness of post-biblical Jews[120]) and recovery/inclusion. It is a profound meditation on the universalism of the Jewish site.

What then are we to make of Paul's lengthy polemic involving Abraham, law, and faith? There is little sense in denying that Paul is resubjectivating Judaism, but, again, it makes all the difference how that resubjectivation is characterized. Does it proceed along the lines of Jeremiah and perhaps Erza, amounting to a restoration or renewal, or along the lines of Bultmann and twentieth-century liberal Protestantism, which amounts to Judaism's replacement by a universal (Protestant) Christianity?

Badiou casts the resubjectivation of Judaism in terms of its Protestant replacement. His reading hinges on the dichotomy of faith and law, embodied in the antithesis of Abraham and Moses in Paul and his conclusion is that "Abraham . . . anticipates what could be called the universalism of the Jewish site; in other words, he anticipates Paul."[121] Notice how this completely effaces the Jews. Abraham is a proto-universalist, whose election is prior to Judaism, whose vision is antithetical to Judaism (faith v. law), and whose blessing is side-tracked by Judaism and must wait until Paul shakes off his particular, Jewish blinders for it to reemerge. The so-called universalism of the Jewish site really has nothing to do with Judaism, which is construed entirely as an obstacle to the emergence of universalism. Between Abraham and Pauline (Protestant) Christianity there is a chasm and what Badiou calls the resubjectivating of Judaism is in fact the replacement of its particular insignificance with the universal significance of Protestantism.[122]

This "resubjectivation as replacement" may be contrasted with the Pauline resubjectivation of Judaism that we might label "renewal" or "restoration" of the Jewish subject as the particular, elect Jewish subject. Thus, in contrast with Badiou, Paul appeals to Abraham and faith, not to establish a

---

120. For more on this, see Bader-Saye, *Church and Israel After Christendom* and Marshall, "Christ and Cultures," 81–100.

121. Badiou, *Saint Paul*, 103. What follows is drawn from here.

122. This replacement may be conceptualized in terms of several shifts: from absolute particular to universal singular, from a particular culture to no particular culture, from difference to indifference, from law to faith, from literal law to a transliteral law that permits anything in the name of love, from a discourse of mastery to one of weakness, from the Father to the Son.

contrast or break with Judaism and law, but in order to argue that Judaism rightly understood was always about faith and always universal in import. This becomes clearer when we consider what Badiou rightly recognizes as the heart of Paul's proclamation—Jesus Christ was resurrected. As Davies and Sanders have pointed out, if one fails to comprehend this core of Paul's gospel, one cannot make sense of Paul's polemic regarding Judaism and the law.[123] In this regard, it is telling that Badiou does very little with this core proclamation—and he does nothing with the messianic assertion (I suppose we are to assume that this is but another instance of Paul's strategic philo-Judaism)—reducing its christological density to an anthropological trope for universal, generic subjective processes.

Paul's resubjectivation of Judaism revolves around the issue of inclusion in Jewish election, membership in the Jewish covenant of salvation. Accordingly, the issue for Paul is not self-reliance ("law") versus reliance upon God ("faith"), but membership in the covenant, which is effected by belonging to the Jewish Messiah, Jesus.[124] And this is precisely a matter of resubjectivation insofar as to be joined to Israel (its election, its covenant) is, according to Paul, a matter of being in Christ, being joined to Christ, who as the Jewish messiah has everything to do with upholding Israel's election.[125] Such a vision of the foundation of covenant membership, such an understanding of the subject of election and covenant will, of course, have consequences for one's construal of the law. But those consequences do not entail either the law's rejection or its dialectical sublimation in a transliteral law that is really not.[126]

To begin with, as Badiou notes in the course of his dialectical overcoming of the law, Paul does not simply discard observance of the law. Indeed, nowhere does Paul tell Jews, even messianic Jews, to cease Torah observance *simpliciter* (we will consider his treatment of Gentiles shortly). Nowhere does he suggest that the advent of the Messiah simply abolishes the law—indeed, he spends significant time arguing against such antinomianism. This

---

123. Davies, *Jewish and Pauline Studies*, 123; Sanders, *Paul and Palestinian Judaism*.

124. Sanders, *Paul and Palestinian Judaism*, 484. It is this that drives the polemic in Galatians. The issue there is not Judaism v. Christianity, but rather what constitutes the "elemental principle" of covenantal inclusion—keeping the Torah or Jesus. See also Harink, *Paul Among the Postliberals*, 78, 92. See also Hays, *The Faith of Jesus Christ*. Note that the issue of inclusion is distinct from the role of the law after inclusion, which will be addressed shortly.

125. See Gal 3:16, where Christ is equated with Israel. See Davies, *Jewish and Pauline Studies*, 202.

126. Is not Badiou's reading of the law finally dialectical, even as he recognizes that Paul is not dialectical? Thesis: "Paul rejects the law." Antithesis: "Paul embraces the law." Synthesis: "Paul proffers a transliteral law."

is the case because the law is not a problem for Paul. As Krister Stendahl pointed out, his theology is not driven by guilt and anxiety before the law.[127] Indeed, Paul boasts of fulfilling the law. What then drives his polemic? The issue is the subject who approaches the law.[128] Quite simply, Paul is critical of all claims made on the law's behalf by subjects who approach the law apart from Messiah Jesus. Such subjects may in fact fulfill the letter of the law, but by so doing they cannot attain the end they seek, namely, life, salvation; such a gift comes only in the Messiah.[129]

This resubjectivation of the one who approaches the law does not overturn the law; instead, it rightly locates observance in relation to the Jewish election and covenant. It has been noted that there is little evidence that Jews believed that the law was a means of earning salvation.[130] Instead, Judaism was characterized by a covenantal nomism; this is to say, covenantal obedience was widely recognized as the response to God's prior and gracious activity of election and not a means of acquiring such blessings.[131] Moreover, such nomism was not without mercy and means of atoning for transgressions, even as it gives rise to the possibility of retribution as well. Paul's polemic with regard to the law upholds the law (retaining notions of mercy, atonement, and retribution as well) even as it secures its location as a grace-enabled response to God's election in the Messiah Jesus. This is to

---

127. See Stendahl, *Paul Among Jews and Gentiles*. See also Sanders, *Paul and Palestinian Judaism*, 482; Davies, *Jewish and Pauline Studies*, 94.

128. See Augustine, *On the Spirit and the Letter*.

129. See Sanders, *Paul and Palestinian Judaism*, 484, 505, 550.

130. Yoder, *Jewish-Christian Schism*, 93–94; Marshall, "Christ and Cultures," 93. How then are we to account for Paul's polemic? Perhaps it is a Gentile distortion of Judaism that Paul attacks? More likely it is a current within what we might call a "diverse popular Judaism," perhaps one that drew heavily from IV Ezra (see Sanders, *Paul and Palestinian Judaism*, 426–28), not unlike the way Christianity is cast with some frequency in a moralizing and legalistic vein in traditions that actually provide no authoritative basis for such a portrayal. The point of this observation is only that whoever Paul is attacking, they are not rightly taken as representative of normative Judaism—in part because there was no monolithic Judaism during Paul's lifetime and in part because there is little evidence that any of the diverse Judaisms of the time held the views Paul attacks. Which does not dissolve Paul's issues with his Jewish sisters and brothers; rather, it only helps reposition the debate to where it should be—conditions of covenant membership.

131. See Sanders, *Paul and Palestinian Judaism*, 75. Note that this counters John Milbank's association of covenant with contract. Although covenant may indeed be distorted into a contract—Hobbes and Spinoza do precisely this by grounding the covenant in human choice—it need not be, and the Jewish covenant, rightly understood, is not. See Milbank, *Theology and Social Theory*, 15.

say, Paul upholds nomism within its proper gracious context of covenant, understood in terms of Messiah Jesus.[132]

There can be no question about replacement, effacement, or even supercessionism in this resubjectivation. Paul's treatment of the law does not exemplify a break or rupture with Judaism. To the contrary, his argument can be interpreted as a gloss on Jeremiah's claims regarding the renewal of the Jewish covenant in terms of a resubjectivation (Jer 31). Likewise, Paul's manner of approaching Torah could be viewed as analogous to the way in which Ezra restored a maculate Torah.[133] In other words, Paul's re-reading of Israel's election and law can be thoroughly situated in Judaism. Moreover, the end result of Paul's argument about Jewish election is a Jewish subject who remains thoroughly and significantly Jewish (in contrast to Badiou's subject who is, at best incidentally and insignificantly Jewish); indeed, if anything, Paul could be considered a Judaizer just to the extent that he universalizes the Jewish subject not by rendering all persons Jewish but by announcing that salvation is universally available to all by means of everyone's affiliation with the Jewish election and covenant.[134] In other words, the universality of salvation does not come to pass by indifferently passing over difference, but by recognizing and affirming the Jewish difference.[135]

Whereas Badiou reads the subject Paul as a subtraction from the Jews, Paul reads the Jews as a subtraction from the nations. The universal

---

132. See Sanders' discussion of Paul and covenantal nomism in *Paul and Palestinian Judaism*, 511–15. He notes the difference that Paul's participationist soteriology makes in designating his ethic a covenantal nomism. We will discuss this more fully below. Here we might mention the charge that Jewish law retains a reactive element advanced by Milbank ("Materialism and Transcendence," 420, see also 425; "On Theological Transgression," 172). Milbank characterizes the Jewish law as reactionary (albeit the least reactionary of laws) in the sense that it assumes sin and death as positive forces possessed of real activity and real subjective appeal. I can agree with this claim if he means by it not that the Jewish law is intrinsically, if mildly, reactionary but that the non-Messianic Jew can only engage the law in such a manner, whereas the subject who approaches the law in Christ finds all reactive elements purged. In other words, this issue is finally not God's gift of the law, but the subject who approaches it. And Judaism and Christianity have different theological anthropologies in this regard; Christians have a more destructive account of sin, which Paul articulates so clearly in his account of the law and sin in Romans 5:12–21.

133. See Halivni, *Revelation Restored*, and Hays, *Echoes of Scripture*, for a more general treatment of Paul's reading strategy as thoroughly Jewish in nature.

134. On Paul as Judaizer, see Yoder, *Jewish-Christian Schism*, 93–102. That Paul might be considered a Judaizer in no way runs afoul of his sharp epistolary attacks on Judaizers. Rather, it is a matter of different uses/connotations of the same term.

135. Which, of course, for Paul, is Messiah Jesus. See Gen 12:1–3, where God declares that the universality of redemption is connected to a people's reaction to Abraham/Israel. See also Zech 8:20–23.

possibility of salvation is irrevocably tied to the break that is the election of this particular people. In other words, Badiou misplaces the break that Paul proclaims. It is not Paul who breaks with the Jews, but the Jews who constitute, by gracious election, a break from unredeemed humanity.

Universalism: The Catholicity of Salvation

To begin with the election of the Jews immediately raises the specter of the reactionary nostalgia for the illusory security of a closed-set, an absolute particularity that Badiou fears and denounces on the grounds that particularity invested with such significance necessarily entails war and massacre. Alternatively, it suggests a capitulation to politically correct moralizing, of the kind that foreswears Christian transcendence of the Jewish legacy in the name of a relativism that stifles action.[136] How is this affirmation of the election of Israel not a call to arms in the name of a closed set or a capitulation to vapid liberal moralizing? An answer entails considering Paul's calling as the apostle to the Gentiles and the gift that is given in the particular differences that constitute humanity.

Paul's call to the Gentiles is typically conceived in terms of a conversion to a new, more universal religion, which is precisely Badiou's reading. Yet, if Paul was convinced that the redemption of all was somehow connected to the election of Israel, then the standard reading collapses. Instead, Paul's apostolic mission must be reconceived as the enactment of the universalism of the Jewish site, of the display of precisely how Judaism is indeed for all, which is frequently called the "Gentile inclusion" but which we might call the "Gentile filiation" as well.

The possibility of such a reconception, however, immediately faces a significant obstacle. Namely, Paul adamantly refused to require that Gentiles become Jews. This is clear in his writings and in the account of the Jerusalem council (Acts 15). However, too much or too little can be made of this. Too much can be made of it in the sense that by pointing to the refusal to require Torah observance, one can cast Christianity as a break with Judaism *simpliciter*; similarly, too little can be made of it in the sense that its refusal to denounce *in toto* the Jewish remainder may be viewed as a mere compromise between the Jewish law and Christian freedom. Both readings miss the dynamics of the Gentile inclusion or filiation with Israel. Such inclusion did not mean that Gentiles were to become Jews; in this regard, Christian practice is rightly distinguished from typical Jewish proselytizing practice.

---

136. Milbank, "Materialism and Transcendence," 399–400. Recall, as well, Badiou's critique of contemporary ethics that collapse into a relativism that undercuts action.

Yet, neither did Gentile inclusion mean that "all things were permitted." To the contrary, Gentiles were expected to abide by the laws that later became known as the Noahide laws,[137] and it is this expectation of some kind of Torah observance that accounts for the appearance of Christian *paranesis* or covenantal nomism, as well as later theological distinctions between laws that pertain to the Jews alone and those that pertain to all. Nor did the inclusion of the Gentiles mean that Jewish Christians were to cease Torah observance themselves, although changes were entailed in some Torah observance, particularly with regard to table fellowship.[138]

The recognition of these changes have led some to speak of the universalism of Judaism in terms of a "shared Israelhood"[139] or a "differential election,"[140] the point being that these changes do not constitute either a replacement of Israel's election or the establishment of two parallel elections. In this regard, it is worth noting that the changes effected in Torah observance (or the understanding of the Torah) with regard to both Jew and Gentile were anticipated and debated within Judaism prior to Paul's arrival and the Christian mission to the Gentiles, which suggests that even alterations in the way Torah observance is practiced do not count as *prima facie* evidence of a break with Judaism. Indeed, the very malleability of Judaism may constitute one of the conditions of its universality; after all, it is precisely such malleability that Paul understood to be a characteristic of his universal ministry (see 1 Cor 9:19). There remains one election; that of the Jews, in which all are invited to share. This is the logic of Paul's and the early church's mission to the Gentiles.

That the election of the Jews is for all but does not entail that all must become Jews suggests that differences are dealt with in a manner other than either their destruction or their erasure through indifference. Here we have a particular that is absolute but at the same time given neither to closure nor to cutting of the flesh. Here is a particular that is universal. This constitutes Israel's break with all the nations; here we have a particularity that is invested with significance without the necessity of positing a rejected, subhuman other.[141]

---

137. Yoder, *Jewish-Christian Schism*, 97, 102, 155.

138. The break between Christianity and Judaism with regard to Torah observance happened later, and as a result of the predominately Gentile character of the church and its mission work. See Yoder, *Jewish-Christian Schism*.

139. Lindbeck, "Postmodern Hermeneutics and Jewish-Christian Dialogue," 110; Lindbeck, "What of the Future?" 362.

140. Harink, *Paul Among the Postliberals*, 183.

141. See Bader-Saye, *Church and Israel After Christendom*, 136.

The Politics of Indifference and the Overcoming of Capital 65

    This recognition of differences, not as a problem to be overcome, but as a gift to be enjoyed, underwrites the Pauline emphasis on reconciliation and unity, on the advent of the peaceable interaction of particularity, which we see displayed in his writings. This is to say, Paul is not the advocate of a generic sameness that is indifferent to difference because differences that matter can only be differences that cut and kill. Rather, Paul celebrates the possibility of the peaceable harmony of differences because those differences can meet in Christ (here we might cite Gal 3:28). Incidentally, here Badiou's dogmatic atheism creates insuperable difficulties, for he cannot read Paul's claims regarding monotheism for what they are—a recognition that what finally unites difference is not creation's generic sameness, but the one Creator. Messiah Jesus is the one who has broken down the dividing walls of hostility, the one who offers a love to each of us that does not render us all the same, but instead in the sharing of that love (the gift of charity) teaches us in turn to share. This is to say, in Christ differences remain but they no longer divide; instead, they become gifts exercised in opportunities of mutual care and service and enjoyment.

    It is this peaceable circulation in accordance with a logic of mutual care and enjoyment that holds out the promise of resistance to capital. Yet, this account of a universalism that stands as an alternative to both Badiou and capital cannot stop here, lest at this crucial juncture it slip back unwittingly into Badiou's vision, becoming an account of a merely human possibility, with Israel as the firstborn example of an otherwise generic event. Moreover, to stop here is to join Badiou in another sense as well, insofar as the claim that Israel's election is a break remains sheer subjective assertion, reminiscent of Badiou's hope for peace, without an account of its ontological condition of possibility. To that condition of possibility, we now turn.

Event: Christ the Concrete Universal

Although I have challenged Badiou's articulation of the advent of truth as well as his reading of Paul from several angles, he is right in highlighting the importance of fidelity in Paul's gospel. Although I have challenged the rendition of Paul that suggests his principal preoccupation was the triumph of faith over law, in fact there is some truth to this claim. Paul is concerned with the triumph of faith; he is simply *not* concerned with the triumph of faith as a human accomplishment. This is to say, the faith that concerns Paul is the faith of Jesus Christ.[142] It is divine fidelity that underwrites Paul's claims for Israel's election and the universality of the Jewish

---

142. See Hays, *Faith of Jesus Christ*.

site via the filiation or inclusion of the Gentiles and the peaceful circulation of differences. It is Christ, the Jewish messiah, who finally upholds the election of Israel and the blessings of all peoples through Israel. Christ is the unsurpassable fullness of God's favor to Israel and its fruition among the nations.[143] Christ it is who makes possible Gentile participation in Israel's election, for differences to interact peaceably without being effaced. And it is his life, death, and resurrection that constitute our hope of deliverance from the malice of capital.

How Christ effects this has already been hinted at. It is a matter of participation, of humanity's being "in Christ." Here the distance separating the contending readings of Paul stretches the furthest. It is the distance between analogical and univocal being and it demarcates precisely the distance between conflicting visions' potential for resisting capital. We can get a handle on Paul's participatory ontology by considering the understanding of incarnation implicit in his work as well as his understanding of Christ's atonement. We begin by considering the incarnation.

Badiou correctly notes that the incarnation is not the object of Paul's direct attention.[144] Nevertheless, the incarnation is implicit in Paul's argument; indeed, Paul's gospel of being in Christ is not intelligible apart from an understanding of the incarnation that corresponds to the church's confession at Chalcedon (451 CE).[145] There the church confessed that in Jesus Christ the antinomy of God and Man has been definitively overcome. Jesus Christ, the fathers of the church declared, is perfect in divinity and perfect in humanity, truly God and truly man. In him are found two natures that undergo no confusion, no change, no division, no separation. Elaborating on this, they state that at no point was the difference between the natures taken away through the union, but rather the property of both natures is preserved and comes together into a single person and a single subsistent being; he is not parted or divided into two persons, but is one and the same only-begotten Son, God, Word, Lord Jesus Christ.

Here the antinomy of God and Man is overcome, not by a defeat of one at the hand of the other nor by means of a synthesis that creates a hybrid. God and humanity (two *ousias*) come together in one person (*hypostasis*), Jesus. Moreover, here God and humanity are joined in the unsurpassable closeness and intimacy ("no division, no separation") of a single life ("he is not parted or divided . . . Jesus Christ") and they are

---

143. Marshall, "Christ and Cultures," 91.

144. Badiou, *Saint Paul*, 74.

145. The text of the "Definition of Chalcedon" can be found in Leith, *Creeds of the Churches*, 35–36. Translation altered slightly.

united in a manner that nevertheless preserves the difference ("no confusion, no change . . . properties of both natures preserved") peaceably. Here is the interplay of robust difference without agony, combat, conflict—a difference that Badiou could not imagine.

More needs to be said, however, if this is to surmount the inevitable rejoinder, one that Badiou would surely issue, that this is but another transcendental One that captures All by means of a divine discipline. Does this not reveal salvation to be just another totalizing discourse that imposes a fixed, transcendental template (order) on an unsuspecting finitude? Is this not the truth of a participatory reading of Paul's soteriology?

A response entails attending to the implications of Paul's claim that redemption comes through one particular person, Jesus. That redemption happens in this particular person means that redemption is not a generalized state of affairs that is ineluctably happening to us.[146] Said differently, redemption is not the capture of finitude within a given totality; it is not the setting of finitude in its assigned place according to a predetermined, transcendental order of fixed essences. Rather, redemption is what happens when people are grafted into the election of Israel by means of an encounter with Israel's messiah. This is to say, redemption is tied to the one whom von Balthasar calls the "concrete universal."[147] The particular, concrete Jew, Jesus, by reason of his being the same person who is the second person of the Trinity, is of universal significance. And this significance is made known, not by means of a transcendental capture but entering into relation with this concrete, particular one. In other words, redemption is not imposed from above or outside the contingencies of history but rather unfolds in the midst of, by means of, the contingent encounters of particulars with this particular Jew. Redemption does not proceed by a fixed organization but by the contingent proliferation of relations with Christ's Spirit in history.

Yet, even if redemption is not imposed from above, it is not yet clear that this redemption is not an order that curtails freedom, even if it advances only immanently, contingently. As previously indicated, the definition of Chalcedon is careful to state that the redemption effected in Christ's person does not destroy the *ousia* therein united. In him is found true humanity and it is not lost in its being brought near to divinity. In Christ, finitude is neither lost nor eclipsed but provided a new way of existing. In particular, and of particular relevance to the matters at hand, in Christ finitude can be lived peaceably. In Christ, finitude no longer need

---

146. Yeago, "Jesus of Nazareth and Cosmic Redemption," 177. Much of what follows draws from Yeago's insightful analysis.

147. Balthasar, *Explorations in Theology*, 1:170.

be scarred by agony, conflict, combat. Rather, finitude can be lived in peace with the infinite God and finite others.

At this point, Aquinas's understanding of the *analogia entis*, the analogy of being, proves helpful. Badiou embraces the univocity of multiple being in the name of liberty, which, it turns out, is either the self-sufficient solitude of the generic or the immortal's indifference to the travails and tribulations that afflict the animal, to which the immortal nevertheless remains susceptible. Aquinas's account of the analogy and univocity of being in the *Summa* helps explain why Badiou has difficulty conceiving of peaceable relations of difference. It also assists in making sense of Paul's understanding of resubjectivation, of our being "in Christ." As Aquinas explains, either univocal being isolates beings (insofar as singularities of univocal being can only be maintained as singulars by some distance) or it dissolves difference altogether (as univocal beings meet they melt together, thus effacing difference). The only mediating position for univocal being is conflict, competition, combat. Univocal being can only maintain difference-in-relation by means of a friction ("cutting of the flesh"). Badiou's work recognizes the third reality and seeks to overcome it by means of the first. He seeks to avoid conflict by the distance of either non-relation or sheer subjective indifference.

In contrast, the analogy of being sustains differences in a way that allows them to be drawn into a relation while preserving (and in the case of the human, enhancing) the liberty of both. Only the analogy of being permits differences to draw near in a mode other than competition and conflict such that in this embrace of intimacy neither being nor its properties are lost. How is this so? What Aquinas accomplishes by positing a qualitative (analogy) and not quantitative (univocal) difference of being, is the drawing near of God and humanity without competition. This is the case because the analogy of being does not posit God and humanity on a single plane, with the result that they are locked in a sort of zero-sum competition as the act/will of one delimits the freedom of the act/will of the other. Instead, the analogy of being permits God an immediate intimacy unavailable to univocal being.[148] It enables God to draw nearer to all things than they are to themselves. Thus, as Aquinas says, "God is in all things, and innermostly ... No action of an agent, however powerful it may be, acts at a distance, except through a medium. But it belongs to the great power of God that he acts

---

148. This is so because were a univocal being to have an unmediated relation, that is, an immediate relation with another univocal being, the "otherness" or difference would dissolve, rendering them one. At which point it no longer makes sense to speak of a relation between different beings. There would no longer be difference or beings, only one being.

immediately on all things. Hence nothing is distant from him."[149] Moreover, this immediate intimacy does not compromise finite freedom (if it did, this would mark a fall to univocity).[150] For God is present to things according to their mode of being.[151] Thus, God's drawing near does not overrule human freedom but enables it: "just as by moving natural causes He does not prevent their acts being natural, so by moving voluntary causes He does not deprive their actions of being voluntary: but rather is He the cause of this very thing in them; for He operates in each thing according to its own nature."[152] Under the influence of this immanent and immediate power that Aquinas calls charity, beings move beyond themselves to embrace others, without the risk of war, in an ever broadening expanse of convivial relations.[153]

The participationist character of Paul's soteriology is further illuminated by his account of Christ's atoning work, an account which also suggests how Christ funds resistance to capital. Again we begin with the caveat that Paul does not spell out in any systematic way a theory of atonement; nevertheless, what he says about Christ's atoning work is consonant with what developed in the church as the substitutionary view of atonement.

The basic outline of the substitutionary account is simple enough, and its Pauline echoes are evident (see Rom 1–5). Through the rebellion that is sin, humanity dishonors God and is thereby indebted in a manner that exceeds humanity's ability to satisfy. Into this situation steps Christ, who makes a sacrifice of atonement by his blood that satisfies the debt and

149. Aquinas, *Summa Theologica*, I.8.1.

150. In this regard it is worth noting that Deleuze fears thinking God will impose a transcendent measure on finitude. Aquinas notes that such could only happen with God thought in the univocal key, that God in analogical relation to creatures is not their measure (*Summa Theologica*, I.13.5).

151. Aquinas, *Summa Theologica*, I.8.1.

152. Ibid., I.83.1. As von Balthasar puts it, "He allows the individual his own will, his choice, his freedom. He does not impose himself from without, but works in the inner source of the created spirit, not as 'another' but as one exalted above all otherness . . . so immanent that he is indistinguishable from the natural spirit" (*Theology of History*, 102–3).

153. Note that the being of finite created beings in relation to other finite created beings is univocal, and their difference is finally quantitative. Two observations spring from this. First, what enables these differences to interact with one another in nonagonistic ways is precisely their mutual participation in God, whose call (in the sense of gathering and sending) both mediates and maintains those differences peaceably. Second, it is these differences in created being that underwrite what are often pejoratively called "hierarchies" among created beings, but when rightly understood and practiced, such relations are non-hierarchical precisely because hierarchy enacts not simply difference but distance, and the analogy of being maintains difference without distance insofar as it permits God an immediate intimacy with all created being—an intimacy that all created beings share with one another via their participation in Christ.

diverts God's wrath. In this way, just as through one person's sin all fell, so through Christ's substitutionary death on the cross, all may be redeemed. Redemption is a result of the payment of a debt incurred through sin by means of a compensatory death that satisfies divine justice.[154]

Actually, this account of the substitutionary atonement is not Paul's. Although it is popularly associated with Paul, it has little in common with the participationist soteriology Paul articulates. Furthermore, this rendition of the atonement does not offer hope of deliverance from capitalism, precisely because it underwrites an economic logic. This is to say, it does not oppose but upholds an order of circulation that operates in accord with a logic of debt, of juridical equity and restitution, of compensatory loss or penal suffering.[155]

From what has already been posited concerning Israel's election and the inclusion of the Gentiles, it is clear that Paul's soteriology is not economic. Likewise, as Badiou notes, suffering, death, and even the resurrection do not play an economic role for Paul. They are not economic compensations. And this holds for faith as well. It is not as if God is in heaven with an adding machine, saying, "Okay, works of the law proved too hard; I'll tell you what. I'll cut your bill in half. All you have to do is have faith."

Paul's participatory soteriology is finally aneconomic. Redemption does not finally rest on an exchange between God and humanity. Rather, redemption is about God's activity, divine fidelity, in which we are graciously invited to participate. It is about the Jewish Messiah and everyone's inclusion in Israel's election. Thus, redemption is not about completing an economic exchange; it is about ontological union. The Messiah's death on the cross was not a payment made to God that zeros out the divine ledger; rather, it is but a display of the depth of the divine love that invites all to join the dance of love that is the life of the blessed Trinity.

This is to say, Paul's soteriology is about the aneconomic bounty of God's goodness. God became human not to overcome a conflict within God caused by sin but so that humanity might be restored to the place of honor that God from the beginning intended for humanity, namely, participation in the divine life. Thus, when Paul says we fall short of God's glory, this is not the calling in of a debt, but an indication of what God desires to give us—a share in the divine glory.

154. The classic example is Aulén, *Christus Victor*.

155. Incidentally, this misreading of Paul's understanding of the atonement is of a piece with the misreading that casts the principal problem of Paul's theology in terms of faith and works. Both are symptomatic of reading Paul through an economic logic—what do we need to do to earn/pay for/acquire/consume salvation.

Paul's vision, from Israel's election to the Gentile inclusion to Jesus' death and resurrection, displays the plenitude of divine charity, of God's giving and giving again. God has always given to humanity in the form of love (creation, election, covenant), and when humanity rejected that gift, God gave again in the form of love incarnate, which is the Son.[156] Christ's work is that of giving again, of communicating God's love and grace (which has never ceased to flow) to humanity again (and again). The work of atonement is God in Christ bearing human rejection and extending the offer of grace again, thereby opening a path for humanity to recover beatitude. In this sense, Christ's faithfulness even to the point of death on the cross marks not a divine demand for retribution, but a divine refusal to hold our rebellion against us. As such, the atonement is not a propitiation offered to God but an expiation effected through Christ's recapitulation enacted for us in our sinful obstinacy.

The atonement is not about meeting the demands of an implacable justice, but about the instantiation of the gift that enables us to return to our source. It is about humanity's being taken up into the divine life of the Trinity through participation in Israel's election by means of Israel's Messiah. There is a sacrifice involved in this atoning work and there is a substitution. But these are not positioned in an economy of equity and retribution, but rather find their true meaning in the aneconomic order of divine plenitude and superabundance where life recovers its true modality of gift, donation, and unending generosity. Thus Christ's sacrifice becomes the donation of obedience and praise (the return of love) offered by the Son to the Father, and his role is substitutionary in that the Son offers the worship that we cannot.

In sum, Paul's gospel is the proclamation of the free gift, Messiah Jesus, that exceeds every debt, that explodes the very calculus of debt and retribution and sets in its place an aneconomic circulation of charity that recovers life in the mode of donation and lavish generosity. Here is the promise of true liberty from capital. As we share Israel's election in Christ, we are set free from an economy whose circulation is ruled by scarcity, debt, retribution and finally death. In Christ, we share in the abundant life of the Immortal, which is not the solitude of self-sufficiency, but life lived as donation, as the ceaseless giving (and receiving) of the gift of love. In Christ, a path is opened up beyond the iron cage of sin, of capitalism, and of the Hobbesian/Weberian world where both appear to rule. In Christ we are liberated from all that would prevent us from giving, that would interrupt the flow

156. Technically this is incorrect. As John Milbank points out, God does not give anything to anyone but establishes all that is as sheer gift. See Milbank, "Can a Gift Be Given?," 134–35.

of divine plenitude that continues through our enactment of love. We are freed from captivity to an economic order that would subject us to scarcity, competition, dominion, and debt, that would distort human desire into a proprietary and acquisitive power.

This is to say, the only way to defeat capitalism is to embrace the gift given in Christ, which is nothing less than the superabundance of grace that repositions our lives within the aneconomic order of love. So repositioned (redeemed) by love, we are enabled to give ourselves, to sacrifice without loss or end, even in the face of an economy that would eclipse gift and plenitude through the imposition of a regime of scarcity, debt, and dominion. Christ defeats capitalism as Christ heals human relations of their economic distortions and renews their circulation as donation, perpetual generosity. Capitalism is overcome as human relations are redeemed from the agony of competition and dominion and revived as the joyous conviviality of love that is the fruit of the proliferation of non-proprietary (that is, participatory) relations. Capitalism is defeated as fear is cast out—the fear of my neighbor that compels me to possess more tightly and acquire more compulsively, the fear that in giving I can only lose, the fear that death and the cross are the end of every sacrifice.

To go further, to articulate specific aneconomic practices, exceeds the parameters of this essay. Nevertheless, such practices can be gestured toward by recalling the rich tradition of the Works of Mercy in Judaism[157] and Christianity. At its fullest, this tradition might be called an instantiation of the divine economy that funds resistance to capitalism, a judgment shared by no less a figure than Adam Smith, who in *The Wealth of Nations* noted that the hospitality and charity of the church were very great, maintaining the poor of every kingdom. He goes on to lament that those practices "not only gave [the church] the command of a great temporal force, but increased very much the weight of their spiritual weapons." Indeed, he observed that the church constituted the most formidable obstacle to the civil order, liberty and happiness that the free market could provide. But, alas, he was glad to report that eventually improvements in "arts, manufactures, and commerce" not only conquered the great barons but undercut the church as well, weakening both its spiritual and temporal authority by rendering its charity merely economic, that is, more sparing and restrained.[158]

---

157. See, for example, Tamari, *The Challenge of Wealth*.
158. Smith, *Wealth of Nations*, Bk. V. Ch. 1. Pt. 3. Art. 3.

Like the scribe whom Jesus lauds as "not far from the kingdom," Badiou discerns in Paul's gospel an event that promises the end of capitalism. Yet, stitched as he is to modernity's defective faith, hope, and love, Badiou finally fails to rightly discern the nature of freedom that Paul declares is ours in Christ, settling instead for a dream of rivaling capital rather than overcoming it. And surely such would more accurately be called a nightmare.

CHAPTER 3

Only Jesus Saves: Toward a Theo-political Ontology of Judgment

For a time it was fashionable in some revolutionary circles to suggest that liberation was to be found only beyond the confines of ontology. If humanity was to overcome the afflictions of this present age then a genuinely revolutionary politics must eschew, indeed escape, the constrictions of ontology. Thus began the quest for a politics shorn of the master narratives of modernity, the grand ontological schemata peddled by the likes of Hegel, Marx, Freud, and their epigones. Now, however, on the far side of the end of history that has opened onto a horizon of terror, the dismissal of ontology is being reconsidered. While totalizing discourse may be anathema and practice celebrated, it is recognized that liberation hinges upon a prior ontology that maps the trajectories of the constitutive power of life.

For a time it was also popular to espouse a militant atheism, to insist that liberation, if it is to be truly liberative, reject appeals to transcendence (and its handmaid, theology) in accord with the received prejudice that transcendence was but a species of opiate. In recent times, this too has been reconsidered. Seeking to ward off a reductive materialism that cannot account for hope, would-be revolutionaries have sought to circumvent the antinomy of God and Man[1] by means of a material vitality (frequently equated with transcendence or theology) conceived in terms of identity, or the Other, or the event, and so forth.

There is much that is praiseworthy and right in the recent effort to recover ontology and overcome the divine-human problematic. The struggle against savage capitalism must be waged at the level of ontology, for capitalism advances not merely by economic victory but also by ontological

---

1. See Foucault, *The Order of Things*. Note that throughout this book I use the descriptor "God and Man" for the antinomy because it is how the authors I engage frame the matter, but the problematic patriarchal connotations of such a way of presenting the God/Human antinomy should not go unremarked.

Only Jesus Saves: Toward a Theo-political Ontology of Judgment

capture. And the divine-human antinomy must be overcome, lest resources of struggle be overlooked and matter be dismissed either as mechanical or inert, and so finally non-meaningful.

But, of course, not just any political ontology will do. Nor will just any effort to incorporate the vitality of transcendence in the material realm succeed in avoiding the dead ends on which modernity's engagement with the finite and infinite foundered, namely inert matter and immaterial theology. Indeed, I will argue that only a robustly theological ontology can found a politics of resistance and hope. However, even this remains insufficient. Today too many false friends invoke a kind of transcendence (even, in some cases "Christ") that can be little more than the figment of a Feuerbachian imagination. Thus, I argue specifically that only Jesus saves. The good news is that in Christ's offering of himself, a political ontology unfolds, a line of flight is opened up beyond the depredations of capitalist organization.

The foil for my argument is the work of Gilles Deleuze. His work garners such attention for several reasons. First, to Deleuze's substantial credit, he was never taken in by the ill-fated efforts to shed ontology. "The death of metaphysics or the overcoming of philosophy," he wrote with Guattari, "has never been a problem for us: it is just tiresome, idle chatter."[2] This is to say, he was among the earliest to recognize that the struggle against capitalism had to be waged at the level of ontology. Second, in a similar vein, before the futility of the modern *episteme* was widely acknowledged, he was laboring to articulate a hylozoism, an ontology that ascribed creative power to matter itself, which he called "pure immanence." While Deleuze's political ontology of pure immanence merits attention in its own right, there is yet a third reason for engaging his work. In a lesser known essay entitled "To Have Done with Judgment," Deleuze drives to the heart of the matter: resistance and liberation turn on the judgment of God. A corollary of the assertion that Jesus saves is that redemption is a gift that exceeds (although it does not arrive simply from outside) *humanum*, even the uber- or para-human.[3] As the venerable Fathers of Chalcedon rightly noted, redemption appears in the truly human, the true human, Jesus Christ. In the aforementioned essay,

---

2. Deleuze and Guattari, *What is Philosophy*, 9. In the course of this essay I refer to several works in which Deleuze collaborated with another author, the most notable example being his work with Félix Guattari. I do not attempt the futile task of sorting out the voices; instead I will simply refer to the texts as being Deleuze's. For Deleuze's remarks on his collaborative efforts, see Deleuze and Parnet, *Dialogues*, 16–19; and Deleuze and Guattari, *A Thousand Plateaus*, 3.

3. The concept "para human" is taken from Surin, "Liberation," 183. It is helpful because it points to Deleuze's disassembly of the very notion of a distinctly human subject. It gestures toward the tendency in Deleuze's work in the direction of the cyborg, which is a result of his critique of organic thought and organism.

Deleuze recognizes that salvation hinges upon Christ as the instantiation of divine judgment on the world. Of course, Deleuze holds that salvation is contingent upon *refusing* Christ and the judgment he embodies and enacts; liberation entails turning on God and God's judgment. And so the gauntlet has been thrown down.

In what follows I will suggest that only in Christ are we finally done with judgment and that Deleuze's vision of pure immanence, far from fleeing judgment can only subject us to the harshest judgment, one that may exceed even that of capital. Accompanying this effort will be an outline of how the practice of the end of judgment that Christ inaugurates opens a space of liberation from the bondage of savage capitalism.

I. The Metaphysics of Madness and Cruelty: Deleuze, Capitalism, and Desire

Because it sets the stage for the constructive argument so well, we begin with a brief consideration of Deleuze's political ontology of pure immanence. Precisely because it is a forthrightly *political* ontology, perhaps the best way into it is at the point of political struggle, which is to say, this survey begins with Deleuze's account of capitalism and desire.

Capitalism and Desire

As revolutionary currents crested and then were turned back in the late sixties and seventies, Deleuze devoted his intellectual acumen to re-envisioning revolutionary politics. Perceiving the inadequacy of both social democracy and actually existing socialisms as means of generating and sustaining resistance to and liberation from the advancing capitalist order, he began to explore new ways of conceiving human relations and revolutionary practice. The result of this effort was a history of capitalism and desire,[4] a history that suggested contemporary capitalism's dominion was not merely an economic affair—concerning modes of production, the efficient manipulation of labor, and the creation of wealth—but was also, indeed especially, ontological. This is to say, Deleuze develops an account of capitalism and its advent that displays its triumph as a matter of the successful capture and disciplining of desire, the constitutive human power. Capitalism, Deleuze

---

4. Deleuze and Guattari, *A Thousand Plateaus*. For a synopsis, see Surin, "Undecidable and the Fugitive," 102–13.

asserts, extends its dominion at the level of ontology, disciplining desire in accord with the golden rule of production for the market.

The recognition that capitalism advances in the ontological and not merely economic register threatens to undo much revolutionary practice. Indeed, Deleuze's history of capitalism is intended in part as a critique of visions of resistance to the capitalist order that amassed their resources on the political-economic front while ignoring the greater horizon on which the ontological struggle was waged (which Deleuze called the "state-form" and I unpack in more detail elsewhere as "technologies of desire"[5]). In particular, it was intended as a critique of then current revolutionary politics that were circumscribed and hence crippled by the "social unconscious"[6]—that ensemble of ideas, institutions, and social arrangements erected and propagated by state, party, class, etc., but attributed a certain fixed, unquestioned status as a "given." Specifically, Deleuze's account of capitalism and desire was meant to dislodge the unquestioned assumption that politics and therefore revolutionary struggle against capitalism are matters of statecraft—that social and political power rests in the state and therefore the key to change is seizing the state and wielding its power for revolutionary ends.

Of course, the suggestion that capitalism's victory is much more insidious and pervasive than mere control of things economic is not necessarily good news to those who seek to throw off its yoke, for it threatens to undo not only much but all revolutionary practice as the realization that by forming and shaping desire capital binds us—ontologically tempts us—to a pessimism that severs the nerve of liberative practice. That capitalism is indeed total, as its advocates proclaim, is not welcome news to those who would resist its advance. Yet, Deleuze certainly intends this analysis of capitalism and desire to aid revolutionary practice. An explanation entails turning more directly to his political ontology of pure immanence.

Pure Immanence

A helpful approach to Deleuze's political ontology passes through the archeology of knowledge he borrows from Foucault.[7] In *The Order of Things*, Foucault maps three *epistemes*: the classical, the modern, and what was for him a yet-to-be-disclosed future formation. According to Deleuze, the classical formation was characterized by infinity, perfection, the God-form.

---

5. See Bell, *Liberation Theology After the End of History*, 12–32.

6. The phrase "social unconscious" comes from Goodchild, *Deleuze and Guattari*.

7. Foucault, *The Order of Things*. For Deleuze's use of this, see his *Foucault*, 124–32.

Everything, including humanity, was cast on a continuum of development that strove to transcend the finite toward the infinite. With the advent of the modern *episteme*, humanity undergoes a mutation as transcendence is eschewed (and God-talk is subjected to suspicion) in favor of finitude. Now humanity is shaped by wrestling with the forces of finitude (life/biology, labour/political economy, and language/linguistics). Under the sign of modernity, the God-form gives way to the Man-form. The passing of the modern *episteme* delivers us to the site/time of Deleuze's work. This final *episteme* is characterized by the dissolution of the antinomies of God-Man or infinite-finite and the emergence of Nietzsche's superman—"the advent of a new form that is neither God nor man and which, it is hoped, will not prove worse than its two previous forms."[8] Here the preoccupations of modernity, namely the forms of finitude, give way to what Deleuze calls an "unlimited finity." This unlimited finity is marked by the proliferation of flows of aleatory, anarchic desire continuously effecting mutations and combinations, multiplicity and difference. It is the realization of a non-reductive materialism, an ontology of pure immanence that attributes to matter an inherent, intrinsic vitality or power. Appreciating the revolutionary potential of this ontology requires delving a bit deeper into what Deleuze calls the "micropolitics of desire."[9]

In constructing his ontology of aleatory desire, Deleuze draws on the medieval theologian, Duns Scotus, who erected an ontology around the univocity of being. Put simply, that being is univocal means that "being" has only one sense and is said in one and the same sense of everything of which it is said.[10] For medievals such as Scotus, this meant that God is deemed "to be" in the same univocal manner as creatures.[11] At first glance, this would appear to be a rather odd way to establish an ontology of difference that celebrates multiplicity, becoming, and flux. If being is univocal, then what could the difference between beings be? Deleuze answers, again echoing Scotus, that difference is a matter of degrees of power, or, rather, degrees

---

8. Deleuze, *Foucault*, 132.

9. Deleuze and Parnet, *Dialogues*, 17; Deleuze and Guattari, *Thousand Plateaus*, 203.

10. Deleuze, "Seminar Session on Scholasticism & Spinoza."

11 For a fuller account of Scotus's theology and its consequences, see Pickstock, *After Writing*, 121–66. For Deleuze's treatment of Scotus and the emergence of the univocity of being along the trajectory of Scotus, Spinoza, and Nietzsche, see Deleuze, *Difference and Repetition*, 35–42. For a helpful narrative of Deleuze's philosophical development in this regard, which unfortunately does little with Scotus, see Hardt, *Gilles Deleuze*.

of desire.¹² Everything is desire, flows of desire. What distinguishes desire, what renders desire distinct, singular, is a matter of degree. Univocal being, desire, is differentiated by degrees of intensity. "Between a table, a little boy, a little girl, a locomotive, a cow, a god, the difference is solely one of degree of power in the realization of one and the same being."¹³

What renders the univocity of being politically potent for Deleuze is the additional fact that this univocal being, the flux of desire that constitute the material realm, is productive. Production constitutes the immanent principle of desire. Thus, desire, according to Deleuze, should not be mistaken for a lack, deficiency, or absence.¹⁴ Desire is not a desire for something; it is not a matter of acquiring or grasping an object. It is not about possession. Nor is it a matter of meeting needs or seeking pleasure; this too would be a lack. Rather, desire produces; it gives. It works. It creates.¹⁵ Desire is a positive force, an aleatory movement that neither destroys nor consumes but endlessly creates new connections with others, embraces difference, and fosters a proliferation of relations between fluxes of desire.

The world, then, is constituted by flows of intensities of desire. The world is constituted as various machines (social machines and their formations of power; semiotic machines and their regimes of signs) capture and organize flows of desire into bodies and institutions and languages. For example, society is an assemblage of desire. A given society or social formation is nothing other than productive desire under determinate conditions. The subject, likewise, is an assemblage of desire. The subject is an assemblage of intensities of desire; it is the result of the capture of desire by a particular regime of subjectification.

---

12. Deleuze, "Seminar Session on Scholasticism and Spinoza," 4.

13. Ibid., 4.

14. Deleuze and Parnet, *Dialogues*, 91; see also Deleuze and Guattari, *Thousand Plateaus*, 154.

15. By positing the ontological primacy of productive desire, Deleuze runs the risk of sounding like a vulgar Marxist who reduces everything to the economic forces of production and their shadows. Indeed, the emphasis on production resonates with the traditional Marxist focus on the modes of production, a focus renewed in Marxist circles in the 1960s and 1970s. However, Deleuze's account of productive desire does not equate, in any uncomplicated way, productive desire with the modes of production. Rather, desire produces the modes of production. Productive desire is what makes the modes possible. Drawing the facile equation "productive desire equals modes of production" overlooks the way in which Deleuze's ontology of desire collapses any distinction between a productive base and a nonproductive superstructure. Everything is desire, hence everything is productive: productions of productions, productions of consumptions. The economy produces, but so too does culture, and religion, and the family, and so forth. See Deleuze and Guattari, *Anti-Oedipus*, 4.

We are now in a position to apprehend the revolutionary potential of Deleuze's political ontology of pure immanence. Every society, every social formation, every subject is constituted by flows of desire, differentials of intensity, that render every assemblage of desire inherently tenuous and every capture congenitally uncertain. Simply by virtue of its being the intrinsically productive, creative, anarchic force that it is, desire is antagonistic to every attempt to capture and assemble it. Univocal, productive desire, reveling in the ceaseless proliferation of new connections and relations, resists any and every end or *telos*, any and every organization and assembly. Resistance and revolution, therefore, are always possible. At any moment desire may discover a line of flight, a crack in a given order and explode it. Every organization, every social formation, every subjectivity is thereby rendered a contingent, unstable assemblage, whose duration is uncertain—lasting a day, a season, a year, a life—and order is nothing but a temporary check on disorder; stability nothing but variation within tenuous limits.[16]

Accordingly, the recognition that capitalism's dominion is extended by ontological capture is not grounds for despair. To the contrary, Deleuze's analysis discloses capitalism's inescapable vulnerability. That capitalism is an always unstable assemblage of flows of anarchic, aleatory desire should reassure all who seek the end of capitalism's reign. Likewise, that power is not finally contained in a center such as the state but is dispersed across the *socius* is reason for hope insofar as it means that resistance can begin at any place and may erupt at any moment. In other words, that capitalism is an ontological and not merely economic discipline does not mean that its victory is in fact total; rather the ontological nature of the struggle broadens opportunities for resistance insofar as it opens up a plethora of fronts on which capitalism may be contested. Deleuze's political ontology opens a horizon of micro politics, of micro revolutions. How such politics may usher in the end of capitalism is our next concern.

Madness and Cruelty

Desire is restless. As the anarchic, creative force that it is, it resists every capture, it eludes every end. And this applies to all desire, not merely to some specifically "revolutionary" desire or privileged subject (generals, workers, academics, the poor). "Desire" writes Deleuze, "is revolutionary in its own right."[17] Even now, in the midst of the triumph of global capital, desire continues to resist (thereby constituting a "war-machine"), eluding

---

16. Massumi, *User's Guide*, 58–59.
17. Deleuze and Guattari, *Anti-Oedipus*, 116.

capture (thus called "fugitive"), seeking cracks in the system and creating lines of flight (hence, named "the nomad").

Thus, revolution, as Deleuze envisions it, is a matter nurturing these flows of desire, encouraging desire's becoming a war-machine, fugitive, nomad.[18] But this revolution has a peculiar characteristic. In keeping with the productive, creative nature of desire, escape from capitalism is not a matter of destruction but of creation, addition, intensification. Liberation is a matter of overwhelming capitalism's ability to capture and adapt desire to the axiomatic of production for the market. Thus, the path beyond capitalism is not one that destroys capitalism so much as it exceeds it. Revolution, in other words, is a matter of achieving absolute deterritorialization. Capitalism advances by means of a pincer movement of deterritorialization and reterritorialization. Capitalism deterritorializes desire, releasing it from prior social formations and codes, only to reterritorialize desire by disciplining it in accord with the axiomatic of production for the market. Hence, although capitalism does liberate desire from various assemblages, it does not permit desire to attain genuine freedom—the anarchic, creative, experimental movement that is the consequence of absolute deterritorialization and that Deleuze labels "schizophrenia." Instead, capitalism's profound potential for absolute deterritorialization is always curtailed by its concomitant reterritorialization of desire.

In its voracious deterritorializing, observes Deleuze, capitalism is a form a madness, and as a way beyond the madness of capitalism, he proposes intensifying the madness, continuing the process of deterritorialization, intensifying the proliferation of aleatory flows of desire, until every order and organization is simply overwhelmed and implodes: schizoid desire, pure *autopoesis*.[19]

At this point, we might ask, but what has this to do with judgment? How does this political ontology of pure immanence, schizoid desire, turn on the practice of judgment, and in particular, on the judgment of God? In the essay "To Have Done with Judgment" Deleuze presents the case against judgment and, in particular, against the Christian doctrine of the judgment of God. There he sketches the development of a "doctrine of judgment" from the ancient Greeks through modernity. In its infancy, Deleuze observes, the doctrine of judgment declared that the gods gave lots to men, and that men, depending on their lots, were fit for some particular form or end.[20] Under this early regime, judgment confines one to one's appointed lot or form and

18. See ibid., 246.
19. Ibid., 373.
20. Deleuze, *Essays Critical and Clinical*, 128.

punishment falls swiftly on deviance or transgression. Christianity soon overtook the Greek doctrine and intensified its effect. Under Christianity, "we are no longer debtors to the gods through forms or ends, but have become in our entire being the infinite debtors of a single God."[21] By this Deleuze means that with the arrival of Christianity, judgment becomes total, infinite, eternal. It is total and infinite in the sense that the debt under which we finite beings toil is now raised to the level of infinity, thereby rendering us totally and infinitely in debt. With the Christian transformation of judgment, there is no longer any sanctuary from judgment; even the restricted space of a lot or form that previously offered some shelter is foreclosed as judgment itself becomes our lot. Christ's appearance announces "nothing is left but judgment" and even the apparent acquittal that is effected through him is in actuality but an "unlimited postponement" that ironically extends judgment to the infinite degree.[22]

What renders such judgment problematic, according to Deleuze, is that it is synonymous with the capture and confinement of desire. The judgment of God, in particular, has served the West as one of the principal paradigms for and instigators of the organization of desire. "Judgment implies a veritable organization of the bodies through which it acts . . . and the judgment of God is nothing other than the power to organize to infinity."[23] Judgment restrains and restricts desire, blocking the proliferation of new connections and relations between flows of desire by subjecting it to transcendent norms or values. In the end, Deleuze declares, "judgment prevents the emergence of any new modes of existence."[24]

As an alternative to judgment Deleuze develops a "system of cruelty." What distinguishes this system from judgment is not that whereas the latter hinges on debt, the former is founded on the forgiveness of debt or debt relief. To the contrary, the system of cruelty too functions according to a logic of debt. Indeed, Deleuze praises Nietzsche for having recognized that exchange between bodies is necessarily a creditor-debtor relation.[25] Rather, what differentiates the system of cruelty is that its debt-cycle is strictly *finite* in scope. One promises and becomes indebted not to a god but to a partner, and redress is obtained through finite relations in the course of time. This, says Deleuze, amounts to a justice "according to which bodies are marked by each other, and the debt is inscribed directly

21. Ibid., 129.
22. Ibid., 129, 127.
23. Ibid., 130.
24. Ibid., 135.
25. Ibid., 128.

on the body following the *finite blocks* that circulate."[26] Under this system, not only is the judgment of God abolished, but even the judgment of man is dissolved as the law is ceaselessly displaced through the vendetta that draws blood or pays with it. This merely finite vendetta Deleuze identifies as combat. Combat, however, should not be equated with a will to destroy or dominate. Rather, the combat of cruel justice is a matter of "a powerful, nonorganic vitality that supplements force with force, and enriches whatever it takes hold of."[27] The example he gives is that of the obstinate, stubborn, indomitable will of a baby—one whose relation to its surroundings is sheer affective, impersonal vitality.

At this point, the connection between the madness that exceeds capitalism and the cruelty that would have done with the judgment of God is apparent. Judgment is but a form of control that would bind desire, just as capitalism disciplines desire for the sake of the market. Both judgment and capitalism constrain the anarchic vitality of desire. And the madness of cruelty or the cruelty of madness is desire released from every such discipline, every such order or organization.

Beyond Madness and Cruelty

We are compelled, however, to ask, are madness and cruelty the way beyond the madness and cruelty of capitalism? Or does such a revolutionary course, such madness intensified, finally collapse in the black hole of nihilism, where vitality becomes necrophilia and an absolute violence is unleashed? Perhaps madness is simply madness and the cruelty that would be done with the judgment of God simply cruelty? Perhaps schizoid desire is nothing but the far side of the madness that is savage capitalism, which makes it that much more savage, and the justice that would be guided neither by God nor human law but only the force of love and hate, the highest injustice?

Deleuze, of course, would vehemently reject such conclusions and counter that his vision is one of affirmation and creativity, not dominion and destruction. Indeed, it was this affirmative desire that prompted him to begin his political ontology with a rupture, with a certain "capture of being."[28] As noted previously, Deleuze recovers from Scotus an ontology of

26. Ibid., 127–28.
27. Ibid., 133.
28. The claim that "politics precedes being" is an instantiation of the univocity of being because it implies a distinction similar to Scotus's "formal distinction," marking a virtual reality between essence and existence, a possible that is not yet actual, a possible that through an act of the will (politics) becomes actual (being). See Deleuze's

the univocity of being, which is a rupture with the Thomistic *analogia entis* or "analogy of being," and is a capture of being in the sense that it renders being knowable, calculable, an "object." The appeal of the univocity of being for Deleuze is precisely the way it secures difference (as degree, intensity) and the interplay of difference that he characterizes as love, joy, playing, and dancing by releasing it from the gaze of a God who imposes a transcendent norm or hierarchical order on being.[29]

Yet, Deleuze cannot get to where he wants to go, starting from where he starts; consequently, his madness is distinguishable only as a difference of degree from the madness that is savage capitalism, and his justice is indistinguishable from terror. It is as if Deleuze has forgotten his own insight—that capitalism's victory is ontological. Hence, by beginning with the univocity of being, he has already suffered ontological defeat. He has already conceded the crucial capture, the capture of being, that leaves desire vulnerable to the ravages of capitalism.

This is the case because relations of desire in the univocal mode can finally only degenerate into the violence of conflict and conquest.[30] In rejecting the analogy of being that preserves ontological difference while nevertheless permitting participation of one in another, Deleuze is left with discrete singularities for whom relations are always external and never constitutive of identity.[31] As a consequence, these singularities can only relate to one another through the formal mechanism of contract (between producer and consumer, between victor and vanquished). Once captured in the univocal code, singularities become "objects" and relations between objects are a matter of capture and possession—combat and sheer assertion. This follows from the fact that the discrete individuals Deleuze celebrates, precisely as discrete individuals, are intrinsically unrelated on account of the absolute and unbridgeable difference (of degree or intensity) that distinguishes them and, hence, they can only form relations either by forcing themselves on

---

discussion of Scotus in *Difference and Repetition*, 39. I owe the phrase "capture of being" to Alliez, *Capital Times*, 197.

29. Deleuze and Guattari, *Anti-Oedipus*, 347; Deleuze, *Nietzsche and Philosophy*, 194; Deleuze, *Expressionism in Philosophy*, 246; Deleuze, *Spinoza*, 126.

30. My understanding of the impact Scotus and the univocity of being relies heavily upon the treatments of Alliez, *Capital Times*; Pickstock, *After Writing*; and Schmitz, "Is Liberalism Good Enough?," 86–104.

31. The proliferation of relations in Deleuze would appear to be more accurately described as a proliferation of "expressions." Desire enters into relations as it expresses itself. The other in this situation resembles a canvass upon which desire expresses itself. Furthermore, the extent to which univocal desire can be genuinely creative is questionable, since new relations are only the old with more added. The already given is simply rearranged.

others (by piercing the sacrosanct veil of analogically unmediable difference and seizing the other) or by entering into a contract with the other (which as a purely external or formal relation rooted in the aleatory coincidence of the calculi of discrete individuals' wills, remains a kind of possession).

The inescapable violence of Deleuze's vision rooted in univocity is perhaps easier to ascertain when approached from the angle of desire's being shorn of any teleology. The development of the univocity of being sundered notions of the good, of love, of justice from the active power of being.[32] Thus it is no surprise when Deleuze de-finalizes desire, casting it as an experimental, anarchic force that defies every *telos* and resists every organization. The question is on what grounds does he assert that when this self-creating, self-asserting desire is released from every organization, the resultant flows of liberated desire will enter into joyful, harmonious relations? From whence cometh the confidence that the flows of desire, deprived of any shared end and barred from analogous participation in the other (which entails desire be understood not merely as assertive or creative, but also as receptive), will not simply collide in absolute war? How does he generate the innocence to assert that justice left in the hands of individuals will not quickly usher in an age of terror, where the only limit to the marking of bodies and drawing of blood (be it in the form of justice or injustice) is finite death? And would this not be the harshest judgment? As was perhaps most famously pointed out by Thomas Hobbes, the sort of nominalist/voluntarist account of desire that Deleuze advocates requires a teleology (whether divinely given or imposed by a secular state) to avoid a state of *bellum omnis contra omnem*. Lacking a shared end and ontologically incapable of entering into non-possessive relations, univocal desire does indeed resemble a "war-machine" and life a cruel combat that is made all the more cruel by insisting that it be called just. Deleuze's assertion otherwise becomes a plea for the miraculous,[33] which remains eternally unanswered because, transcendence having been banished, the heavens are empty. Thus, Deleuze's championing of assertive, creative desire looks more like the advancement of arbitrariness, and portends not the proliferation of joy and harmony but the endless spilling of blood and shedding of tears.

Having embraced the univocity of being, Deleuze is delivered to an account of desire that in the name of securing difference ensures that relations of desire will be conflictual. In this way, Deleuze does not escape capitalist discipline, for capitalism has so construed the market that it too mediates all relations of desire agonistically. Capitalist discipline distorts desire into

32. Alliez, *Capital Times*, 211–12; Pickstock, *After Writing*, 157.
33. Pickstock, *After Writing*, 132.

a competitive force—competing for resources, for market share, for a living wage, for the time for friendship and family, for inclusion in the market, and so forth. Of course, Deleuze's capitulation to savage capitalism comes as no surprise, given that, as his analysis masterfully shows, capitalism is erected on the same ontology of univocal desire shorn of any particular *telos*.

In the end, then, Deleuze's vision does not dismantle capitalist discipline. But this was never really his goal; his objective was to envision a way beyond capitalism and there is a sense in which he has accomplished this. The revolution of schizoid desire, of absolute deterritorialization, promises to surpass capitalism in the sense that were it to succeed, we would be delivered to a world that exceeds even the savagery of savage capitalism. *Bellum omnis contra omnem*. Absolute war. After all, there is some truth to the long standing claim that capitalism has a pacifying effect. Deleuze's revolution would leave us without even this, and as terrifying as capitalism is, this is a truly hideous prospect.

If Deleuze finally does not free us from madness, neither does he succeed in being done with the judgment of God. Far from being done with it, he only sets it aside, leaving us to our own deadly devices, to the (in)justice of our loves and hates. But there is a judgment of God and (fortunately) we are not left to our own devices. And there is a way to be done with that judgment; although that occurs not by setting it aside but only by passing through it. And it is in this passing through that desire discovers the hope of escaping the cruel madness that is capitalism. To the hope that is ours by having done with the judgment of God we now turn.

II. Christ and the Judgment of God

The "doctrine of judgment" Deleuze sets forth, which reaches its climax with debt being extended infinitely and judgment totalized in Christianity, is a truly horrific spectacle. In this it is of a piece with the exposition of the Christian practice of judgment, confession, Foucault offers, which reveals a logic of torture, death, and self-destruction.[34] Confronted with such an account, the temptation is to dismiss it out of hand as a caricature of Christian theology. After all, one might note, in vain does one search the corpus of Deleuze's work for sustained and vigorous engagement with orthodox Christian thought. Such a dismissal, however, would be disingenuous, for the ethos of debt and judgment he portrays permeates significant segments of the Christian imagination. Moreover, as a host of modern and contemporary theologians will attest, such a logic of infinite debt and judgment

---

34. Foucault, "About the Beginning of the Hermeneutics of the Self," 215.

does ring true to the orthodox heart of the Christian faith. In particular, such a logic finds a prominent niche in the Christian imagination by way of St. Anselm's (in)famous treatment of the atonement of Christ. Indeed, in his treatise *Cur Deus Homo*, the doctrine of divine judgment constructed around an infinite debt is laid out with such stark clarity that one cannot help but wonder if, although never mentioned, Deleuze had Anselm in mind when he set out to have done with the judgment of God.

Cur Deus Homo *Revisited*

In his treatise, Anselm sets forth how the judgment of God is brought to bear on the world through Christ. In summary form, the well-known argument unfolds something like this: As creatures, we owe the Creator perfect obedience. The failure to render this obedience is an offense against God's honor, thereby increasing the debt infinitely, since the one offended against is infinite. Because God must uphold justice, God cannot simply remit the debt. Indeed, humanity is required to restore more than was taken in order to make satisfaction. But, alas, finite humanity possesses nothing with which it might satisfy this infinite debt. In this circumstance, only a God-man will do: one who as God can make an infinite payment and who as man needs to. Thus, Christ emerges to pay the infinite debt on the cross with a compensatory death that satisfies divine justice. As a result, anyone who has faith in him, and abides in that faith, may avoid the infinite judgment of God.

Here we have all the components the doctrine of judgment that Deleuze set forth: totalized judgment (creatures subjected to a regime of perfect obedience); a debt elevated to infinity; and an acquittal become unlimited postponement—in the sense that a loss of faith entails the reinstatement of the regime of judgment. If this is indeed what Christ is about, then there is no escaping Deleuze's judgment. Nor will it do to invoke a heterodox current of the Christian tradition, for such a move would only be an evasion of and not a refutation of Deleuze's charge. Deleuze must be confronted head on. Does an orthodox understanding of atonement, as articulated by Anselm, embody a doctrine of judgment founded on the logic of infinite debt and omnipresent judgment?

Recently, theologians such as David Hart and Hans Urs von Balthasar[35] have offered readings of Anselm that suggest, precisely to the extent that his account of the sacrifice and death of Christ on the cross has been used to underwrite a doctrine of infinite and totalized judgment, it has been

---

35. What follows draws heavily on Hart, "A Gift Exceeding Every Debt," 333–49; Balthasar, *Glory of the Lord*, 2:211–59; Milbank, "Forgiveness and Incarnation," 92–128.

distorted—its aneconomic logic of charity, plenitude, and ceaseless generosity transposed into an alien and merely economic logic that trades on debt, lack, and loss. This is to say, read rightly Anselm displays the beauty of sacrifice, of life in the mode of donation and gift, which promises to free us from the horror of the merely economic, from the terror of capitalism and the cruelty of justice.

Read rightly, Anselm's account of the atonement is finally not economic. It is not a matter of debt, of juridical equity and restitution, of compensatory loss or penal suffering. As Anselm says, in accord with the standard precepts of medieval theology, God needs nothing and no necessity compels God to act as God does in redeeming us from sin.[36] Likewise, God does not demand bloodshed, divine justice is not in conflict with divine mercy, and God's power and dignity cannot be diminished by human insurrection.[37] That Anselm continues to be read in terms of this economic logic (debt, equity, retribution) and these distinctions (justice versus forgiveness) reflects less the deficiencies of his Augustinian vision of sacrifice than it does the way we modern readers of Anselm have been disciplined by an economy that functions in accordance with such logic and such distinctions.[38]

Shorn of such economic distortions, Anselm's account of the atonement reveals the splendor of the aneconomic bounty of God's goodness. God became human not to satisfy an infinite debt, but so that humanity might be restored to the place of honor that God from the beginning intended for humanity, namely, participation in the divine life. The injury to God's honor that is effected by sin is a matter of the absence of humanity from full communion with its creator.[39] Thus, rightly understood, God's honor is not a barrier to humanity's reconciliation with God, one that creates an infinite debt, rather it is the origin of God's free act to provide humanity with a path to renewed communion.[40] The atonement, the judgment of God, is not about a juristic reckoning stretched to infinity, but ontological union.[41] As

36. Balthasar, *Glory of the Lord*, 2:240, 245, 250, 246.

37. Ibid., 2:247; Hart, "Gift Exceeding Every Debt," 343, 349.

38. Note Milbank in "Forgiveness and Incarnation" suggests that Anselm does at times attempt too much and thus is guilty of occasionally slipping in the direction of this economic logic. He goes on to argue that one must read Anselm aesthetically, which is precisely what von Balthasar does—one of the sections of his treatment of Anselm is labeled, "aesthetic reason."

39. Balthasar, *Glory of the Lord*, 2:248.

40. In this regard, Alasdair MacIntyre notes that with the loss of a thick conception of the common good, the notion "honor" degenerates into merely a "badge of Aristocratic status." See his *After Virtue*, 232.

41. Thus we can see why sheer negative "pardon," although possible as Anselm and others such as Aquinas make clear, is nevertheless not "fitting." And it explains Anselm's

such, it displays not the scarcity of finitude in the face of the infinite but the plenitude of divine charity, of God's giving and giving again. God has always given to humanity in the form of love, and when humanity rejected that gift, God gave again in the form of love incarnate, which is the Son.[42] Christ's work is that of giving again, of communicating God's love and grace (which has never ceased to flow) to humanity again (and again). The work of atonement is God in Christ bearing human rejection and extending the offer of grace again, thereby opening a path for humanity to recover beatitude. In this sense, Christ's faithfulness even to the point of death on the cross marks not a divine demand for retribution, not the settling of a debt, but a divine refusal to hold our rebellion against us. (In this sense, *pace* Deleuze, the Book of Life is the book of *life* precisely because it does not record debt.[43])

The atonement is not about infinite debt and totalized judgment, but about the instantiation of the gift that enables us to return to our source. It is about humanity's being taken up into the divine life of the Trinity through participation in Christ. There is a sacrifice involved in this atoning work and there is a substitution. But these are not positioned in an economy of debt and retribution; rather they find their true meaning in the aneconomic order of divine plenitude and superabundance where life recovers its true modality of gift, donation, and unending generosity. Thus Christ's sacrifice becomes the donation of obedience and praise (the return of love) offered by the Son to the Father, and his role is substitutionary in that the Son offers the worship that we cannot. As Hart explains,

> [A]s Christ's sacrifice belongs not to an economy of credit and exchange, but to the trinitarian motion of love, it is given entirely as gift, and must be seen as such: a gift given when it should not have been needed to be given again, by God, and at a price that *we*, in our sin, imposed upon *him*. As an entirely divine action, Christ's sacrifice merely draws creation back into the eternal motion of divine love for which it was fashioned. The violence that befalls Christ belongs to our order of justice, an order overcome by his sacrifice, which is one of peace.[44]

---

intriguing claim that he would prefer to be in hell without sin than heaven with sin. Sheer negative pardon would result in humanity gaining entrance to heaven but still in need and thus devoid of blessedness. As a result, heaven would be hell. Conversely, hell with complete virtue would be heaven. See Balthasar, *The Glory of the Lord*, 249.

42. Technically this is incorrect. As John Milbank points out, God does not give anything to anyone but establishes all that is as sheer gift. See "Can a Gift Be Given?" 134–35.

43. Deleuze, *Essays Critical and Clinical*, 128.

44. Hart, "Gift Exceeding Every Debt," 348.

In sum, God became human as a gift that exceeded every debt, that exploded the very calculus of debt and retribution and set in its place an aneconomic order of charity that recovers life in the mode of donation and lavish generosity. In Christ, we are done with the judgment of God; in Christ we reach the end of judgment.

True God and True Human

It is worthwhile to linger a bit longer over Christ's atoning work, for Christ's enactment of the judgment of God as the end of judgment is the ground of our hope for being free of the bondage of capital. Previously it was noted that contemporary efforts to articulate a political ontology could be mapped in terms of several *epistemes*. Deleuze, we will recall, positioned his work beyond the antinomy of the infinite and finite, God and Man, such that the vitality of transcendence is reclaimed for the material via the pure immanence of the uber- or, more accurately, para-human. In turn, my critique suggested that the effort to articulate a pure immanence on the basis of the univocity of being could only deliver us to the worst violence, the harshest judgment. Now it is time to indicate how Christ, and only Christ, overcomes the antinomy of God and Man in a manner that is full of the promise of freedom, which is to say, that neither sacrifices the finite to the infinite (a concern that drives both Deleuze's critique of the "doctrine of judgment" and his advocacy of a schizo desire beyond every order and organization) nor abandons the finite to the agony of unlimited, if still only finite, combat and cruelty.

Following the Apostle Paul's lead when he wrote, "God was in Christ reconciling the world to himself" (2 Cor 5:19), at Chalcedon (451 CE) the church stated once and for all that what it professed when it professed Jesus Christ is precisely that in this particular person the antinomy of God and Man that Foucault traced has been definitively overcome.[45] Jesus Christ, the fathers of the church declared, is perfect in divinity and perfect in humanity, truly God and truly human. In him are found two natures which undergo no confusion, no change, no division, no separation. Elaborating on this, they state that at no point was the difference between the natures taken away through the union, but rather the property of both natures is preserved and comes together into a single person and a single subsistent being; he is not parted or divided into two persons, but is one and the same only-begotten Son, God, Word, Lord Jesus Christ.

45. The text of the Definition of Chalcedon can be found in Leith, *Creeds of the Churches*, 35–36. Translation altered slightly.

Here the antinomy of God and Man is overcome, not by a defeat of one at the hand of the other nor by means of a synthesis that creates a hybrid (although in the long argument preceding and following the council, such victories were attempted and such mutants proposed). God and humanity (two *ousias*) come together in one person (*hypostasis*), Jesus. Moreover, here God and humanity are joined in the unsurpassable closeness and intimacy ("no division, no separation") of a single life ("he is not parted or divided... Jesus Christ") and they are united in a manner that nevertheless preserves the difference ("no confusion, no change . . . properties of both natures preserved") peaceably. Here is the interplay of difference without agony, combat, conflict—a difference that in Deleuze's univocal pure immanence can only be imaginary, virtual.[46]

More needs to be said, however, about Jesus's overcoming of the divine-human antinomy, if it is to surmount the inevitable rejoinder, one that Deleuze would surely issue, that this orthodoxy is but another form of organization, another transcendental theory that descends from on high to enclose all of reality in its grasp by means of a divine discipline. Does this not reveal salvation to be just another totalizing discourse that imposes a fixed, transcendental template (order) on an unsuspecting finitude? If so, then the definition of Chalcedon notwithstanding, Christ is but the instantiation of the defeat of the human/finite at the hands of the infinite and no freedom is forthcoming.

A response entails attending to the implications of Chalcedon's claim that redemption comes through the particular person Jesus. That redemption happens in this particular person means that redemption is not a generalized state of affairs that is ineluctably happening to us.[47]

Redemption is not a generalized process, a fixed order that is always already around all of us acting on us all, to which Jesus is uniquely transparent, as some sort of symbol or signifier, or which Jesus manifests in an unusual degree, as an example or leader, perhaps. Although such general theories of salvation, with corresponding images of Jesus as symbol or exemplar, are popular in some theological tributaries, it finds no repose in the orthodox Christology of Chalcedon, where salvation is not associated with a generalized process but with the goings on of a particular person. Said differently, redemption is not the capture of finitude within a given totality; it is not the setting of finitude in its assigned place according to a predetermined, transcendental order of fixed essences. Rather, redemption is what

---

46. Univocal difference is not a difference of being, thus it is virtual. On this, see Smith, "Doctrine of Univocity," 179.

47. Yeago, "Jesus of Nazareth and Cosmic Redemption," 177.

happens in the life, death, and resurrection of one particular person, Jesus Christ. This is to say, redemption is tied to the one whom von Balthasar, calls the "concrete universal."[48] The particular, concrete human, Jesus, by reason of his being the same person who is the second person of the Trinity, is of universal significance. And this significance is made known—redemption is incarnate—not by means of a transcendental capture or overcoding that is laid upon us all simply by virtue of our being finite beings who live in the inescapable shadow of the infinite but rather as finite beings enter into relation with this concrete, particular one. In other words, redemption is not imposed from above or outside the contingencies of history but rather unfolds in the midst of, by means of, the contingent encounters of particulars with this particular one named Jesus. In this regard, it is worth recalling Anselm's assertion that no necessity compels God as a reminder that redemption does not proceed by a fixed organization but by the contingent proliferation of relations with Christ in history.

Granting all of this, there is still the question of freedom. Even if redemption is not imposed from above, a fixed template pressed onto humanity, it remains to be seen how this redemption does not entail a loss of freedom, and so is still a defeat of the finite by the infinite. Does it not remain an order, organization or discipline that restricts the movement of desire, even if it advances only immanently, contingently?

As previously indicated, the definition of Chalcedon is careful to state that the redemption effected in Christ's person does not destroy the *ousia* therein united. In him is found true humanity and it is not lost in its being brought near to divinity. In Christ, finitude is neither lost nor eclipsed but provided a new way of existing (of which Deleuze's "unlimited finity" is finally only a parody). In Christ, finitude is lived in a new way. In particular, and of particular relevance to the matters at hand, in Christ finitude can be lived peaceably. "My peace I give to you" (John 14:27 NRSV). In Christ, finitude no longer need be scarred by agony, conflict, combat. Rather, finitude can be lived in peace with God and one another (see Eph. 2:14).

At this point, in order to spell out how this new way of living finitude does not eclipse freedom but instantiates it (Gal. 5:1), it is necessary to supplement Chalcedon with Aquinas on the *analogia entis*, the analogy of being. Deleuze embraced the univocity of being in the name of nurturing difference and freedom. Yet as Aquinas lays out the analogy and univocity of being in the *Summa*, it becomes clear that the univocity of being cannot preserve difference, at least it cannot preserve difference peaceably, which means that it cannot preserve freedom. Either univocal being does not

---

48. Balthasar, *Explorations in Theology*, 1:170.

Only Jesus Saves: Toward a Theo-political Ontology of Judgment 93

bring beings closer (insofar as differences can only be maintained by the distance of differing degrees of intensity) or it dissolves difference altogether (as univocal beings meet they melt together, thus effacing difference). The only mediating position for univocal being is conflict, competition, combat. Univocal being can only maintain difference-in-relation by means of a friction (agony) created between different degrees of intensity that necessarily mediates the encounter or clash of otherwise univocal beings.

In contrast, the analogy of being maintains difference in a way that allows differences to be drawn into a relation while preserving (and in the case of the human, enhancing) the freedom of both. Only the analogy of being permits differences to draw near in a mode other than competition and conflict such that in this embrace of intimacy neither being nor its properties are lost (recall Chalcedon, or the Thomistic principle that grace does not destroy but perfects nature). How is this so? Aquinas's account of the analogy of being begins with what at first glance would appear to be a univocal claim, namely that all created beings participate in God, who is the first and universal principle of all being. This, however, is not tantamount to univocal pantheism, for Aquinas is quick to point out that God's presence to all things is not as a univocal agent[49]; rather, the relation is one of analogy.[50] What Aquinas accomplishes by positing a qualitative (analogy) and not quantitative (univocal) difference of being, is the drawing near of God and humanity without competition. This is the case because the analogy of being does not posit God and humanity on a single plane, with the result that they are locked in a sort of zero-sum competition as the act or will of one delimits the freedom of act/will of the other. Instead, the analogy of being permits God an immediate intimacy unavailable to univocal being.[51] It enables God to draw nearer to all things that they are to themselves (to paraphrase Augustine). Thus, "God is in all things, and innermostly . . . No action of an agent, however, powerful it may be, acts at a distance, except through a medium. But it belongs to the great power of God that he acts immediately on all things. Hence nothing is distant from him."[52] Moreover, this immediate intimacy does not compromise finite freedom (if it did, this

---

49. Aquinas, *Summa Theologica*, I.4.2.

50. Ibid., I.4.3.

51. This is so because were a univocal being to have an unmediated relation, that is, an immediate relation with another univocal being, the "otherness" or difference would dissolve, rendering them one. At which point it no longer makes sense to speak of a relation between different beings. There would no longer be difference or beings, only one being.

52. Aquinas, *Summa Theologica*, I.8.1.

would mark a fall to univocity).⁵³ For God is present to things according to their mode of being.⁵⁴ Thus, God's drawing near does not overrule human freedom but enables it: "just as by moving natural causes He does not prevent their acts being natural, so by moving voluntary causes He does not deprive their actions of being voluntary: but rather is He the cause of this very thing in them; for He operates in each thing according to its own nature."⁵⁵ Under the influence of this immanent and immediate power that Aquinas calls charity—love—desire moves out beyond itself to embrace others in an ever broadening expanse of friendship, a dance of conviviality that takes place in the very heart of the Triune God.⁵⁶ Here, finally, is desire, not disciplined and defeated but healed and set free. Beatitude.

The True Sacrifice

Aquinas's account of the analogy of being provides a way of envisioning the interplay of difference that maintains difference and freedom yet is full of the promise of peace, of the genuine communion that eludes the madness and cruelty of Deleuze's pure immanence. But Aquinas's account of the analogy of being is no general theory of salvation. For Aquinas, no less than for Anselm and the luminaries of Chalcedon, the possibility of the free and peaceable communion of difference is anchored in the concrete universal, Jesus Christ. So we are compelled to inquire: How do we joint this dance?

53. In this regard it is worth noting that Deleuze fears thinking God will impose a transcendent measure on finitude. Aquinas notes that such could only happen with God thought in the univocal key, that God in analogical relation to creatures is not their measure (Aquinas, *Summa Theologica*, I.13.5).

54. Aquinas, *Summa Theologica*, I.8.1.

55. Ibid., I.83.1. As Hans Urs von Balthasar puts it: "He allows the individual his own will, his choice, his freedom. He does not impose himself from without, but works in the inner source of the created spirit, not as 'another' but as one exalted above all otherness . . . so immanent that he is indistinguishable from the natural spirit" (*Theology of History*, 102–3).

56. Note that the being of finite created beings in relation to other finite created beings is univocal, and their difference is finally quantitative. Two observations spring from this. First, what enables these differences to interact with one another in nonagonistic ways is precisely their mutual participation in God, whose call (in the sense of gathering and sending) both mediates and maintains those differences peaceably. Second, it is these differences in created being that underwrite what are often pejoratively called "hierarchies" among created beings, but when rightly understood and practiced, such relations are non-hierarchical precisely because hierarchy enacts not simply difference but distance, and the analogy of being maintains difference without distance insofar as it permits God an immediate intimacy with all created beings—an intimacy that all created beings share with one another via their participation in Christ.

Where do we enter into the aneconomic fold of plenitude opened up by Christ's sacrifice? When do we encounter the particular one who is of universal significance, yet who died some two millennium ago?

The orthodox claim is that the one who died on the cross as an atonement for sin was raised from the dead and through the Spirited fire of Pentecost gathered unto himself a community, the church, that eucharistically becomes his body and as such continues his atoning work in the world. This is to say, we meet the one who redeems in the particular, contingent event of the Eucharist. Augustine describes this encounter, and the union thereby effected, in a profound passage from book ten of *The City of God*. There he is discussing the nature of true sacrifices, and about them he writes that they are "done that we may be united to God in holy fellowship" and they have as their reference "that supreme good and end in which alone we can be truly blessed." Then he continues with a lengthy description that takes us to the altar:

> Since, therefore, true sacrifices are works of mercy to ourselves or others, done with a reference to God, and since works of mercy have no other object than the relief of distress or the conferring of happiness, and since there is no happiness apart from that good of which it is said, "It is good for me to be very near to God," it follows that the whole redeemed city, that is to say, the congregation or community of the saints, is offered to God as our sacrifice through the great High Priest, who offered himself to God in His passion for us, that we might be members of this glorious head, according to the form of a servant. For it was this form he offered, in this He was offered, because it is according to it He is Mediator, in this He is our Priest, in this the Sacrifice . . . This is the sacrifice of Christians: we, being many, are one body in Christ. And this also is the sacrifice which the Church continually celebrates in the sacrament of the altar . . . in which she teaches that she herself is offered in the offering that she makes to God.[57]

Here the strands of my argument come together in a manner that gestures toward a conclusion. Christ's work of atonement is the true sacrifice, which did not pay a debt but rather draws us unto God. As the true sacrifice, Christ is the mediator, the one who overcomes the antinomy of God and Man in a way that delivers beatitude. Moreover, this beatific communion is realized through the contingent encounter with one person, Christ, whom we do

---

57. Augustine, *City of God*, 10.6.

meet and with whom we are intimately joined (but not lost) in the church's celebration at the altar.

Yet there is something odd about Augustine's account. Christ, the true sacrifice, does not stand alone, in stark solitude, a transcendent totality that has no room for mere finite sacrifices. To the contrary, the one true sacrifice unleashes a multitude of sacrifices. Not only in the proliferation of eucharistic enactments, but also, Augustine notes, as the Body receives the form of a servant who enacts other true sacrifices.

To the sacrifices of this servant, and how such sacrifices, non-identical repetitions of the one true sacrifice, extend the effect of this sacrifice—like a rhizome of redemption across the rough terrain of sin—we turn. For herein lies the promise of freedom from capital.

III. Practicing the End of Judgment: Sacrifice and the End of Capitalism

Christ enacts the judgment of God as the end of judgment, overturning the economy of debt, loss, and death, healing the breach between the infinite and finite, opening a horizon of harmonic concord. In the celebration of the Eucharist we are joined to Christ and consequently released from judgment for communion. But this release takes a peculiar form. Insofar as we are set free, we become a servant who extends the effect of the one true sacrifice by making true sacrifices. But is this not a contradiction? By Christ's final and sufficient sacrifice (Heb 7:27; 10:10–12), we are done with judgment; and yet now we go forth to sacrifice? Are we then truly done with judgment? (And has not the infinite debt reappeared?) This is to say, is not to sacrifice to be reinscribed in the agonistic logic of debt and retribution and so of the very economic order we seek to escape? How, then, is it that such sacrifices portend the fall of capital?

Practicing the End of Judgment

For the beginning of an answer we return to Anselm's aneconomic reading of Christ's work of atonement. His account of the atonement revealed that Christ bears God's judgment but he does so in such a way that God's judgment marks the end of judgment. Christ, in other words, is God's judgment of judgment. If judgment is as Deleuze holds, a matter of debt, loss, and compensatory agony, then Christ's sacrifice is God's refusal of every such judgment. God's judgment then is paradoxically revealed to be a non-judgment precisely because it refuses to record debts or exact compensation.[58] In non-paradoxical terms, echoing Augustine's suggestion that true sacrifices are ultimately about mercy, we might call this a judgment of mercy or grace, which contravenes the logic of infinite as well as merely finite debt and retribution.[59] In more traditional theological language, this judgment of mercy, which is the end of judgment effected by Christ's sacrifice, is named "forgiveness."

How does this forgiveness that is the end of infinite judgment come to bear on the finite agony of capital? How does the end of judgment that is forgiveness contravene both the logic of infinite as well as merely finite debt and retribution? Recall that even as Deleuze rejects infinite judgment (whether rendered by a god or human law), he embraces a purely finite justice. Yet because he cannot unthink the economic logic of debt and retribution, he can only think of a different economy, which is to say, the difference between infinite judgment and finite justice can only be a difference of degree or intensity (the only kind of difference his univocal ontology permits). Thus, his alternative to infinite judgment is finite cruelty—the vendetta—and in the end, this is no escape from judgment; it is only judgment of a different degree or intensity. And, as argued previously, it is no escape from the economic logic of capital.

If Deleuze's univocal ontology finally traps him in a logic of judgment—albeit the finite judgment of a cruel justice—Christ sets us free from infinite judgment and finite justice insofar as his true sacrifice inaugurates a flow of forgiveness in the form of the finite sacrifices of those pneumatologically connected to him at the altar. In place of an economy of justice, Christ's Spirit releases the aneconomic flow of forgiveness (thus, contra Foucault, confession and penance are not an embodiment of judgment, but its end). At first glance, this appears an absurd claim. After all, Christianity has not forsaken justice; indeed, it is one of the cardinal virtues! This objection is deceptively true. It is such because what Christianity calls justice is a justice that has been transformed or redeemed by its being relocated from the univocal order of combat to an aneconomic order of charity. As a result, it would no longer be recognizable as justice at all to the likes of Deleuze. What is forsaken (absolved) is the economic justice founded on scarcity, debt, and retribution and that in turn founds combat and cruelty. What is given in its place is a justice formed by charity, tempered by mercy, that nurtures the

---

58. Note that this is opens the space for accounts of final judgment that suggest such judgment is not something that finally God inflicts, but rather is self-inflicted by the sinner in the sense that it is not God's turning away from the sinner but the sinner's final refusal of God's eternal offer.

59. See Jones, *Embodying Forgiveness*.

sociality of desire in love precisely by absolving debt, instead giving. For this reason, both Aquinas and Anselm insist that there is no opposition between divine justice and mercy; mercy implements perfect justice (Aquinas) and the rule of God's justice is mercy (Anselm).[60]

What, then, happens at the Eucharist as we are provided a new way of living, which includes the poetic continuation of true sacrifices, is not the reinstatement of an order of judgment or justice that adjudicates debt, loss, and retribution. Rather, insofar as these sacrifices flourish as a consequence of a pneumatological connection with the one true sacrifice of Christ, they repeat (although non-identically, because the particular, contingent finite matters, which is to say, because the finite is a difference that is not obliterated by this connection but preserved in accord with the analogy of being) or extend the line of flight from the economic logic of both judgment and justice that was initiated by Christ and is sustained across time and space by his Spirit. In other words, true sacrifices are the continuation of the end of judgment. They are the practice of the end of judgment. To make true sacrifices is to have done with judgment, in both infinite and finite forms.

Sacrifice Contra Capital

Anselm's aneconomic reading of Christ's atonement also provides several intimations of how true sacrifices, the practice of the end of judgment, may fund resistance to capitalism. It does so as it creates a space that allows us to distance true sacrifice from all pernicious forms of sacrifice, all forms of sacrifice that correspond to an economy of debt, scarcity, and competition.[61] According to such an order, all sacrifice is implicated in violence as it necessarily entails a loss—a loss of self, a loss of dignity, a loss of identity, a loss of life. Pernicious sacrifice is always a giving up or a surrender of the lesser to the greater—the present to the future, women to men, men to the state/corporation, all to the greater good (market). Thus, morality under the sign of modernity oscillates between egoism and altruism, between self-preservation and self-destruction. And, perhaps unsurprisingly, modern Christian ethics has tended to embrace altruism and "self-sacrifice."[62] But in so doing, it is rightly censured by liberationists and others, for altruism and self-sacrifice remain circumscribed by scarcity, loss, and death—sacrifice always entails a loss. For this reason, as Ayn Rand reminded us, altruism is immoral.

60. See Bell, "Sacrifice and Suffering," 349–51.
61. I am indebted here to Milbank, "Stories of Sacrifice," 27–56.
62. See Woodhead, "Love and Justice," 44–61.

Conversely, Deleuze's univocal *autopoesis* gravitates toward the other pole, egoism, as it refuses the participation in the other offered by the analogy of being and consequently construes relations as effects of sheer self-assertion. Indeed, Deleuze's account of difference in combat, again in spite of his hopes otherwise, cannot avoid becoming a Darwinian struggle for self-preservation. And here too we see how Deleuze's economic logic cannot resist but only surpass the madness of capital.

Yet Anselm's account of Christ's sacrifice suggests that true sacrifice is not pernicious. The sacrifice of Christ, and hence of those who would follow him, does not belong to an economy that forces one to decide between self and neighbor, with a decision for one necessarily entailing a loss of the other. To the contrary, Christ's sacrifice births an aneconomic space where the divine plenitude spills over with the result that sacrifice becomes gain (Luke 9:24; John 12:25) and we can give ourselves as a gift of love to our neighbors without end and without loss (Matt 22:39; Mark 12:31). In Christ's sacrifice nothing is lost and everything is gained. Through his sacrifice sin, which as *privatio* is precisely nothing, is lost. The "nothing" that is lost is the modern illusion of the isolated, alienated self (or postmodern dissolute self) that only has the eyes to see and ears to hear the sacrifice of love as loss. The "nothing" that is overcome is the masculine fantasy of an absolute self-possession that can only be lost in giving, sharing, participating in and receiving from others. What is gained in Christ's sacrifice is abundant life,[63] life lived as donation, as the ceaseless giving (and receiving) the gift of love, life as participation in the dance of charity that is the Trinity.

Moreover, to cling to the economic vision of pernicious sacrifice is to refuse the aneconomic gift of Christ's sacrifice. Said ethically, it is to renounce the gift of the theological virtues of faith, hope, and love that animate Christian sacrifice. For it is precisely the theological virtues that save us from the futility of pernicious sacrifice. It is faith in Christ's resurrection (1 Cor 15:17) and the hope that we shall share it in (Rom 6:5) and the love that casts out all fear (1 John 4:18) that sustain us in the conviction that infinite self-giving is truly an expression of the fullness of love and is not gratuitous self-annihilation or masochistic self-renunciation.[64]

We can now appreciate how Christ's work of atonement creates the possibility of release from capitalism. Through Christ's sacrifice a path is opened up beyond the iron cage of sin, of capitalism, and of the Hobbesian/Weberian world where both appear to rule. In Christ we are liberated from all that would prevent us from giving, that would interrupt the flow

---

63. Milbank, "Midwinter Sacrifice," 31.
64. Milbank, "Socialism of the Gift, Socialism by Grace," 546.

of divine plenitude that continues through our enactment of love. We are freed from captivity to an economic order that would subject us to scarcity, competition, dominion, and debt, that would distort human desire into a proprietary and acquisitive power. We are released from the agonistic logic of rights that envisions only a world where atomistic individuals compete for access to the goods necessary for the pursuit of private ends.

This is to say, the only way to defeat capitalism is to embrace the gift given in Christ, which is nothing less than the superabundance of grace that repositions our lives within the aneconomic order of love. So repositioned (redeemed) by love, we are enabled to give ourselves, to enact true sacrifices without loss or end, even in the face of an economy that would eclipse gift and plenitude through the imposition of a regime of scarcity, debt, and dominion. Christ's sacrifice defeats capitalism as that sacrifice, and every true sacrifice that flows from it, opens a way for desire to be healed of its economic distortions and renewed in the mode of donation, of perpetual generosity. Capitalism is overcome as human relations are redeemed from the agony of competition and dominion and revived as the joyous conviviality of love that is the fruit of the proliferation of non-proprietary (that is, participatory) relations. Capitalism is defeated as fear is cast out—the fear of my neighbor that compels me to possess more tightly and acquire more compulsively, the fear that in giving I can only lose, the fear that death and the cross are the end of every sacrifice.

Works of Mercy

In terms of specific aneconomic practices, the practice of the end of judgment which is true sacrifice prompts us to reassess the Christian practice of charity. Of course, by charity I do not mean the anemic contemporary practice of contributing two or three percent of one's disposable income to worthy causes, which many rightly critique as falling short of the gospel. Likewise, charity as the concretion of life lived as an outpouring of the divine donation has but the faintest resemblance to tech millionaires pledging the "earnings" they accumulate from a day's "play" on the stock market (Mark 12:41–44). Rather, again recalling Augustine ("true sacrifices are works of mercy"), charity as an incarnation of true sacrifice takes shape in the ancient tradition of the Works of Mercy, at the heart of which are almsgiving and hospitality. Accordingly, charity as an aneconomic practice animated by the theological virtues is manifest not in the hobby of philanthropy, but in lives lived in accord with Matthew 25:31–45, one of the traditional Scriptural warrants for the Works of Mercy. Although it does not compare to the witness of the lives of countless saints, from Francis and Clare to Day and Romero, Martin Luther captured the profundity of the aneconomic life of charity as well as anyone when he wrote, "We should devote all our works to the welfare of others, since each has such abundant riches in his faith that all his others works and his whole life are a surplus with which he can by voluntary benevolence serve and do good to his neighbor."[65] Having received all that we need in Christ, we are freed to devote our lives in their entirety to meeting the needs of others. By opening our hands to give freely of our resources to those in need and by welcoming them into our homes and communities, by becoming, as the Latin American liberationists say, "friends of the poor," we display the aneconomic order of divine charity that is overcoming the agony of the capitalist economy.[66] It is worth noting, however, that placing the emphasis on the Christian embodiment of charity via the Works of Mercy does shift the focus of Christian confrontation with economic sin away from where it is principally located today, namely, in public policy pronouncements by bureaucratic arms of ecclesial bodies that do not themselves adhere to their own "official" pronouncements. Instead, it suggests that Christians confront economic sin, systemic and otherwise, first by enacting (or receiving) this aneconomic order in their own life together.

At this point, some may object that, to paraphrase Jon Sobrino, speaking of charity and works of mercy is too soft, even too dangerous, an expression of what those who suffer under the capitalist economy need.[67] Interestingly enough, Adam Smith did not share those doubts concerning the potency of the church's aneconomic practice of charity when he penned his famous economic treatise, *The Wealth of Nations*.[68] There he noted that the hospitality and charity of the church were very great, maintaining the poor of every kingdom, and he laments that those practices "not only gave [the church] the command of a great temporal force, but increased very much the weight of their spiritual weapons." Indeed, he goes on to observe that the church constituted the most formidable obstacle to the civil order, liberty and happiness that the free market could provide. But, alas, he is glad to report that eventually improvements in "arts, manufactures, and

---

65. Luther, *Freedom of a Christian*, 74.

66. The risk in positing charity as the central aneconomic practice of the faith is that it may appear to treat symptoms of injustice and poverty while overlooking (systemic) causes. Charity and the Works of Mercy rightly practiced, however, do not preclude but rather demand confronting sin. One of the spiritual works of mercy, for example, is "admonishing sinners." In this regard, I find the lives of the saints, such as Romero and Day, the best "explanations" of Christian charity.

67. Sobrino, *Principle of Mercy*, viii.

68. Smith, *Wealth of Nations*, Bk. V. Ch. 1. Pt. 3. Art. 3.

commerce" not only conquered the great barons but undercut the church as well, weakening both its spiritual and temporal authority by rendering its charity merely economic, that is, more sparing and restrained.

∾

Beyond capital there is plenitude. Beyond madness there is hope. Beyond cruelty, joy. Beyond judgment, peace. At that altar of God we approach this "beyond." There we behold the true sacrifice—the Lamb of God who takes away the sin of the world—and beholding, we are beholden. But this implies no debt, for this sacrifice is a pure offering, defying every necessity, exceeding every economic calculus. This mutual beholding is the gaze of love—beatitude—that fires a multitude of other true sacrifices. And as this conflagration spreads, blowing where it will, we are set free.

A fading, flickering neon sign interrupts an urban moonscape announcing a rescue mission to the nomad, the fugitive, the veteran, to the homeless and destitute: Jesus saves. Only Jesus overcomes the hostility between God and humanity, the infinite and finite, in a way that is full of promise, that is full of the promise, not of the nihilistic madness and cruelty postmodernity barely wards off, but of the joyous conviviality that is love.

CHAPTER 4

The Law Exceeding Every Madness

Excess and the Law of Love Beyond Capital

Among the leading lights of the postmodern/Continental philosophical tradition there is a striking consistency with regard to law. In one form or another they all acknowledge what Giorgio Agamben calls the contemporary "crisis of law." This shared sense of the crisis around law, however, is not a matter of the law's breakdown or abandonment, as some have mistakenly suggested. Rather, the crisis is faced by those who live (and die) under the force of law even as their illusions regarding its benevolent and protective character are shattered, as their bodies are subjected in Kafkaesque[1] style to the force of law even as the letter of the law is suspended with a regularity approaching normalcy.

In other words, the crisis is one effected *by* the law, but it is not so much a crisis *of* the law. To the contrary, one might argue, again following Agamben, that the contemporary crisis of law is but the (imperial) expansion of the force of law beyond the confines of the letter of the juridical-legal order that was assumed to contain it but that turns out only to express it. This is to say, the crisis of law is in fact not the decimation of law, but its crossing a threshold in the extension of sovereign power.

Indeed, these authors share a sense that the crisis of law is but the latest symptom of the further erosion of life under capitalist dominion (although none would reduce the problems of contemporary life to a single cause, such as capitalism). Insofar as they share a political vision of the emancipation of life in its singular brilliance from all that would capture or contain the flow of singularities, they share an opposition to law.[2] In other words,

---

1. See Franz Kafka's "In the Penal Colony," where the prisoner feels the force of law on his skin without knowing his crime.
2. Derrida's position in this regard is disputed. I am reading him as opposed to capitalism both on the grounds of the general nature of his thought as concerned with

the crisis of law does not elicit support for law and its reinforcement, but a renewed attack on law in the name of life beyond law, in the hope that the crisis effected *by* law actually becomes a crisis *of* law.

In what follows I consider the nature of law and its relation to the capitalist captivity of life. I begin by presenting the treatment of law and "law beyond law" in the work of Derrida, Deleuze, Agamben, Badiou, and Žižek. Then I evaluate the emancipatory potential of their respective visions of life beyond law, arguing that a certain isomorphy between their visions of freedom from law and capitalism in its neoliberal form does not bode well for human emancipation. Finally, I consider the Christian law of love. Here we behold law not in a nominalist but analogical mode that invites participation beyond the clash of sovereign wills, thereby transfiguring the subject and economy in accord with universal charity and so holding out the promise of life beyond the chains of capitalism.

I. Freedom From Law

We begin with the problem of law. Each thinker presents law as in some way an obstacle to the full expression of life. Taking a cue from Žižek, I consider them in order of the degree to which they assert life can be free from law—beginning with Derrida, for whom freedom from law is finally unrealizable, and concluding with Žižek, for whom freedom is *always* realizable in the negative moment of the "no," of the subject's refusal of the law.

Derrida: The Double Bind of Law

Derrida's treatment of law can be approached by means of the fundamental orientation of his philosophical-political vision. Although deconstruction is frequently dismissed as a purely negative movement of critique or, worse, as apolitical aestheticism, such characterizations miss the mark, insofar as Derrida's vision is fundamentally a vision of *responsibility*, which is made clear in his treatment of the sacrifice of Isaac:

> Abraham's decision is absolutely responsible because it answers for itself before the absolute other ... If God is completely other, the figure or name of the wholly other, then every other (one) is every (bit) other ... It implies that God, as the wholly other,

---

exclusion and marginality and on the basis of his work *Specters of Marx*, which is an appropriation of Marx against dogmatic Marxism. Although, it is worth noting that Derrida would resist such a bald claim, insofar as he did not think capitalism was monolithic and thus so easily dismissed.

is to be found everywhere there is something wholly other. And since each of us, everyone else, each other is infinitely other in its absolute singularity, inaccessible, solitary, transcendent, nonmanifest, originarily nonpresent to my *ego* ... then what can be said about Abraham's relation to God can be said about my relation without relation to *every other (one) as every (bit) other*.[3]

Clearly Derrida is deeply indebted to Levinas.[4] He is also drawn to Kant on the grounds that Kant, by effectively announcing the death of God, intensified human responsibility.[5] This is to say, Kant represents Christianity's full moralization, its embrace of full responsibility without falling back on God to shoulder or share that responsibility, something that, Derrida suggests, Judaism or Islam, the last two monotheisms, refuse to do.[6]

Furthermore, it is not unimportant that this responsibility is an "oath before the letter," which is to say, a responsibility placed on human shoulders prior to the written law, and so "a debt before every contract or loan."[7]

How does this relate to the problem of law? The problem of law emerges at the intersection of the ethics of responsibility (or hospitality) and politics, at the intersection of the absolute, unconditional, universal call of infinite responsibility and the conditions of particular, historical, quotidian demands of contemporary political life.[8] This is to say, if responsibility is that which is called forth by the face of the other, the problem of law arises in the context of the advent of the third. The arrival of the third, Derrida says, is the beginning of justice, at once as law and beyond the law.[9]

---

3. Derrida, *Gift of Death*, 77–78.

4. Derrida offers a criticism of Levinas, writing that he "never gave in to a democratizing rhetoric but actually subjected or subordinated freedom in accordance with responsibility that makes me the hostage of the other in an experience of absolute heteronomy, although without servitude." Indeed Levinas placed responsibility before and above "difficult freedom" (*Rogues*, 42). Derrida appears to distinguish himself from Levinas by means of his invocation of a "democracy to come" that does not renounce responsibility but situates it. Thus he writes of democracy's "vocation for hospitality" (*Rogues*, 63), desires to do the impossible of separating democracy and autonomy (*Rogues*, 84) and describes democracy as the opening of a public space for the experience of freedom "with the necessarily excessive responsibility of which no one may be resolved" (*Rogues*, 92).

5. See Derrida, *Acts of Religion*, 50–51.

6. Ibid., 51.

7. Derrida, *Adieu to Emmanuel Levinas*, 34.

8. See the preface to Derrida, *On Cosmopolitanism and Forgiveness*, xi–xii. See also 45.

9. Derrida, *Adieu*, 29.

This reference to justice "as law and beyond law" brings us to the heart of the matter. As a matter of law, justice is about the political codification of responsibility with founding violence (the "mystical foundation of authority") and the perpetual force of enforcement.[10] Yet, here Derrida suggests that "the justice of law, justice as law, is not justice."[11]

The source of this *aporia* is the inevitable loss or exclusion that occurs when responsibility expands from two to three (or more) in the form of law. Derrida states the problem thus: "How to reconcile the act of justice that must always concern singularity, individuals, groups, irreplaceable existences, the other or myself *as* other, in a unique situation, with rule, norm, value, or the imperative of justice that necessarily have a general form . . . ?"[12] Something of the singular is always lost in the general as it becomes calculable, regulated, or programmable,[13] and the external imperative, not unlike religion before the death of God, unavoidably diminishes responsibility as it becomes a decision that does not pass through the test and ordeal of the undecidable.[14]

At this point one might think that the solution to this problem is simply to abstain from law, to abjure law but according to Derrida that is not possible.[15] Granted, as noted above, he writes of a justice "beyond law" and of a politics "to come"[16] but they will never exist as more than a promise that "swoops down and seizes me *here and now*" in the form of the injunction that is the unforeseeable coming of the other.[17]

He identifies this with a kind of eschatology[18]—the trace of a messiah who will never arrive because he is already here, like a Job who would like to be more just than justice, yet who can only utter the sigh of the just, "What have I to do with justice?"[19]

Thus justice beyond the law, pure unconditional responsibility or hospitality, is finally not possible because of what Derrida calls the double bind

---

10. Derrida, *Acts of Religion*, 233, 264, 268–69. On 242 he notes that there is "a silence walled up in the violent structure of the founding act," which he identifies as the mystical.
11. Ibid., 240.
12. Ibid., 245.
13. Ibid., 251.
14. Ibid., 252.
15. Ibid., 243, 364, 380, 381.
16. Ibid., 281.
17. Derrida, *Rogues*, 84, 86.
18. See Derrida quoted in Smith, *Jacques Derrida: Live Theory*, 68.
19. Derrida, *Adieu*, 34, 30.

of responsibility.[20] On one hand, the appearance of the third undermines the purity of one's response to the other who is the second, tarnishing its immediacy and uniqueness; on the other hand, the absence of the third would "threaten with violence the purity of ethics in the absolute immediacy of the face to face with the unique," which Derrida identifies with the impossibility of discerning between good and evil, love and hate, giving and taking, the desire to live and the death drive, the hospitable welcome and the narcissistic closing within oneself.[21]

In the end, there is no beyond the law, only a between, only deconstruction as the movement between justice and law, exercising a constant vigilance and naming the inevitably occluded other.[22]

Deleuze: Pure Vitalism and the End of Judgment

Deleuze devotes relatively little time in his work to treating the problem of the law and he did not make the "turn to religion" that most of the thinkers considered here do in the sense that he does not draw upon religion for resources in resolving the problem of law.

Nevertheless, where he does engage the law it is clear that he considers it a problem to the extent that it is part and parcel of that which organizes desire according to resemblance, equivalence, and generality and so inhibits the flow of singularities that Deleuze calls "repetition."[23] Thus, he writes:

> If repetition is possible, it is due to miracle rather than to law. It is against law: against the similar form and equivalent content of law. If repetition can be found . . . it is the name of a power which affirms itself against the law, which works underneath

---

20. Ibid., 33. In *Rogues*, where he treats sovereignty and democracy to come, the double bind is synonymous with the aporetic (86), paradox (101), autoimmunity (e.g., democracy is open to anti-democrats and so open to its own destruction), and "threat in promise" (82). Likewise he sets sovereignty over against the "unconditional" even as he argues that democracy is not simply opposed to sovereignty (158) but seeks to undermine nation-state sovereignty (157) in the name of a supersovereignty (100, 101). Or see the dialectic of human rights and unconditional justice (151), which are not related as a future horizon or *telos* that is deferred, which Derrida rejects (86).

21. Derrida, *Adieu*, 32.

22. Derrida, *Acts of Religion*, 251.

23. Deleuze, *Difference and Repetition*, 2. Note that there is an effort in legal scholarship to rehabilitate the law in Deleuze by appealing to Deleuze's contrast between law and jurisprudence, where the latter is a matter of decisions of singularities. Alexander Lefebvre, for example, exploits Bergson to redeem law by rendering it virtual. I find such efforts unpersuasive and basically evasions of Deleuze's ontological argument for singularities. See Lefebvre, "A New Image of Law," 103–26.

laws, perhaps superior to laws . . . In every respect, repetition is a transgression. It puts law into question, it denounces its nominal or general character in favour of a more profound and more artistic reality.[24]

Law, then, stands unequivocally opposed to the unorganized flow of singularities that Deleuze advocates.

Deleuze's treatment of moral law is brief but it follows the trajectory of this passage. The moral law is but another instance of the capture of desire by a transcendent Idea or unity. As he puts it, the classic conception of law, perfectly expressed in Plato and universally accepted in Christianity, is that of the law construed as the representation or image of a transcendent Good, on which the law is dependent.[25]

But of course the classic world is long gone, even in Christianity, and the force of modern moral law no longer is suspended from a transcendent Good. Here Deleuze turns to Kant as the paradigmatic thinker of the moral law under the sign of modernity. Kant earns this honor, as Deleuze puts it, because "Kant discovers the modern way of saving transcendence."[26] While Deleuze is specifically referring to Kant's transcendental subject (for whom the field of immanence is only as it is a reflection of the self back to itself), his point applies equally to the Kantian transformation of law. Commenting on the *Critique of Practical Reason*, Deleuze marks the fateful change wrought by Kant in the moral law: "Kant reverses the relationship between the law and the Good, and thereby raises the law to the level of a pure and empty uniqueness. The good is what the Law says it is—it is the good that depends on the law, and not vice versa."[27]

What is significant here is the effect of becoming self-founding upon the law. When the law no longer depends on the Good but rather determines the Good, the law becomes formless. "It is a pure form that has no object, whether sensible or intelligible. It does not tell us what we must do, but what subjective rule we must obey no matter what our action."[28] Kant's categorical imperative is the perfect example of this. It is a pure form that is independent of content or object, spheres of activity or circumstance.[29]

---

24. Deleuze, *Difference and Repetition*, 2–3.
25. Deleuze, *Coldness and Cruelty*, 81.
26. Deleuze and Guattari, *What is Philosophy*, 46.
27. Deleuze, *Essays Critical and Clinical*, 32. See also Deleuze, *Kant's Critical Philosophy*, x.
28. Ibid.
29. Deleuze, *Coldness and Cruelty*, 83.

Thus, says Deleuze, Kant added the essential dimension of modern moral law: the object of the law is by definition unknowable and elusive.[30]

The unknowable and elusive character of modern moral law is essential to what Deleuze denounces as "the doctrine of judgment," the binding of singularities together by means of the consciousness of an infinite and unpayable debt.[31] Deleuze explains this infinite and unpayable debt thus:

> If the law is no longer based on the Good as a preexisting, higher principle, and it is valid by virtue of its form alone, the content remaining entirely undetermined, it becomes impossible to say that the righteous man obeys the law for the sake of the Best. In other words, the man who obeys the law does not thereby become righteous or feel righteous; on the contrary, he feels guilty and is guilty in advance, and the more strict his obedience, the greater his guilt.[32]

Although it is has been lamented that Kant stormed the heavens and put God to death,[33] Deleuze was not taken in by Kant's supposed deicide. He asserts that far from banishing the power of God and transcendence, Kant saw to it that the organizing power of the transcendent Good was not only replaced but even intensified as the law took its place and by becoming pure form, increased its territorializing power (not unlike Bentham's Panopticon, we might note).

At this point it is worth noting the role that religion, specifically Judaism and Christianity, had in this development, if only for the sake of appreciating why Deleuze did not make the "turn to religion," and why he would be less than sanguine about contemporary efforts to use Paul against law. In the few places where he treats religion in any detail, it is clear that Deleuze thinks Kant has expressed not only the essence of modern moral law but the heart of Judaism and Christianity as well.

What is striking in his treatment of Judaism and Christianity is that even as he follows the commonplace interpretation of the move from the former to the latter as a shift from the local to the universal,[34] unlike many modern interpreters, Deleuze sees this evolution as a move from bad to worse. Likewise, whereas it is not uncommon to attribute the best and most refined treatment of law to the Jewish prophets, Deleuze counters that it is Jewish prophetism that contributes most significantly to the sense of per-

---

30. Ibid.
31. Deleuze, *Essays Critical and Clinical*, 126.
32. Deleuze, *Coldness and Cruelty*, 84.
33. Heinrich Heine, quoted in Schnädelbach, *Philosophy in Germany*, 17.
34. Deleuze, *Essays Critical and Clinical*, 40.

petual judgment by means of indefinite postponement.[35] Christianity—in the combination of Jesus, Paul, and John of the Apocalypse—intensifies this perpetual judgment and debt to the point that judgment and debt become infinite.[36] Together Jesus, Paul, and John capture all singularities—individuals and collectives—in a regime of infinite judgment, suicide and death:

> Between Christ, Saint Paul and John of Patmos, the chain closes in on itself: Christ the aristocrat, the artist of the individual soul, who wants to give this soul; John of Patmos, the worker, the miner, who lays claim to the collective soul and wants to take everything; and Saint Paul, who closes the link, a kind of aristocrat going to the people, a kind of Lenin who will organize the collective soul, who will make it an "oligarchy of martyrs"—he gives Christ the aims, and the Apocalypse the means. Was not all this essential to the formation of the system of judgment? Individual suicide and mass suicide, with self-glorification on all sides. Death, death, this is the only judgment.[37]

Christianity renders judgment compete, total, infinite and inescapable. Over against this Deleuze wants to be done with judgment, which entails a rejection of law. This rejection of law is to be carried out by means of the struggle and combat of the will to live that constitute the flows of desire that connect with other flows in an anarchy of loving singularites. This is a struggle against law, a struggle to subvert law, in one of two directions. First, there is the Sadian hero who rises above the law not in the direction of God or the Good but in the direction of evil and wickedness.[38] This is the line of anarchic transgression. Second, there is the masochist, whose attack is a matter of descending in the sense that she submits to the law to the extreme, exposing its absurdity and so provoking contempt and resistance (work-to-rule, following the letter rigidly, etc.).

Agamben: Pure Potentiality and the Deactivation of Law

The question of law is front and center in Agamben's work as he takes up the challenge of envisioning a new form of life, a new politics of freedom or

---

35. See Deleuze and Guattari, *Thousand Plateaus* 123–24; Deleuze, *Essays Critical and Clinical*, 40.

36. See Deleuze, *Essays Critical and Clinical*, 36–52.

37. Ibid., 51.

38. Deleuze, *Coldness and Cruelty*, 86–87. See also Deleuze, *Difference and Repetition*, 5.

democracy, where pure singularities interact in a common life as the expression of potentiality instead of the imposition of sovereignty.

By placing the question of sovereignty at the center of his work, Agamben positions his work as a supplement and corrective to biopolitical models of power, such as that famously developed by Foucault. Specifically he seeks to expose the "hidden point of intersection" of biopolitical power with juridico-institutional power; that is, with the paradoxical power of sovereignty that is simultaneously the force of law and its exception.[39]

Indeed, what is particularly striking is how Agamben does not focus on the force of law per se, that is, on what the sovereign law succeeds in internalizing. This is the case because that dimension of law is everywhere in crisis. He observes that all societies and all cultures today have entered into a crisis of legitimation in which the law is in force as the pure "nothing of Revelation."[40] This is an allusion to the outside of law that is the state of exception and that is the norm today.[41]

It is important to note that this state of exception is not so much *outside of the law*, in the sense of separate and free from it, but rather it is *the outside of law*. The state of exception is the outside of law in the sense that it is the legal-juridical space created by sovereign power's suspension of the law. It is not simply an exclusion but is an inclusive exclusion.[42] The state of exception is the state of life under law without content; it is life under law that is empty.[43] And its paradigmatic example is the Nazi *Lager*.[44]

At this point we are faced with an interesting conundrum. Law is an expression of sovereign power and as such it is a problem. Yet as Agamben suggests there is no "outside of the law," no simple escape from the sovereign power embodied in law for the "outside" has now been incorporated into the political as the state of exception. Indeed, the outside of law has become the norm. How, then, is the sovereign force of law overcome?

For an answer Agamben "turns to religion" in the form of a commentary of sorts on Paul's letter to the Romans. What prompts this turn is Agamben's realization that Paul's text is "the fundamental messianic text

---

39. Agamben, *Homo Sacer*, 6, 15.

40. Ibid., 51. Giorgio Agamben, *Potentialities*, 171 makes explicit the association of the "nothing of Revelation" with the State of Exception.

41. Ibid., 20; Agamben, *Means Without End*, 113.

42. Agamben, *Time That Remains*, 105.

43. Agamben, *Homo Sacer* 52; Agamben, *State of Exception*, 6.

44. Ibid., 123.

for the Western tradition."[45] Although, he goes on to note, the church has succeeded in neutralizing the messianic both in Paul and in its life.[46]

Drawing on Benjamin, Agamben defines the messianic in terms that clearly echo what he previously described as the state of exception. Thus, he writes, "the messianic event above all signifies a crisis and radical transformation of the entire order of law . . . *The Messiah is, in other words, the figure through which religion confronts the problem of Law, decisively reckoning with it.*"[47]

The parallel between the Messianic and the sovereign state of exception becomes clearer as one considers Paul's treatment of the law. Agamben analyzes this first in terms of Paul's calling as a slave of Christ and the callings of the messianic community. His central insight revolves around the Pauline "as not" of 1 Corinthians 7:29–32, where members of the messianic community are encouraged to remain in the status they are currently in, but they are to occupy those positions as if not in that status. Thus the messianic vocation is the revocation of every vocation.[48] This revocation, however, is not a matter of transgression but of hollowing out, nullification.[49] The Messiah does not call one out of one's vocation but rather to occupying a vocation "as not."

The similarity with the state of exception should now be clear. Just as the state of exception is not the absence of law but its suspension, its presence without form or content, so too the messianic does not abolish vocations but maintains them in hollowed out form, without form or content.

Against the backdrop of the messianic evacuation of vocation, Agamben turns to Paul's treatment of the law. Unsurprisingly, it follows the same pattern. Paul's argument, he says, is not with the law itself but rather *within the law*.[50] Specifically, Paul's quarrel is with the normative, dividing[51] aspect of the law. Thus, he does not present the messianic as the abolition or destruction of the law but rather as the rendering of the normative function of law inoperative. The law remains but it is de-activated.[52]

45. Agamben, *Time That Remains*, 1.
46. Ibid.
47. Agamben, *Potentialities*, 162–63. Italics in original.
48. Agamben, *Time That Remains*, 23.
49. Ibid., 24.
50. Ibid., 94–95, 118.
51. Agamben argues that the principle of the law is division (*Time That Remains*, 47), and argues that Paul negates that principle as he "divides the divisions" (50, 52), of Jew and non-Jew. This "cut" creates a tension that is not resolved in identity (53) but leaves us instead with a "remnant," the "non-non-Jew" (50–51).
52. Agamben, *Time That Remains*, 98.

However, the messianic finally is not synonymous with the current state of exception. Indeed, Agamben writes, "we can compare the situation of our time to that of a petrified or paralyzed messianism that . . . nullifies the law, but then maintains it as the Nothing of Revelation in a perpetual and interminable state of exception, 'the "state of exception" in which we live.'"[53]

This is to suggest that merely living "as not" is not yet living the fullness of which the Pauline messiah is the advent. If the "as not" were the permanent state of affairs, then it too would be a sign or symptom of a petrified or paralyzed messianism. So, Agamben, elaborates,

> The Messiah's task becomes all the more difficult from this perspective. He must confront not simply a law that commands and forbids but a law that . . . is in force without significance. But this is also the task with which we, who live in the state of exception that has become the rule, must reckon.[54]

What remains of law when both the law that commands and the law that is in force without significance have been confronted? Is this not a covert antinomianism and so a clear break from Paul? Agamben thinks not, for what is to come, the labor of the time that remains, is not that of the destruction of law, but that of creating a space for "pure law," which is law after its nexus with power and violence has been broken.[55] This is law shorn of its binding, commanding, prohibitive dimension.[56] It is non-normative law, law in its promissive[57] dimension alone, which corresponds to the potentiality of singularities and their actions as pure means (hence the "deactivation" of law).[58]

---

53. Agamben, *Potentialities*, 171.
54. Ibid.
55. Agamben, *State of Exception*, 63, 88.
56. Ibid., 88.
57. Agamben, *Time That Remains*, 95.
58. Agamben, *State of Exception*, 88. This is decidedly not a return to the state of "prelaw," where word and law combined in the oath (or covenant), which as a personal contract or obligation was indeed a form of "pre-law." Instead the messianic restores the two halves of prelaw in unison by means of an experience of the pure performative word (*The Time That Remains*, 114, 135). Furthermore, it is a matter of weakness insofar as it is a word that is utterly gratuitous and free, devoid of the sovereign power to enforce it (*The Time That Remains*, 136). This is a non-normative law.

Badiou: Pure Chance and the Subtraction of Law

As was the case with Deleuze, the problem of law does not occupy a prominent position in Badiou's work. Yet in the course of thinking toward an emancipatory politics characterized by the flourishing of universal singularities and generic multiplicities, of a universalism of indifference to difference, Badiou treats the law in its relation to the truth-events that are the points of this politic's emergence. He does this most significantly in his work on Saint Paul, whom, he says is the "poet-thinker of the event."[59]

An event is the irruption of generic multiplicities that break from the conformity, the repetition, of the existing situation.[60] As such, an eventual site is "the edge of the void,"[61] a kind of tearing or punching a hole[62] in the regularity of a situation—be that a regime of place and totality (Greek wisdom) or observances and rites (Jewish law).[63] It is non-denumerable, uncontrollable, and gratuitous.

Given the singular, interruptive character of the event, it is perhaps unsurprising that Badiou would set the event and the generic multiplicities that initiate it over against law, which he does by drawing upon Paul's polemic against Jewish and Greek law. Describing Paul's "general procedure," he notes that "since truth is evental . . . it is singular. It is neither structural, nor axiomatic, nor legal. No available generality can account for it, nor structure the subject who claims to follow in its wake. Consequently, there cannot be a law of truth."[64]

As Paul makes clear, law and the event are juxtaposed, at odds. This is the case because, Badiou asserts, law is intrinsically "statist" in character:

---

59. Badiou, *Saint Paul*, 2. Badiou's difficult and lesser-known work *Theory of the Subject* deals with the order of law through an engagement with Lacan and psychoanalysis, German idealism, and Greek tragedy in a manner that is clearly a precursor to his idea of "the event." His *Logics of Worlds* deals with the law indirectly by continuing the argument begun in *TOS* in terms of treating terror, anxiety, courage, and justice. See Badiou, *Logics of Worlds*, 86.

60. In his *Logics of Worlds*, Badiou nuances the nature of this break such that the sharp dualism presented in *Being and Event* is softened a bit. He does this by introducing a logical theory—"a logic of appearing"—alongside his ontological theory, which was the focus of *Being and Event*. The former privileges coherence and correlation, the latter localization and singularity. Or as he puts it "a point [event] is the binary dramatization of the nuances of appearing." See *Logic of Worlds*, 399. The quote is from 437. He discusses this change briefly in the preface to the English translation of his *Ethics*, lvi–ii.

61. Badiou, *Being and Event*, 175.

62. Badiou, *Ethics*, 42–43. The expression "punching a hole" is Lacan's.

63. Badiou, *Saint Paul*, 57.

64. Ibid., 14.

it enumerates, names, and controls. It governs and so contains multiplicity under the rule of the count.[65] It subsumes the multiple under the whole, rendering difference merely a part.[66]

As such, the law becomes, as Paul points out, a figure of death that fixes or binds the inconsistent gratuitousness of desire so that it flows involuntarily, so that it is now sin, that is, the automatism of repetition.[67] Or, put a little differently, Badiou says that the law kills by separating thought from power, by rendering thought powerless, unable to prescribe action.[68]

Against this law, Paul declares Jesus Christ as the pure event, pure beginning.[69] His resurrection is pure excess over law that relieves us of law and its guilt.[70]

This freedom from law, however, does not place us in an antinomian situation, for the event's overcoming of the law is not simply a matter of transgression or negation. After all, as Paul suggested, transgression is not emancipation. Rather, the event is a matter not of negation but of subtraction. It is "beneath good and evil."[71] An event subtracts a subject from the law. Subtraction is not a matter of destruction but of extraction; it is a matter of sapping the law not of its existence but of its power to hold thought and so check action.[72]

What does a law look like that has been emptied of its power to check the proliferation of generic multiplicities? It is a nonliteral law, a transliteral law of the spirit. It is love as the law beyond law. Badiou explains it this way. Love is the eventual declaration that a new assemblage of life is possible.[73] On its own, in the passing of the moment, however, this event is useless.[74] The novelty of the event is quickly subsumed and the tear that was the event is stitched up by the reactive subject who seeks to destroy the trace of the event, or the obscurantist who uses the weight of the existing order to conceal the event in silence and so deprive it of existence.[75]

---

65. Ibid., 76, 78, 10.
66. See Badiou's critic of identitarian ethics in *Ethics*, 20–25.
67. Badiou, *Saint Paul*, 27, 79.
68. Ibid., 83.
69. Ibid., 48–49.
70. Ibid., 48, 57, 72.
71. Badiou, *Ethics*, 59, 85.
72. Badiou, *Saint Paul*, 73, 83.
73. Ibid., 88.
74. Ibid., 91.
75. Badiou, *Logics of Worlds*, 54–62.

What the event requires, if it is to endure, is the faithful subject, the subject of fidelity to the truth-event. This fidelity, this consistency, this public militancy of the event is the transliteral law of love.[76] About this return of law, Badiou writes,

> Love underwrites the return of a law that, although nonliteral, nonetheless functions as principle and consistency for the subjective energy initiated by [the event]. For the new man, love is fulfillment of the break that he accomplishes with the law; it is the law of the break with law, law of the truth of law.[77]

Thus, the solution to the problem of law is not its negation but its subtraction. It is the emptying of law of the power to thwart either by reaction or obscurantism the post-eventual unfolding of truths.

Žižek: Pure Will beyond Law

Of those considered thus far, Žižek's politics of freedom is arguably the most radically autonomous, and, perhaps somewhat ironically given that it is also the most negative, the most realized.

Žižek's vision of freedom revolves around the act of pure willing. Whereas other thinkers rooted their ontologies in a materialist vitality or pure potentiality or pure chance, Žižek founds his vision in pure will, pure voluntarism.[78] Adapting F. W. J. Schelling's creation myth for the emergence of reason out of chaos, Žižek holds that in the beginning was pure impersonal Willing that wills nothing.[79] Pure primordial freedom. When this Will made the primordial decision, when it acted, and so differentiated itself, the vortex of drives, of antagonistic forces that constitute the innermost base of all reality, is born. Our freedom (the freedom of the subject), is the freedom of pure will, the will to act in the midst of and as part of this vortex of antagonistic forces that define life as such.

As pure will, this freedom is more than simply getting in touch with and following the dictates of one's nature, giving free reign to one's drives, or hedonistically pursuing pleasure.[80] After all, where action is prescribed

---

76. Badiou, *Saint Paul*, 87.
77. Ibid., 89.
78. Žižek, "Thinking Backward: Predestination and Apocalypse," 196.
79. What follows is drawn from Žižek, "Schelling-in-Itself," 251–65.
80. Note Žižek, following Hegel, does not have a static notion of nature. See Žižek, *Interrogating the Real*, 328. It is not clear that Žižek finally succeeds in distancing his ethic from hedonism, albeit a patient or more utilitarian hedonism that does not necessarily define pleasure narrowly in terms of sensual desires. See also Žižek, *Puppet and Dwarf*, 113.

by nature or drives, it is not genuinely free. It follows, as well, that this freedom is not synonymous with liberal freedom of choice according to one's psychological propensities and subjective preferences or even democracy, where citizens are free to choose within the coordinates of existing power relations.[81] Certainly it has nothing to do with and indeed is actively opposed to global capitalism's freedom to consume, which is freedom withered to a trifling whim.[82] Likewise, this freedom is not compatible with submitting the will to a big Other, be it a God, an ideology, or a party line.[83] It is not even compatible with the freedom to respond to a little other; that is, to the imperative imposed upon us by the presence of the Levinasian Other, the neighbor. Indeed, Žižek argues, the imperative pressed upon us by our neighbor's presence actually diminishes our freedom to the extent that it reduces our responsibility to decide in the face of our neighbor.[84]

A correlative of freedom as pure will is the heightening of risk. Freedom as pure will amounts to the decision made without the security or guarantee offered by a big Other. It is an unscripted decision, a courageous risk; it is a leap into the void.

Accordingly, it is fundamentally a negative act,[85] freedom from.[86] Freedom as radical negativity.[87] As Žižek argues, one can always say "no."[88] It is freedom as antagonism, as a break with the symbolic order. Žižek associates it with Badiou's truth-event, although he heightens the negative and even potentially violent nature of the event's uncoupling from its social surroundings—speaking of ruthless power and ruthless war, resignifying terror, the necessity of more hatred, murder, excessive cruelty, vengeful blind justice, and so forth.[89] "Freedom," he writes, "is not a blissfully neutral state

---

81. Žižek, *On Belief*, 116, 122.

82. See Žižek, *Welcome to the Desert of the Real*, 86.

83. One of the reasons Žižek has embraced Christianity is that he sees Christ's death on the cross and the death of God as the death of transcendence, of the big Other. See Žižek, *On Belief* and Žižek, "The Fear of Four Words," 24–109.

84. Žižek, *Interrogating the Real*, 331.

85. Žižek, "Holding the Place," 311.

86. Žižek, "Fear of Four Words," 36.

87. Žižek "Neighbors and Other Monsters," 186.

88. Ibid., 140.

89. Žižek, *Fragile Absolute*, 127; Žižek *Desert of the Real*, 68; Žižek, "Holding the Place," 326. Žižek, *Fragile Absolute*, 11, Žižek, "Dialectical Clarity," 302; Žižek, "Neighbors and Other Monsters," 185–90. Part of his plea for ethical violence involves the "violence" done to the liberal vision of equality and universality when one attends to the particularity of the singular—not unlike the tension inherent in medical ethics when one is charged with attending to the needs of the particular patient without consideration for others. See also his essay, "From Democracy to Divine Violence," where he

of harmony and balance, but the violent act which disturbs this balance."[90] Indeed, Žižek is explicit in rejecting any assertion of a natural desire for peace and harmony.[91]

The violence of freedom brings to the fore the inherently conflicted nature of the exercise of freedom. Insofar as reality is fundamentally antagonistic and conflicted, insofar as antagonism is inherent in universality itself, the exercise of freedom can only mean choosing sides in the struggle.

In essence there are two sides to the conflict.[92] On one side there are the false concrete universalities that legitimate the existing divisions of the whole into functional parts and on the other side, there is the impossible real abstract universality, which is the void that is the meaningless multiplicity of the Real.[93] Žižek describes the division that the free act (the truth-event) mobilizes thus:

> The existence of the true Universal (as opposed to the false "concrete" Universality of the all-encompassing global Order of Being) is that of an endless and incessantly divisive struggle; it is ultimately the division between the two notions (and material practices) of Universality: those who advocate the positivity of the Order of Being as the ultimate horizon of knowledge and action, and those who accept the efficiency of the dimension of Truth-Event irreducible to (and unaccountable in terms of) the Order of Being.[94]

More specifically, the free political gesture is to act with and on behalf of the point(s) of exception or exclusion from the false concrete universal order(s)—like illegal immigrants or homeless. Such an act is nevertheless a universal one because it is antagonistic on behalf of the real universal, which is itself antagonistic.

---

defends violent popular self-defense—the example he uses is impoverished Haitians "necklacing" folks with burning tires—suggesting this violence is but the popular correlative of the sovereign state of exception (115–16).

90. Žižek, "Neighbors and Other Monsters," 186.

91. Žižek, "Dialectical Clarity," 245. See also 291, where he argues that action is not about transforming misery into a rose garden but looking for a rose in the midst of the misery.

92. What follows is drawn from Žižek, *Ticklish Subject*, 223–27.

93. Žižek, "Fear of Four Words," 80, 95, 97. It is worth nothing that Žižek speaks of the ontological incompleteness of reality, of its openness, which precludes the capture or containment of multiplicity in any whole or order of being. See Žižek, "Fear of Four Words," 90 and Žižek, "Dialectical Clarity," 240. See also Žižek, *On Belief*, 102 where he says life cannot be totalized; Žižek, "Thinking Backward," 94 argues reality is not constrained by the positivity of being. See also Žižek, *Puppet and Dwarf*, 94, 98, 143.

94. Žižek, *Ticklish Subject*, 227.

Such is the context and content of freedom that is the setting of Žižek's treatment of law. Given this construal of freedom it should be thoroughly unsurprising that Žižek is opposed to law. In keeping with the antagonistic character of the social field, and in the midst of arguing for a leftist suspension of the law, Žižek points out that the law is not neutral, that just as reality is fundamentally conflicted, the law too plays a part in the conflict and takes sides.

To understand the dynamics of law and how it thwarts freedom, Žižek devotes significant energy to the interrelation of Judaism and Christianity, and he draws heavily from Badiou's account of Saint Paul, who, we will recall, overcame the law not by means of simple negation—which remains in the cycle of transgression—but by means of subtraction; that is, by evacuating it of force. Žižek makes the same point by contrasting perversion, which remains bound to law as transgression and crime, with hysteria and "traversing the fantasy," both of which amount to breaking the passional attachment to law.[95]

Žižek, nevertheless, differs from Badiou in a few significant details. First, he has a much more dialectical and hence positive reading of Judaism, at times—although not consistently—suggesting that Judaism actually effected the same kind of subtraction of the law as Paul.[96] Second, in keeping with his negative ontology, he has a much more positive construal of sin. Whereas Badiou casts sin as the creation of law, Žižek interprets sin as an act of freedom. Thus, he makes the startling claim that the Fall into sin is Redemption, the explosion of freedom.[97] Third, he has no interest in retaining law, even as the law of love. Indeed, he suggests that a "law of love" would actually prompt him to want to hate and hurt his neighbors.[98] Instead, he is forthright in arguing that we must break out of law, that there is no way to "line up" law and love, that what matters is love beyond the law.[99] Thus, Christ's fulfillment of the law is a matter of completely voiding love from the law and so Christ's suspension of the law is actually its demise.[100]

Fourth, when Žižek speaks of love he means something different from Badiou's indifference to difference, which Žižek suspects too easily collapses into apoliticism.[101] Rather, by love Žižek means picking sides in the onto-

---

95. Žižek, *Ticklish Subject*, 247–48, 265.
96. Žižek, *Puppet and Dwarf*, 113.
97. Ibid., 118; Žižek, "Dialectical Clarity," 273.
98. Žižek, "Dialectical Clarity," 282; Žižek, "Neighbors and Other Monsters," 183.
99. Žižek, "Dialectical Clarity," 246; Žižek, *Puppet and Dwarf*, 114.
100. Žižek, *Puppet and Dwarf*, 117; Žižek, *On Belief*, 140.
101. Žižek, *On Belief*, 125–26.

logical struggle. Love is not a matter of desire[102] or a sentimental (pagan) cosmic feeling of oneness.[103] Indeed, love is ready to kill the neighbor.[104] Accordingly, love is neither reciprocity nor generosity but rather willed faithfulness to the imperfect other whom one elects from among all the others.[105] Thus, love is not universal but particular. It is a matter of violently cutting into the multitude and privileging one.[106]

II. Capitalism and Freedom

Having considered these philosophers' rejection of law in favor of a life beyond law, we must now ask if this freedom beyond the law can indeed bear the emancipatory expectation with which it is endowed by these philosophers. In particular, does such a freedom beyond the law trace a line of flight beyond the terror of capitalism?

The allusion in the section heading to the well-known book by Milton Friedman, one of the leading lights of the contemporary neoliberal capitalist order, is not accidental, for the argument that follows is that capitalism too embodies a kind of freedom beyond the law. Indeed, I argue that these philosophers' visions of freedom beyond the law do not offer a path beyond our current capitalist captivity, but are circumscribed by the capitalist (dis)order. This can be seen in at least two ways.

First, these visions remain trapped within what might be called the "dialectic of modern sovereignty" whereby even as they attempt to overcome the sovereign One of the state-form and its force of law, they do not succeed in escaping the multiplicity or multitude that is capitalism. Second, there is a striking isomorphy between neoliberal capitalism as a form of freedom beyond the law and particular features of life beyond the law as variously envisioned by these thinkers.

---

102. Ibid., 90; on this point, see Depoortere, "The End of God's Transcendence?" 497–523.
103. Žižek, *Puppet and Dwarf*, 119.
104. Žižek, "Dialectical Clarity," 254.
105. Milbank, "Double Glory," 122.
106. Žižek, "Neighbors and Other Monsters," 182. He goes on to say that justice is the attention given to those not selected. It is worth noting that this appears in the midst of an extended critique of Levinas' other as too narrowly defined, in such a way that it overlooks "monsters"—those whom we exclude from even the category of other.

The Dialectic of Modern Sovereignty

The crisis of law that initiates postmodern philosophical attention to the intersection of the juridical and the biopolitical is finally a question of sovereignty. After all, as Carl Schmidt famously declared, "the sovereign is he who decides on the exception,"[107] and as Agamben reminds us the exception is not the end of the force of law but a threshold whereby the force of law exceeds the letter.

It has become commonplace to assert that the current age is undergoing a transition from modern sovereignty centralized in the nation-state to a postmodern imperial sovereignty exercised by decentralized, transnational bodies.[108]

Yet as Adrian Pabst has argued, such a mapping of the matrix of sovereignty misidentifies the truly significant shift. The fundamental difference in rival modes of sovereignty, he argues, is not between the modern and postmodern but between the modern and pre-modern.[109] This is the case because the postmodern is but an extension and intensification of modern modes of sovereignty, with the transnational merely reinforcing the national subordination of the local under the universal. Indeed, as Foucault's work on modern biopolitical power has shown, modern sovereignty is not simply a matter of a centralized national sovereignty exerted over against the many but rather was equally a matter of sovereignty exercised in a decentralized mode as technologies of the self and economic "government through freedom." Thus modern sovereignty is not quintessentially centralized and national. Rather it is a dialectic of one *and* the many, of a juridical *and* biopower, of law *and* the state of exception, of the state *and* the market, of the Leviathan and the Multitude.[110]

What has this to do with postmodern freedom beyond the law? Put simply, the aforementioned efforts to escape both the juridical state and its law as well as the biopolitical force of law that is the state of exception fail to address adequately the sovereignty of the market. Tracing the political genealogy of the Spinozan multitude, Malcolm Bull has observed:

> Contemporary champions of the multitude remain trapped within this history, committed to a position that is ultimately either Hobbesian or Hayekian. Seeking a route out of the impasse posed by the global market and its reactive populisms,

---

107. Schmidt, *Political Theology*, 5.
108. See Hardt and Negri, *Multitude*.
109. Pabst, "Modern Sovereignty in Question," 572–73.
110. See Bull, "The Limits of Multitude," 19–39.

> they have retraced the path that led to it. The difficulty comes from starting with the multitude as an aggregation of individuals, and then proceeding to dichotomize the one and the many. Agency is then turned into a choice between general will or general intellect, state or society. Rather than being an agent of limitless potential, the multitude contracts political possibility to the primitivisms of the security state and the free market.[111]

In other words, the juridical state and its biopolitical law are not the only obstacle to freedom. Alongside the state, one must also contend with the market.

This is not to deny that the capitalist market still requires the state's law and the force of its law as the state of exception and that challenging this sovereignty as these postmodern philosophers do is necessary and worthwhile. Neither do I deny that setting sovereign singularities against the force of law may break (or at least resist) one pole of the modern dialectic of sovereignty.

However, freedom construed as beyond the law—even if it is attained—does not escape the other (arguably stronger) pole of the modern dialectic of sovereignty, namely, the free market of capitalism. Indeed, if we recall Deleuze and Guattari's history of capitalism, capitalism was born of such escapes and thrives under such conditions.

Hence such freedom may simply deliver the bearer even more firmly into the grasp of capitalism even as it prompts a mutation in the state-form. Which brings us to the isomorphy between capitalism and these visions of freedom beyond the law.

Capitalism as the Practice of Freedom

It is perhaps unsurprising that theologians and philosophers concerned with the brutal and exclusionary effects of the current global regime would approach capitalism as a form of bondage. We might even say that such a disposition comes naturally for those whose intellectual lineage includes Marxism and/or Christian socialists and liberationists. For such persons, it is counter-intuitive to suggest that capitalism is a practice of freedom.

Nevertheless, this is indeed how capitalism in its neoliberal form sees itself. Milton Friedman's work is finally not a testament to profit-maximization but to freedom, and his efforts on behalf of the capitalist market are in response to "the great threat to freedom" that is "the concentration

---

111. Ibid., 39.

of power."[112] Thus he is an advocate of the multitude, of decentralized power and the proliferation of variety over against oppressive uniformity, of the voluntary cooperation of individuals in the capitalist market place over against the centralized and coercive power of the state.

At first glance, one may be inclined to dismiss such a description as mere ideology or propaganda, but in fact this description finds significant *support* among most of the thinkers we have considered. After all, as Deleuze notes, capitalism itself is a freedom "beyond the law" insofar as its deterritorializing force liberates constitutive human power (whether it be Deleuze's desire or Žižek's drive) from the force of the state-form's law and its coding. Deleuze is not alone in praising capitalism's liberating force. Agamben and Badiou do so as well, and it would likewise appear amenable to both Žižek's[113] and Derrida's thought.

Of course, all of these thinkers finally turn against capitalism because its deterritorializing promise is unfulfilled.[114] Fidelity to the event of capitalist decoding is not sustained, we might say. As Deleuze argues, capitalism's deterritorializing power is not quite absolute; it finally effects a reterritorialization, associated with rendering desire amenable to insertion in capitalist processes, which Badiou associates with "the count."

Yet this alleged reterritorialization is not the imposition of law. It remains a freedom beyond law insofar as this reterritorialization is not a matter of a new law but, as Deleuze argues, an utterly flexible axiomatic[115] of decoded flows of desire: produce for the market.

112. Friedman, *Capitalism and Freedom*, 2.

113. Jason Glynos argues that Žižek embraces capitalism's deterritorializing power. See Glynos, "'There is no Other of the Other," 79.

114. Žižek argues that capitalism, like Lacan's analysis of the *object petit a*, structures subjectivity according to a failure to satisfy desire, which he calls "subject of desire." The object of desire is an imaginary lure concealing the substanceless void that is the real cause of desire. See Glynos, "There is no Other," 87, 90. A driving question of Žižek's work is, Why does capitalist deterritorializing generate new anxieties instead of individuals enjoying the creative process of shaping and reshaping their fluid multiple identities (see Glynos, "There is no Other," 88; Žižek, *Ticklish Subject*, 341)? The subject of desire cannot handle fulfillment and so creates new obstacles to fulfillment, *object petit a*, outsides, enemies, as well as big Others (Glynos, "There is no Other," 90). What holds us is not a false narrative but a mode of enjoyment made possible (Glynos, "There is no Other," 95). Žižek seeks a new subjectivity and an ethic of drive/ethic of the real that breaks from capitalist mode of enjoyment by exposing the absence of the big Other, the imaginary obstacle become scapegoat (like immigrants and refugees) (Glynos, "There is no Other," 96–97). Glynos argues that Žižek's alternative ethic is at this point entirely negative because it is nothing less than a new subjectivity that lives by passing through the fantasy, that lives without being bothered by lack of the big Other (Glynos, "There is no Other," 100).

115. Derrida might call it a "postulation." See his *Rogues*, 142.

Capitalism as Pure Means

Moreover, it is increasingly *less* clear that capitalism is defined by the rigidity of "the count." Increasingly it appears capable of marketing anything, be it of a transgressive, perverse, or even oppositional nature. (Think of Che Guevara as a brand logo.) As Hayek notes, "the cosmos of the market neither is nor could be governed by such a single scale of ends; it serves the multiplicity of separate and incommensurable ends of all its separate members."[116] This is to say, even the way Deleuze puts the axiomatic as "produce for the market" is perhaps too teleological. As many economists insist, the market is a pure means, facilitating and accommodating a multiplicity of human ends.[117] In this regard, Hayek notes that a capitalist society is "means-connected" and not "ends-connected."[118]

Moreover, as Friedman insists, the market is voluntary and not coercive—people are "free to choose"—and as Deleuze argues, desire is inherently productive. In other words, it is not clear that capitalism does reterritorialize desire. Instead, it may only facilitate "what comes naturally," as Adam Smith suggested when he observed that humanity has a natural propensity to "truck and barter."[119] This possibility is heightened by the appearance of shopping (not purchasing or acquiring) as an kind of end-in-itself; a pure desire that (contra Žižek) does not exist by being thwarted because it literally desires nothing beyond desire.[120] If this is true, then capitalism can be characterized as, to twist Augustine's famous saying, the freedom to produce and exchange as you please. It may yet be that capitalism is the freedom of crowned anarchy and so finally compatible with a self-governed life beyond law, with freedom as pure means.[121]

Capitalism and Free Relations

This possibility is further suggested by a certain isomorphy between capitalist relations and human relations beyond the law as construed by philosophical visions we have considered. To begin with, the neoliberal understanding

---

116. Hayek, *Mirage of Social Justice*, 108.
117. See Marglin, *Dismal Science*, 173–75.
118. Hayek, *Mirage of Social Justice*, 110.
119. Smith, *Wealth of Nations*, 1:17.
120. See Wannenwetsch, "The Desire of Desire," 315–30, and Sedgwick, *Market Economy and Christian Ethics*, 149.
121. Agamben, *Means Without End*, 115–17.

of market exchange as beyond law and so as voluntary, as a matter of pure uncoerced will, is well-known.[122]

There is a striking parallel between this and the kinds of relations beyond law envisioned by the postmodern philosophers we have considered, which are likewise purely voluntary. Indeed, if anything, several of these thinkers portend a purer capitalism or freer market insofar as they abjure even the circumscribed reciprocity of the contract in favor of relations of sheer gratuitousness and use without return.[123] As such, they resemble—even as they exceed—the libertarian voices who eschew any juridical interference in the market.[124]

Several other shared features of the relations between these free singularities and multiplicities bear mentioning. Michael Novak, a well-known Christian advocate of capitalism, describes the character of capitalist relations thus: "Individuals wander alone, in some confusion, amid many casualties" on the "wasteland at the heart of democratic capitalism [that] is like a field of battle."[125] It would be a mistake to interpret this condition as a matter of isolation, for the capitalist subject can and does engage in common endeavors and collective action. Voluntary associations and the multitude are at the heart of this capitalist vision.

In this brief description of capitalist relations we find several similarities with the vision of life beyond law offered by Derrida et al. First, there is the alienation of these singularities. Von Hayek is well known for arguing that the capitalist market is a spontaneous order ("catallaxy") that emerges in response to the intrinsic alienation that separates individuals. The market is an adaptive response to the fact that we are intrinsically opaque to one

---

122. Note that voluntary choice is not synonymous with unlimited choice. Freedom is freedom within constraints. This is not unlike Žižek's account of freedom as the ability to say "No" in any circumstance.

123. Agamben, *Time That Remains*, 119, 135–36; see also Derrida's well-known rejection of exchange and gift-eliciting-a-return. In this he is following Levinas, who is subjected to a withering critique on this point by David Hart in *The Beauty of the Infinite*, 81–83. Hart points out that the refusal of return is a kind of elevated self-denial and self-torture that becomes a moral heroism as it really seeks to preserve the purity of the agent's intention, a kind of self-aggrandizement that effaces anything distinctive about the Other, rendering it merely the same, "nothing before the infinite orientation of my ethical adventure." Žižek makes a similar point with regard to Derrida actually defacing the otherness of the Other. See his "Neighbors and Other Monsters."

124. One might think that the market depends on the force of enforcement and that without it, the market would collapse. While force certainly enhances the efficiency of the market, as Adam Smith noted, it is sympathy that drives the market (which is a kind a concern for reputation), something noted more recently by Francis Fukuyama in *Trust: The Social Virtues and the Creation of Prosperity*.

125. Novak, *Spirit of Democratic Capitalism*, 54.

another, not sharing in a common good beyond the contingent intersection of the sheer force of our wills. Thus, the market functions in essence as an epistemological tool, that by means of price and demand communicates knowledge about the desires of the impenetrable others.[126] Here we may recall Derrida's "double bind of responsibility" that leaves one unable to discern how to respond to the other in the absence of the law. There is perhaps no better description of this fundamental alienation between singularities than that offered by Žižek, when he writes about the paradox of human freedom:

> There is no freedom outside the traumatic encounter with the opacity of the Other's desire: freedom does not mean I simply get rid of the Other's desire—I am, as it were, thrown into my freedom when I confront this opacity as such, deprived of the fantasmic cover that tells me what the Other wants from me. In this difficult predicament, full of anxiety, when I know *that* the Other wants something from me, without knowing *what* this desire is, I am thrown back into myself, compelled to assume the risk of freely determining the coordinates of my desire.[127]

In both the capitalist vision and the vision of life beyond the law, singularities are fundamentally and intrinsically strangers, relating without empathy, "doing what is to be done in a weird coincidence of blind spontaneity and reflexive distance, helping others while avoiding their disgusting proximity."[128] Given this distance and aversion, one might wonder what kind of "help" can be given and one can appreciate Derrida's admission that apart from the law, discerning responsibility is impossible. Nevertheless, this distance is called freedom.

Second, and unsurprisingly given the alienation that characterizes singularities beyond the law, the free relations that characterize capitalism and these postmodern philosophical visions are marked by conflict. Thus Novak equates capitalist society with a battle field. Although capitalism is frequently defended as an alternative to war for bellicose passions, a claim refuted in a variety of ways,[129] it is nonetheless an agonistic vision of human relations: strangers struggling to assert their wills and accumulate the resources necessary to achieve what they will. Likewise, the freedom beyond the law espoused by these philosophers is an agonistic vision. Žižek is perhaps the most forthright in this regard, openly embracing conflict, struggle,

126. See Hayek, *Constitution of Liberty*, 29; Hayek, *Fatal Conceit*, 77, 81.
127. Žižek, *Puppet and Dwarf*, 129.
128. Žižek, "Dialectical Clarity," 303.
129. See Perelman, *The Invention of Capitalism*; Wood, *Empire of Capital*.

and violence, which correspond to the fundamental nature of reality. But it is not absent in the others, even in Badiou, whose efforts to espouse a non-competitive vision of relations fails under the weight of his own account of the event and the clash of worlds.[130]

III. Freedom in Christ: The Law of Love Beyond Capital

The implication of the previous section is neither that there is no freedom beyond law nor that such a freedom cannot escape the bonds of capitalism. Rather, it is that the vision of life beyond law offered by Deleuze and company lacks the resources to effect that line of flight. Their efforts to escape law and one pole of the "dialectic of modern sovereignty" only sends them into the clutches of the other pole: the multitude that is capitalism and the "liberation" accomplished by its deterritorializing power.

Escaping both the capitalist state and the capitalist market requires more than rejecting the law, which merely leaves us struggling to remain afloat in a turbulent sea of singularities contending with one another by the pure means of capitalism. What is needed is a law that can guide us through the valley of death, shadowed as it is by the state and market, to the promised land of charity, where the law is finally deactivated. To one such vision of law we now turn. First we consider the transfiguration of law, then the transfiguration of the subject under law, and then finally the transfiguration of economy.

The Transfiguration of Law

Judaism and Christianity share a liturgical proclamation, "Happy are those who delight in the law of the Lord."[131] Of course, such an exclamation could be dismissed as the cry of the conquered, of those who have internalized the force of law and so quenched the spirit of life that they delight in their captivity. Such a dismissal, however, can draw no support from Agamben and company, for theirs is uniformly a vision of the law as coercion of the will. Yet the Jewish and Christian claim is that the will can *delight* in the law, that is, the will can *freely* will the law's end. Here is a vision of law that is shorn of

---

130. See Žižek's review of *Logics of Worlds*: "On Alain Badiou and *Logiques des mondes*."

131. Ps 1 NRSV. The Psalter is a liturgical book of both Jews and Christians.

the force of law, a law that neither inaugurates a crisis nor constructs death camps. How is this possible?

In the *Summa*, Aquinas begins what is known as the treatise on law by noting that law pertains to reason and not to the will simply.[132] For Aquinas and the analogical-intellectualist tradition of which he is a part, law is a matter of practical reason, of *iudicium*, judgment, that involves *both* the will and the intellect working in harmony.[133] In other words, law is a "rule and measure of human action" in which the will participates. It is not simply a matter of *imperium*, of the execution of a judgment already made in which the will has no participation and which confronts the will with the stark choice: obey or disobey.

With this simple statement we have moved beyond the dialectic of force of law and no law. Here is a law that is not founded on violence, that is not dependent upon the coercive force invested in law by the sovereign. Here is a law that does not require either external motivation to coerce the will into obedience nor an endless proliferation of particular laws until finally we are submerged in the totalizing morality of the Kantian axiom (or Kakfa's penal colony) that renders us guilty, indebted, under judgment in the absence of the law's letter. As Daniel Westberg notes, Aquinas was content to address the law in a general way, to address the first few principles, to refer to the Decalogue, and leave the rest to Christian prudence, where reason and will combine in discerning, judging, and deciding.[134]

What traps the likes of Deleuze in the dialectic of modern sovereignty is their indebtedness to the nominalist/voluntarist vision of law associated with Scotus and Ockham, as well as Suarez, who though not a nominalist inadvertently strengthened the voluntarist vision of law.[135] According to this vision, law is strictly a matter of the will. When one is confronted with law, one is confronted by the codification of the sovereign's (inscrutable) will. And the only choice is either to obey or disobey, with the motivation for that choice provided by the coercive force invested by the sovereign in law.

Since law is by definition a matter of the will, and the force of law is by definition a coercive, external imposition and not a shared deliberative practice of both the will and intellect and of many persons, the only truly liberative practice is not transgression, but the rejection and evacuation of law.

---

132. Aquinas, *Summa Theologica*, I–II, 90.1.
133. Ibid., I–II, 91.3.
134. Westberg, "Reason, Will and Legalism," 434.
135. See Westberg, "Reason, Will and Legalism."

To be fair I do not mean to suggest that the likes of Žižek are simply wrong in their account of law. To the contrary, capitalist law may well function in a nominalist/voluntarist mode, as the forceful imposition of will upon will.

Where these thinkers err is in holding that such is the only mode of law's operation. As a result, when they move beyond law they are left naked before the other pole of the dialectic of modern sovereignty, namely, the multitude that is capitalism.

The alternative, as I have suggested, is a more analogical, participatory practice of law in which the will can delight; that is, freely participate. What is more, it is this analogical or participatory mode of law that finally portends the deactivation of law. To make sense of this claim we must return to Aquinas and the transfiguration of law.

Already we have suggested that Aquinas' vision of law is not coercive. Yet, as Žižek notes, neither is it neutral. But unlike our philosophers who are only capable of viewing law negatively, the possibility of *delight* in the law suggests that law can be positive. Indeed, insofar as the law is not coercive but is something that the will or desire can actually *delight* in, it must be positive; that is, it must embody something toward which the will by its nature freely moves. As Aquinas notes, this positive dimension of law is its being ordered to humanity's (super)natural end, which is the friendship of humanity in and with God.[136]

Here it is important to note that the law is *not* our end. Obedience to the law is not the end of human desire. Nor is abject submission to the will of an alien, inscrutable other (think of Derrida and Žižek) the end of law. Rather, the end of law is the free communion of all in charity. Thus, the law is a kind of temporary measure, a guide or pedagogue that is "deactivated" when the *telos* of law and of humanity is attained.

More specifically, the law is deactivated as it is transfigured, as its end becomes neither submission to the coercive force of a sovereign will, nor the proliferation of specific laws that eventually festers into a generalized guilt but participation in the communion of the Trinity through Christ. Law is transfigured as it becomes a figure, as it finds its end in the figure of the Messiah, Christ, who by renewing the possibility of the joyous conviviality of all in charity, fulfills the law, not by setting it aside but by exceeding it in the way that all true virtue (which is to say infinite charity, the sum of all virtue) exceeds the law.[137] (Think here of Kierkegaard's suspension of the ethical or the "higher righteousness" of the Gospel of Matthew's Christ.)

---

136. Aquinas, *Summa Theologica*, I–II, 99.1.ad 2.
137. See Milbank, "Double Glory," 168.

This transfiguration of law is behind Aquinas' remarkable logic of the divine law whereby the Mosaic Law is still observed by Christians (including Jewish Christians) who do not abide by its ceremonial and judicial precepts. This is the case because Christ is the fulfillment of Torah, the communion that is the law's end. Therefore, being joined to Christ is the perfect fulfillment of law.[138] Here, finally, we have a law that neither bites nor commands, a law that is indeed beyond law.

The Spirit and the Letter: The Transfiguration of the Subject

The nominalist/voluntarist vision of law must coerce the subject by forcing the will. Already it has been suggested that the Jewish-Christian transfiguration of law creates the possibility of a non-coercive law, of a law whose principle is not the *force* of law but *delight*. It has been further suggested that such a possibility hinges upon not only a different notion of law but a different understanding of the subject, one in which the will participates in the deliberation and judgment that is law.

To better understand this transfigured subject and how it too finally deactivates the law, we turn to Augustine and his treatise *On the Spirit and the Letter*. In this treatise, Augustine proposed to treat the law and in particular, Paul's charge that through the law sin has abounded.[139] What is quickly apparent, however, is how Augustine never views the law as a problem, as anything other than good, holy and just (following Paul in Rom 7:12).[140] Rather the problem resides in the subject whose will refuses the

---

138. On this point, see Levering, *Christ's Fulfillment of Torah and Temple*. The question of supersessionism is complicated, in part because much depends on how the term is understood. For a helpful treatment of this question, see Marshall, "Christ and Cultures," 81–100. There is a kind of complex supersessionism in the sense that the Old Law (exterior conformity) is superseded by the New Law (associated with the grace of the Holy Spirit that effects interior change). Yet as Aquinas says, the New Law was found in the state of the Old Law (see Levering, *Christ's Fulfillment*, 22–23) and the present state of the New Law will be done away with and surpassed by the heavenly state. See Aquinas, *Summa Theologica*, I–II 106.4, especially ro1. I am inclined to argue that Judaism, no less than Christianity, is not and will not be superseded so much as fulfilled. The church between the times is the fulfillment of neither Judaism nor Christianity. Rather Christ, the Jewish Messiah, is the fulfillment of both.

139. See also Augustine's unfinished commentary on Romans, published as *Augustine on Romans*.

140. The challenge is Romans 7:7–13 and especially v. 9, "I once was alive apart from the law." The error occurs when one reads this contrast between life and law as biographical and chronological. The "I" clearly does *not* correspond to Paul's biography—see Phil 3:5–6; Gal 1:14—nor does it refer to the Adamic state of paradise before

gift of participation in its own good and so separates itself from the intellect (and others).[141] Thus the treatise begins with a defense of those who claim that it is possible for humanity to advance steadily toward and live in the perfect righteousness signified by the law. What Augustine warns against is the supposition that the subject through the "mere power of human will itself" can be righteous, that the human will alone can use the law to attain righteousness.[142]

Here our philosophers are exposed. In a sense their entire argument against law is that it would coerce the will and impose an alien *telos* upon it. Yet Augustine, following in Paul's footsteps and foreshadowing Aquinas, suggests that the problem our philosophers identify with the law is in fact not a problem of law at all but a problem of the subject, and in particular of the will.[143] In other words, the problem of law is finally not a question of law at all but of the subject who appropriates the law.

This is to say, the problem is the subject's transformation of the law. As Augustine makes clear, the law cannot prevent sin; it cannot coerce the will. But this does not signify the failure of the law, for the law is good. It simply reveals that the law was never meant to prevent sin or coerce the will. In a sense the law in its pure form is "deactivated."

The problem of law surfaces when the subject hijacks the law, activates it by wedding it to sovereign violence, and uses it in the futile attempt to prevent sin and conquer other wills. In particular, when the subject that appropriates law is first and foremost the autonomous will, the will that claims to be free by refusing the gift of participation in corporate, rational judgment concerning the good, the law becomes the "letter that kills."

Whereas when the subject that appropriates the law is first and foremost the subject of a unified intellect and will, and so capable of participating in, deliberating over, and finally delighting in the good, the law is no problem at all. Far from coercively confronting the will as an external other,

---

the fall. It is a literary device (see 1 Cor 13 for similar move) contrasting two states of law, law without the Spirit and law under the Spirit. See Byrne, *Romans,* 216–24; Johnson, *Rereading Romans,* 112–23.

141. This is not so much argued as presupposed in *On The Spirit and the Letter.* For an explication of Augustine on freedom and the will, see the excellent essay by Schindler, "Freedom beyond Our Choosing: Augustine on the Will and Its Objects," 67–98.

142. Augustine, *On the Spirit and the Letter,* chapter 4.

143. I do not mean to imply that the problem is *only* of the will's making. Certainly, human reasoning is also corrupted by sin. What I mean to suggest is that the problem is of the will as a power distinct from reason, with reason functioning at best as a kind of "advisor" as in Suarez. In contrast, in Augustine and Aquinas the intellect and will are unified as a kind of rational desire. On this, see Westberg, "Reason, Will and Legalism."

the law is, as previously suggested, itself the product of the will's participation in the apprehension of the good. Thus as Herbert McCabe notes, "A totally obedient community would be one in which no one was ever compelled to do anything."[144]

But, of course, the presupposition of both Augustine's and Paul's account of law is that such a subject no longer naturally exists. Instead, postfall, we inhabit a world that resembles the nominalist/voluntarist vision of our philosophers, a world where law seems inherently connected to force and life is but a struggle of wills—wills that, having forsaken the labor of reasoning[145] and the attraction of the good, are left to the fate of the inevitable conflict that characterizes not merely contingent (with which the Christian tradition has no truck) but finally utterly arbitrary relations.[146] Life is reduced, as Badiou and others would have it, to a throw of the dice.

It is at this point that the Spirit comes into play in Augustine's argument. The law is good but the (fallen) subject has renounced the gift of participation in the good and so confronts a law that now bites (not because the law has changed but because the subject has). To this fearful, disconnected, and divided[147] subject the Spirit comes with the offer of healing and renewed participation in its good, through union with Christ, who is the good incarnate. So by grace the subject is transfigured, joined to Christ's body, and the law is (once again) deactivated, no longer commanding anything; only giving testimony to the form of our freedom,[148] which is the end of law, Christ himself. As Augustine says, "love and do as you please," with love not being a command at all but rather simply what we please, what pleases us, the source of our delight.

---

144. McCabe, *God Matters*, 229.

145. What I mean by the labor of reasoning is the will's participation with the intellect in discerning, deliberating, and deciding on action in accord with its good. See Westberg, "Reason, Will and Legalism."

146. David Schindler ("Freedom beyond Our Choosing") points out that a truly autonomous free will renders the will's choices utterly arbitrary because the will's autonomy precludes its being influenced by externals, for such external influences are by definition an infringement of the will's autonomy. Schindler notes that even where some influence is permitted, the aporia between the influence that is not determinate and the decision of the will can only be arbitrary.

147. The reference to a divided subject is a reference to the disorder of the subject's intellect, will, and desires internally as well as the conflict with God, neighbors, and the rest of creation.

148. As Milbank notes, love has a form. Milbank, "Double Glory," 156. For more on law as the form of our freedom, see Hütter, "The Twofold Center of Lutheran Ethics," 31–54, and Yeago, "Martin Luther on Grace, Law, and Moral Life," 163–91.

Economy Transfigured: The Law of Love Beyond Capitalism

A transfigured law that elicits the will's participation in its good and a transfigured subject that delights in a deactivated law that is the form of its freedom. How do these portend the end of our capitalist captivity?

The economic corollary of the modern dialectic of sovereignty is that of a command economy or the *laissez-faire* market, with a welfare-state/regulated market occupying the threshold at their juxtaposition. At first glance one might be inclined to associate this rehabilitated law and subject with citizens of this modern between, and certainly Christian social ethics has its share of voices who stake out this nether-ground as the space of the Gospel's law of love.

Yet as both Pabst and Bull remind us, the "or" of the modern dialectic of sovereignty (state or market) is but a secret collusion between the two poles (a hidden "and") so that, as Pabst argues, the real cut, the real between lies elsewhere.

Why is this the case? Because the regulated market and the welfare state do not resolve anything; here I am tempted to invoke (and perhaps twist) Žižek's notion of the "parallax view" and suggest that the reconciliation projected upon that middle ground is a reconciliation that reconciles nothing.[149]

The state-regulated market does not fundamentally change the nature of economic relationships in the market. They remain a contest of autonomous wills, only now those wills are coerced by the force of law. Likewise, the welfare state with its redistributionist efforts does not alter the nature of the market in the direction of justice. It does not stop the economic war of wills. At best it merely compensates for the worst injustices—sort of like an economic Red Cross on the battlefield of the capitalist *socius*—and at worst it prepares its customers for further incorporation into and expropriation by the market.

In contrast, the transformed law and transformed subject of Christianity point beyond the mere moderation of the commercial war of wills. At home neither in the modern One nor Multitude, nor in a hybrid of the two, the transformed law and subject are part and parcel of the divine economy born of the event of Christ and lived in fidelity to that event. This is to say, Christ's new command/new law of love subtracts those who hear it from the age of warring wills, the force of law, and the state of exception[150] and inaugurates an economy of love.

---

149. See Žižek, *Interrogating the Real*, 213–25.

150. It is beyond the scope of this paper to argue that Jewish and Christian

This economy of love lies between the state and the market. It is between them in the sense that it involves *both* market and state. As such it is not a command economy simply coercing and containing the chaos of the multitude nor is it the "free" market in the perverse sense of the agony of "free" wills that it is commonplace to celebrate today.

Yet neither is it a hybrid welfare state/regulated market that does not fundamentally challenge the antagonism of the One and Many. Rather, it brings the state and the market both under the good in which they, and the persons who constitute them, participate. In other words, it envisions the state and market as expressions or practices of the common good.

Concretely, this economy of love involves laws. After all, as Aquinas notes, reflecting on the economic precepts of the Mosaic law, the law aids people in loving their neighbors by accustoming them to giving and coming to one another's aid.[151] This is seen as well in the New Law, which takes shape in, among other things, the works of mercy and the economy that such work nurtured in the life and history of the church.[152]

But at the same time it is beyond the law in the sense that the law of love is finally transfigured, fulfilled and so deactivated in the presence of the virtue that is the law's end—namely, charity.

This creates the space for a truly free market, one that aids persons in loving their neighbors as a practice of love. Another name for this free market is a virtuous or moral market. Here is economy transfigured so that in the very processes and practices of production and distribution, justice and love are served as human communion is nurtured. The economy itself becomes an opportunity for love and service instead of a field of contention and bitter tears that needs ever tighter regulation (voluntarist accounts of law require endless proliferation and ever greater specificity of law[153]) and ever greater supplementation in the form of forever expanding safety nets.

This is the economy toward which Pope Benedict XVI gestured in *Caritas in veritate* and which is glimpsed in what Bruni and Zamagni call the "civil economy," and John Milbank calls "the real third way."[154] Such visions

---

Messianism has nothing to do with the "state of exception" that our philosophers identify with the messianic, following Benjamin.

151. Aquinas, *Summa Theologica*, I–II 105.2 r01, 4.

152. For more on the Works of Mercy as constituting an economy and even a full-fledged way of life, see Keenan, *The Works of Mercy*; Broadman, *Charity and Welfare*; Broadman, *Charity and Religion in Medieval Europe*; Henderson, *Piety and Charity in Late Medieval Florence*; Black, *Guild and State*; Mollat, *The Poor in the Middle Ages*; Tierney, *Medieval Poor Law*.

153. See Westberg, "Reason, Will and Legalism."

154. Bruni and Zamagni, *Civil Economy*; Milbank, "A Real Third Way," 27–70.

and efforts foreshadow the divine economy where we plant and harvest, build and inhabit, and all gather around the Lord's Table to share in his bounty, and none go hungry any more.

5

"The Fragile Brilliance of Glass"

Empire, Multitude, and the Coming Community

> Is it wise or prudent to wish to glory in the breadth and magnitude of an empire when you cannot show that the men whose empire it is are happy? ... The joy of such men may be compared to the fragile splendor of glass: they are horribly afraid lest it be suddenly shattered.
>
> —Augustine[1]

This essay takes up the political questions of empire, sovereignty, and democracy by means of an engagement with the thought of Michael Hardt, Antonio Negri, and Giorgio Agamben. The work of these thinkers merits engagement not the least because they are among a handful of contemporary philosophers whose thought of the political proves simultaneously most salutary and vexing for the task of articulating a postliberal Augustinian/radically orthodox political theology. At the risk of artificially separating the salutary from the vexing—for finally they are one and the same—their accounts of the political problem of the early twenty-first century West are most helpful while their anticipation of democracy raises serious questions about the viability of the church as a political formation capable of escaping the clutches of the current terror.

After considering their respective accounts of the biopolitical production of postmodern empire, I take up their constructive visions of what comes next: the coming community, the multitude, the common, and so forth. I then compare and contrast those democratic hopes with that embodied in an Augustinian political ecclesiology, an ecclesial politics of

---

1. Augustine, *City of God Against the Pagans*, 4.3.

pilgrimage, considering in particular how this theopolitics foreshadows the advent of a new kind of democracy. In the end, I argue, the hope nurtured by Agamben, Hardt, and Negri fails to hold out the promise of life beyond empire and this because finally they, and not an Augustinian church, are insufficiently democratic.

I. Sovereignty, Empire, and the Camp

Over the last several decades much has been made of the new world order announced by the first Bush administration. In an attempt to make sense of this novel political situation, various concepts and labels have been applied, such as "the end of history," the advent of a post-political age, the establishment of a *pax americana*, or empire lite, to name just a few. Such terms are interesting not the least because they suggest a situation that is simultaneously old and new. The current political situation is understood as both something novel—the end of history, a post-political era—as well as a return of the old—the *pax romana* and empire. The work of Hardt and Negri as well as Agamben is helpful because it aids us in making sense of this simultaneously novel yet ancient moment.

The ancient or continuous aspect of the current political situation is described by both in terms of sovereignty, the power of rule. The novelty of the current situation is, again for both, a matter of the particular form that the exercise of sovereignty takes today. Hardt and Negri treat this complex of the old and new in terms of empire. Agamben approaches it in terms of the state of exception and the camp.

The Postmodern Sovereignty of Empire

At least since the second Bush administration's assumption of power in 2001 and subsequent military (mis)adventures, it has been fashionable in some circles to argue over whether or not the United States constitutes an empire. In their work, *Empire*, Michael Hardt and Antonio Negri cut through the debate in a manner that intends to leave both sides of the debate chastened. On one hand, they affirm that the current global order can indeed be conceptualized in terms of empire. "Empire is materializing before our very eyes," they wrote in 2000, pointing to the irresistible and irreversible globalization of capitalist production and exchange overseen by a political subject that governs this world.[2] Moreover, by virtue of its formal as well as

---

2. Hardt and Negri, *Empire*, xi.

material constitution the U.S. holds a privileged position in this empire.³ On the other hand, however, this imperial subject is not in any simple manner properly identified either with the Bush administration or the United States. "The United States does not, and indeed no nation-state can today, form the center of an imperialist project."⁴ This is the case because the current imperial order is unlike previous empires and imperial logics, which is to say that it embodies a distinctly postmodern form of empire.⁵ Hardt and Negri identify several features of this new, postmodern sovereignty.

First, in conjunction with the advance of capitalist globalization, the sovereignty of nation-states has declined. The modern form of sovereignty embodied in nation-states has given way to the postmodern sovereignty of empire, which has no origin in a single nation-state or figure but instead is composed of a series or network of national and supranational organisms, including major capitalist corporations.⁶ Mind you, this is not to suggest that nation-states are irrelevant. To the contrary, imperial administration today continues to be conducted largely by the structures and personnel of the dominant nation-states.⁷ The point is rather that nation-states are no longer sovereign in the sense of serving national interests but are increasingly oriented toward the ends of the global capitalist market.⁸ Moreover, as we shall see momentarily, the military force of the nation-state remains vital to the perpetuation of this empire.

Second, this empire is not governed by a linear logic that extends power outward from a sovereign center by means of conquest and destruction, thereby enlarging its borders and subsuming countries within the closed space of its sovereignty. Rather, this new empire exercises a postmodern sovereignty that eschews boundaries and recognizes no territorial limits. It is decentered and deterritorializing.⁹ It expands by rearticulating open space and reinventing incessantly diverse and singular relations in networks across unbounded terrain.¹⁰ Hence, the catchphrases of this imperial logic include "contingency," "mobility," "flexibility," "fluidity," and "difference."

---

3. Ibid., xiv. By "formal constitution" they mean the written document along with its various amendments and legal apparatuses; by "material constitution" they mean the continuous formation and re-formation of social forces.
4. Ibid., xiii–xiv, italics deleted.
5. See Wood, *Empire of Capital*.
6. Hardt and Negri, *Empire*, xii.
7. Hardt and Negri, *Multitude*, 60.
8. Ibid., 163.
9. Hardt and Negri, *Empire*, xii.
10. Ibid., 182.

Third, even as this empire is perhaps most visible in its global extension, weakening national sovereignty and incorporating economies in a global capitalist market, at least as significant is its intensive extension into all areas and aspects of life itself. Not only does this new mode of imperial sovereignty breach national and economic boundaries for the sake of capitalist production and exchange; it also subsumes life itself. Here we touch upon the biopolitical dimension of postmodern empire, familiar to readers of Michel Foucault, upon whom Hardt and Negri draw. They observe that the new empire is not satisfied with political and economic sovereignty; it claims life as well. Its scope exceeds territory and population to embrace the depths of the social world.[11] This is to say, it is not satisfied with the formal subsumption into capitalism of a vital power that originates outside of its gaze (whether that be non-capitalist modes of production or the reproduction of its labor force). Now it seeks the real subsumption of the productive power that is life. Accordingly, under this new imperial order, production is no longer conceived in merely economic terms but now encompasses what might be called social production—not only the production of material goods but also the production of communications, relationships, and forms of life.[12] In other words, production is now not merely economic but has become biopolitical as capitalist logic encompasses not only the production of material goods in a strictly economic sense but all facets of social life, the economic, cultural, and political.[13]

Empire accomplishes this real subsumption by supplementing the heavy, spatial disciplines of modernity (the factory, the school, the hospital, the barracks, the prison) with the exercise of a "lighter" and more defuse biopower through various socio-cultural practices aimed at rendering not only the body's product (labor) but the body itself susceptible to capitalist incorporation. Hardt and Negri summarize the modes of biopolitical control as "the bomb, money, and ether."[14] By "ether" they mean communication, education, and culture. Think of the manifold ways culture, fashion, consumption, communication, sports, entertainment, and education are permeated by capitalist significance and capitalist imperatives. Now even when we are not working or are otherwise engaged in activities only tangentially related to the market we are in fact being more deeply enmeshed in the bonds of capital as it becomes the very fabric of our life and being.

11. Ibid., xv.
12. Hardt and Negri, *Multitude*, xv.
13. Ibid., xvi.
14. Hardt and Negri, *Empire*, 345.

Fourth, war is inevitable in this new empire. War has become a generalized state, global and interminable.[15] Indeed, Hardt and Negri declare that under this new imperial regime, war functions as an instrument of rule; military force must guarantee the conditions for the functioning of the world market.[16] At first glance this may appear to contradict the claim that this empire differs from past empires precisely because it eschews invasion, conquest and the seizure of territory. Yet the contradiction is resolved when it is realized that the point of this war is not territorial conquest and the enlargement of national boundaries—clearly defined goals with a terminal point—but the sheer assertion of dominance.[17] This is the war of smooth space; a war without end in the sense of war that is both continuous and devoid of any *telos*, whose goal rather is the removal of boundaries and ends that would obstruct or block the flow of capital. This is war for a generalized but nebulous and elusive condition called "security" that is fittingly captured in the concept of "preemption." War to ward off that which does not (yet) exist; war as distraction,[18] obstructing the potential emergence of alternatives to the current order of things.

The State of Exception and the Camp

Turning to the work of Giorgio Agamben, one is immediately struck by the very different, if ultimately complementary, focus of his work.[19] Although broadly concerned with similar issues of sovereignty and power in the contemporary political milieu, the political problematic that draws Agamben's attention is more narrowly focused than that of Hardt and Negri. Instead of concentrating on the broad and fashionable problematic of empire, Agamben interrogates the "state of exception" that, he holds, is the condition of

---

15. Hardt and Negri, *Multitude*, 3.
16. Ibid., xiii, 177.
17. This insight is Wood's, but it comports well with Hardt and Negri.
18. See Klein, *The Shock Doctrine*, for a compelling account of how capitalism advances by means of exploiting crises and disasters provoked by war.
19. Although I treat these thinkers as complementary in this essay, I am not denying that differences exist. For the purposes of this essay, however, the similarities are far more important than the differences. For one instance of how they understand their differences, see Negri, "Political Subject and Absolute Immanence," 234–37, and Agamben, *Homo Sacer*, 243–44. Negri says Agamben's focus on the margin and the refusal of sovereignty does not provide a positive account of being's productivity; Agamben suggests that Negri cannot adequately distinguish constituting power from sovereign power because in the end he lacks an adequate ontology of potentiality.

possibility of all sovereignty and the hidden foundation of Western politics, of which the current imperial age is but the latest manifestation.

His starting point is familiar. His work is, in part at least, "a response to the bloody mystification of a new planetary order" and the contemporary dissolution of "the great State structures."[20] Likewise, he embraces Foucault's account of modern biopolitics, in which life itself becomes a principal object of the projections and calculations of State power.[21] In fact, he attributes the eclipse of political thought in this post-political age to a failure to reckon with this "foundational event of modernity."[22]

However, Agamben deliberately positions his work as a supplement to or completion of Foucault's efforts insofar as he suggests that the biopolitical turn in itself is neither as novel nor as decisive as Foucault's work might suggest. Agamben argues that biopolitics has ancient and not merely modern roots, that the subsumption of life by the political is the original, if concealed, nucleus of sovereign power: "It can even be said," he writes, "that the production of a biopolitical body is the original activity of sovereign power."[23] He supports this claim by pointing out that the Western political tradition has always asserted that true life, the good life, was not natural life, life in a state of nature, but rather political life. Thus Western politics always aimed at the subsumption of life, even if it has only approached that goal under the sign of (post)modernity.

Agamben's supplementation of Foucault, however, extends beyond pushing back the history of biopolitics. He also challenges the significance of Foucault's insights. Not because Foucault is wrong, or that his work is not of crucial importance, but because only considering how the state-form has gone biopolitical and now so thoroughly and intensively manages life risks distracting would-be revolutionaries from the underlying problematic of sovereignty.

Pressing beyond the significance of the biopolitical character of contemporary politics, Agamben holds that what is decisive for acting politically today is the recognition that the *arcanum imperii* (the secret of rule) lies not in the state-form, with its disciplines and techniques of the self, but

20. Agamben, *Homo Sacer*, 12.
21. Ibid., 3, 9; Agamben, *Means Without End*, 7.
22. Ibid., 4.
23. Ibid., 6. Hardt and Negri make a similar point when they argue that whereas Foucault contrasts sovereignty with modern biopolitics, which he captured with the concept of "governmentality," they prefer to conceive of this shift as a passage within the notion of sovereignty. See Hardt and Negri, *Empire*, 88.

in an underlying logic of sovereignty, a logic of the state of exception, which is the hidden foundation of the entire political system.[24]

What is this logic of sovereignty? Agamben's answer begins with an enigmatic figure in ancient Roman law, the *homo sacer*.[25] The *homo sacer*, or "sacred man," is one who, being found guilty of crime, is not to be sacrificed even as his killing goes unpunished. As such, this figure is doubly excluded. Excluded from divine law—he cannot be sacrificed—and from human law—he is neither under a capital sentence nor is his killing a homicide. He is subject to a double excess, a violence beyond law and sacrifice.[26] Agamben calls the condition of the *homo sacer* "bare life" and argues that the production of bare life is the originary activity of sovereignty.[27]

In other words, political sovereignty is not the power of life; the logic of sovereignty is not redemptive; it does not seek to produce, protect, and reproduce life. Sovereignty is not about contractual belonging or identity; it is not about preserving rights.[28] Biopolitics may be the original activity of sovereignty, but it is not the foundation, its originary act. Rather the originary act of sovereignty is the subjection of life to the power of death; it is the power to kill; the power to expose life, render it bare, naked and abandon it as *homo sacer*.[29] For this reason Agamben states that the *homo sacer* is the originary political relation.[30] Political life begins not with the protection and (re)production of life but with death: "the first foundation of political life is a life that may be killed, which is politicized through its very capacity to be killed."[31] It is as if Agamben is reminding us that the significance of biopolitics notwithstanding, Hobbes is still right; sovereignty is not a matter of protecting life but of an unconditional exposure to death.[32]

We are now in a position to consider how Agamben's account of sovereignty as the power to decide the *homo sacer* relates to the state of exception and, further, to the contemporary political context. Put simply, the power of sovereignty that creates the *homo sacer* is the power to decide the state of exception.[33] Sovereignty is the power of exception; the power to

24. Ibid., 9.
25. Ibid., 71.
26. Ibid., 86.
27. Ibid., 83.
28. Ibid., 181, 126–35.
29. Agamben, *Means Without End*, 5–6.
30. Ibid., 85.
31. Ibid., 89.
32. Ibid., 5.
33. Agamben, *State of Exception*, 1. Agamben cites Carl Schmitt on this point.

place persons outside the juridical-political order, to decide that one may not be sacrificed but that their killing is not homicide. The *homo sacer* is in a state of exception because he is excepted, excluded from the law, both human and divine.

It is perhaps worth noting that this differs from dictatorship insofar as a dictatorship is a kind of fullness or excess of law whereas the state of exception is the absence or emptiness of law.[34] Unlike dictatorships, which function through the proliferation of laws that effectively legalize the state's war on its citizens, the state of exception is not a special kind of law, but law's threshold or limit, the moment of the law's suspension. As such it is an anomic state, where one feels the force of law without the law.[35] Like the Nazi *Lager*.

Agamben lifts up the concentration camps as the paradigmatic exemplification of the state of exception created by sovereign power.[36] He notes that the concentration camps do not have their origin in criminal or even penal law but in colonial war and preventative detention, both of which are extra-judicial states of exception. The camps were spaces of exception, where the normal juridical order was (permanently) suspended. They were not ordinary prisons populated by ordinary jailers and inmates, subject to criminal and penal law. They were outside the juridical order, overseen by the SS and (de)populated by persons who were first stripped of citizenship rights and finally denationalized.[37] The camps were exceptional spaces where life shorn of political status was reduced to bare life and confronted by bare sovereignty, the naked, unmediated power of death.

Because the camps were exceptional it would be easy to dismiss them precisely as exceptions from which one should not draw conclusions about the nature of the contemporary political order. Yet, this is exactly what Agamben does when he asserts that the camps expose the power of sovereignty that underwrites Western politics. As he puts it, the camp is "the hidden matrix and *nomos* of the political space in which we still live."[38] He argues that the camps are not historical artifacts but remain with us in both their political structure and practice. The state of exception that the camps

---

34. Ibid., 48.
35. Ibid., 39.
36. See ibid., 37–45.
37. Agamben notes that between 1915 and 1933, almost all European states passed laws on denationalization. See Agamben, *Homo Sacer*, 175.
38. Agamben, *Means Without End*, 37; Agamben, *Homo Sacer*, 166.

embody is becoming the dominant paradigm of government in contemporary politics.[39] He writes,

> Indeed, the state of exception has today reached its maximum worldwide deployment. The normative aspect of law can thus be obliterated and contradicted with impunity by a governmental violence—while ignoring international law externally and producing a permanent state of exception internally—nevertheless still claims to be applying the law.[40]

The state of exception is no longer an exception. Rather, it has become the norm, the rule. The empire has no clothes; sovereign power, the power to decide the *homo sacer*, to kill in a way that is neither sacrifice nor homicide, is laid bare, naked.

Fifty years ago perhaps such a claim would have sounded preposterous. But unfortunately today it no longer sounds so outlandish. In an era that has seen the advent of rape camps, the USA Patriot Act, and Guantanamo, the persistence become permanence of the state of exception is increasingly, painfully obvious. To these rather glaring examples, Agamben adds as well practices such as the treatment of refugees, the eclipse of parliamentary and congressional power by executive power, the detention of persons without access to the judicial system, the outskirts of great postindustrial cities, and even gated communities in the United States.[41]

What is noteworthy here with regard to the discussion of democracy that follows is that in offering this assessment of the condition of contemporary politics, Agamben does not distinguish between democracies and totalitarian states but instead notes the "contiguity" or "inner solidarity" between them.[42] This contiguity is a matter of the biopolitical character of the sovereignty exercised in both states. Reflecting on the otherwise incomprehensible rapidity with which democracies become totalitarian, Agamben observes that both political forms rule over bare life; what distinguishes them is the manner in which this biopolitical rule is pursued. He writes, "the only real question to be decided was which form of organization would be best suited to the task of assuring the care, control, and use of bare life."[43] We might say, to follow Foucault, that openly totalitarian states opt for the heavier technologies of power like the disciplines and law whereas democracies opt for the lighter technologies of the self, associated with the

---

39. Agamben, *State of Exception*, 2.
40. Ibid., 87.
41. Agamben, *Means Without End*, 42.
42. Agamben, *Homo Sacer*, 121, 10.
43. Ibid., 122.

social sciences, culture and so forth. And, as the twentieth and twenty-first centuries suggest, democracies have shown themselves more than capable of voluntarily creating a permanent state of exception.

II. The Coming Community

Empire and Camp. A dark vision of the way things are. A commonplace criticism of biopolitical accounts of political power, such as those offered by Hardt and Negri as well as Agamben, is that they foreclose any possibility of resistance. By conceiving power in such a totalizing manner, they are thought to strangle hope by drawing the chains of sovereignty even tighter. If sovereignty's rule is all-pervasive, biopolitical, then the space of resistance appears to have evaporated.

The Primacy of Resistance

Hardt, Negri, and Agamben, would contest any such construal of their treatments of sovereignty. Although sovereign power aspires to such comprehensive reach, it cannot succeed. To echo Augustine, they would suggest that the glory of empire is indeed little more than the fragile splendor of glass, always susceptible to being shattered. This is the case because resistance is ontologically primary.

As Hardt and Negri write, "dominance, no matter how multidimensional, can never be complete and is always contradicted by resistance."[44] Resistance is primary with respect to power; insurgency comes first and counterinsurgency is always a reaction, a response.[45] Put differently, the multitude precedes empire:

> The revolting masses, their desire for liberation, their experiments to construct alternatives, and their instances of constituent power have all at the best moments pointed toward the internationalization and globalization of relationships, beyond the divisions of national, colonial, and imperial rule. In our time this desire that was in motion by the multitude has been addressed (in a strange and perverted but nonetheless real way) by the construction of Empire. One might even say that the construction of Empire and its global networks is a *response* to the various struggles against the modern machines of power, and

---

44. Hardt and Negri, *Multitude*, 64.
45. Hardt and Negri, *Empire*, 64.

specifically to class struggle driven by the multitude's desire for liberation. The multitude called Empire into being.[46]

Consequently, empire may aspire to the real subsumption of life into the capitalist network, but it is always already playing catch-up. It is finally an empty, parasitical or vampiric machine whose power is a privation of being and whose production is the empty trace of the prior constituent power of the multitude that it manages to capture and harness.

This is to say, life is elusive and any capture effected is always already unstable. Thus, recognizing the biopolitical character of empire today has precisely the opposite effect in their work than what the critics take it to imply. Far from foreclosing resistance, it opens up a multitude of sites and opportunities for resistance and attack. For example, with specific reference to the phenomenon of globalization, they write:

> There are two faces of globalization. On one face, Empire spreads globally its network of hierarchies and divisions that maintain order through new mechanisms of control and conflict. Globalization, however, is also the creation of new circuits of cooperation and collaboration that stretch across nations and continents and allow an unlimited number of encounters.[47]

Their name for this collaborative network that may give birth to resistance is "multitude" and what is discovered and produced in this collaboration is "the common."

Agamben, likewise, does not think that sovereignty's death grip on life is inescapable. Far from a fatalistic resignation to the nihilism of the age, his work is an effort to articulate the conditions of possibility for answering "yes" to the question, "Is it possible to have *political* community that is ordered exclusively for the full enjoyment of worldly life?"[48] The animating force of his work is entirely positive—the conviction that it is possible to organize life politically around something other than the power to decide the *homo sacer*, that life can be included in politics by means other than the exception.[49] Hence, starting from the uncertain terrain of bare life, of the permanent state of exception, Agamben attempts to shed light on the path of exodus from the state and sovereignty to another politics.[50] What illuminates the path to be cleared, he believes, is not so much the multitude

---

46. Ibid., 42–43.
47. Hardt and Negri, *Multitude*, xiii.
48. Agamben, *Means Without End*, 114. Italics in original.
49. Agamben, *Homo Sacer*, 11.
50. Agamben, *Means Without End*, 8–9, 139.

connected by globalization as it is the concept of the refugee, which is nothing less than a limit-concept that induces a radical crisis in the principles of the nation-state and the sovereignty it enacts.[51]

A New Democracy

What we behold in these thinkers is the possibility of a global democracy as an alternative to the politics of sovereignty. Yet, as Agamben in particular suggests, democracy is implicated in the problematic that is to be overcome. In fact, "democracy" is not a term Agamben ever uses to describe his efforts. Part of an explanation for this anomaly is that clearly democracy does not mean one thing. It is an ambiguous—some would say meaningless—term.[52] The adjectives that adhere to it and the forms equated with it are legion— liberal, communicative, deliberative, strong, communist, underdeveloped, protective, developmental, equilibrium, participatory, direct, representative, republican, aggregative, and (my favorite) Pavlovian are just a few.[53] Hence, what these thinkers mean by "democracy" as well as the forms and possibilities of its emergence bear examining.

The Multitude and the Common

Hardt and Negri's account of democracy can be succinctly captured in two concepts: the multitude and the common. The multitude is an emergent subjectivity, which they describe first in terms of what it is not.[54] It is not the people. A population is composed of different individuals and classes who when they become a people are synthesized into one identity. The multitude, in contrast, is a set of singularities, social subjects whose differences cannot be reduced to sameness. Thus, however the multitude connects, it is not unified but remains plural and multiple. Likewise the multitude should not be confused with the working class, another unitive and exclusive identity. In this sense it is not a rehashing of Marxist eschatology. On the other hand, although the multitude remains multiple, it is not fragmented, anarchical, or incoherent. Not everything is permitted.[55] It

---

51. Ibid., 16, 22–23. See also Agamben, *Homo Sacer*, 134.
52. See Orwell, *Orwell Reader*, 359–60.
53. On the multitude of democracies, see, for example, Benhabib, *Democracy and Difference*; Macpherson, *The Real World of Democracy*; Macpherson, *The Life and Times of Liberal Democracy*; Young, *Inclusion and Democracy*.
54. Hardt and Negri, *Multitude*, xiv, 99.
55. Ibid., 204.

is not merely spontaneous and improvised but organized.[56] Consequently it should not be equated with the crowd, the masses, or the mob. Although these social subjects consist of different individuals and groups, the differences are inert, which is to say that these are indifferent, indistinct conglomerates. Moreover, these groupings cannot act by themselves but must be led. In contrast, the multitude is an active social subject that acts on the basis of what the singularities share in common.

That the multitude is not anarchical or incoherent suggests that even as its multiplicity and difference remain irreducible to a unity, it nevertheless embodies a teleology. Specifically, it embodies a collective, material teleology[57] expressed in the notion of the common. This "common," however, is not a *telos* in any ordinary sense of the term; it is neither predetermined nor pregiven. Hardt and Negri oppose any "ideal final goal of history" that draws resistance forward "through some natural evolution or in some preordained linear march toward absolute democracy."[58] In this regard, they are forthright in rejecting any sense of divinity or transcendence, and, thinking of Augustine, they explicitly deny that the earthly city belongs to or is subject to a city of God, which, they declare, has lost all honor and legitimacy.[59] Thus they write:

> The multitude today ... resides on the imperial surfaces where there is no God the Father and no transcendence. Instead there is our immanent labor. The teleology of the multitude is theurgical; it consists of the possibility of directing technologies and production toward its own joy and its own increase of power. The multitude has no reason to look outside its own history and its own present productive power for the means necessary to lead toward its constitution as a political subject.[60]

Along these same lines, they argue that the common should not be equated with community, identity, or authority. The common is not the name of a sovereign authority that imposes a moral unity on the multitude, as if it were a community or a recognizable political body.[61] The multitude is a plurality that refuses to be reduced to a *unum*.[62] It refuses the organic unity of

---

56. Ibid., 354.
57. Hardt and Negri, *Empire*, 405.
58. Hardt and Negri, *Multitude*, 93.
59. Hardt and Negri, *Empire*, 396.
60. Ibid.
61. Hardt and Negri, *Multitude*, 204.
62. Ibid., 310.

the body.⁶³ "The multitude," they write, "is composed of radical differences, singularities, that can never be synthesized into an identity."⁶⁴

Instead of a kind of sovereignty that constrains differences and squelches the expressiveness of singularities, the common is the name given to the way the singularities that constitute the multitude are able collaboratively to organize themselves.⁶⁵ Accordingly, Hardt and Negri suggest that the common is "not so much discovered, as if it were given all along, but produced."⁶⁶ In this regard, the common is perhaps better understood as "becoming common."⁶⁷

At one point they liken the common to an orchestra without a conductor, "an orchestra that through constant communication determines its own beat and would be thrown off and silenced only by the imposition of a conductor's central authority."⁶⁸ Such an image highlights the way in which the common encompasses all that which allows the multitude to communicate and act together. It includes shared knowledges, language, affections, images and ideas, production processes, but also the pleasures, desires, capacities and needs we all share.⁶⁹ Hence, the common is neither a procedural means nor a predefined end but a communication and collaboration that produce a common project, a common existence, a life.⁷⁰

The Coming Community, the Spectacle, and the Common

Agamben's vision of a new politics, like that of Hardt and Negri, revolves around the activity of singularities that constitute what he calls the "coming community." The activity of this new politics is, likewise, identified with "the common." The similarities between these two visions continue as Agamben articulates the conceptual possibilities for a democratic politics that forms community even as it is non-statist, does not possess any identity or bond of belonging that could be represented as a kind of unity, and shares no historical, spiritual, or biological vocation or destiny that humans must enact

---

63. Ibid., 162.
64. Ibid., 355.
65. Ibid., 337.
66. Ibid., xv.
67. Ibid., 114.
68. Ibid., 338.
69. Ibid., 148.
70. Ibid., 127.

or realize.[71] Furthermore, while this politics is not determined by a *telos*, neither is it simply indeterminate, anarchic. Agamben writes about this lack of vocation or *telos*,

> This does not mean, however, that humans are not, and do not have to be, something, that they are simply consigned to nothingness and therefore can freely decide whether to be or not to be, to adopt or not adopt this or that destiny (nihilism and decisionism coincide at this point). There is in effect something that humans are and have to be, but this something is not an essence nor properly a thing: *It is the simple fact of one's own existence as possibility or potentiality*.[72]

Unpacking the meaning of this statement and its importance for Agamben's political vision requires considering the ontology that underwrites his project.[73]

His is an ontology of potentiality. It begins with singularities, by which he does not mean "individuals." Rather, singularity is a matter of what Agamben, drawing on Scholastic thought, calls "whatever" being (*quodlibet ens*).[74] At the same time, "whatever" being does not refer to generic, indifferent or universal being either. Instead, Agamben writes:

> Whatever [being] is constituted not by the indifference of the common nature with respect to singularities, but by the indifference of the common and the proper, of the genus and species, of the essential and the accidental. Whatever being is the thing *with all its properties*, none of which, however, constitutes difference.[75]

Whatever being is being without identity; it is singularity related to the totality of its possibilities.[76] Granted, as such whatever being is empty space because it is not possible to simultaneously enact all of one's possibilities. That this is the case, however, does not render it synonymous with the void. Instead, it is like a halo[77] that hovers around the singularity that has crossed the threshold from the totality of its possibilities to particular predicates. The "whatever" lingers beside being that has crossed the threshold to actuality.

71. Agamben, *Coming Community*, 85–86, 43.
72. Ibid., 43.
73. Wall, *Radical Passivity*, 115–62, offers a helpful digest of Agamben's ontology.
74. Agamben, *Coming Community*, 1.
75. Ibid., 19.
76. Ibid., 67.
77. Ibid., 53.

It lingers not like the hollow exoskeleton of a bug that has been shed but like the light of the halo, shining with the radiance of possibilities that remain possibilities. Singularities have halos because the passage from potentiality to act, the individuation of a singular existence, is not a punctual fact but a line of continuous movement, an incessant emergence that constitutes the expressivity of life. Agamben puts it this way:

> The passage from potentiality to act, from language to the word, from the common to the proper, comes about every time as a shuttling in both directions along a line of sparkling alternation on which common nature and singularity, potentiality and act change roles and interpenetrate. The being that is engendered on this line is whatever being, and the manner in which it passes from the common to the proper and from the proper to the common is called usage—or rather, *ethos*.[78]

This passage returns us to the question of what humans have to do or be. What they have to do, their ethics, is be their own possibility or potentiality. This does not constitute a vocation or destiny in the ordinary sense of those terms because it is not in any way a limitation on the human.[79] It is not a binding but a perpetual unbinding, a constant leaving open of possibilities, an affirmation of whatever being, of the totality of being's possibilities. Moreover, when those possibilities are actualized is not predetermined, pre-given or preordained. It is a matter of the undetermined will, a dice throw.[80]

At this point we can begin to discern a difference between Agamben's political vision and that of Hardt and Negri, a difference that revolves around the centrality of language in Agamben's account of this new politics.

To begin with, in Agamben's vision language is essential to the individuation of the singular, to the singular's move from potential to actual. This is to say, individuation is a linguistic practice. Specifically, individuation

---

78. Ibid., 20.

79. In his later work there is a similar notion in the idea of a "pure" law. See Agamben, *State of Exception*, 87–88.

80. The reference to a dice throw comes from Wall, *Radical Passivity*, 162. It echoes an idea that is prominent in the work of Alain Badiou. According to Badiou, the chance of every event is absolutely distinct, meaning that every chance is ontologically distinct from every other chance and thus incapable of being composed into a series or totality of the count that would render it susceptible to calculations of probability. Every event is the chance occurrence of a chance. This is in contrast with Deleuze, for whom chance is the play of the One-All, the vitality of univocal being, such that chance is expected and hence open to calculations of probability, etc. See Badiou, *Deleuze*, 67–77.

happens by means of "being-called."[81] The singular is individuated by being-called. Not, for example, by "being-red," but by "being-*called*-red." The former actually effaces singularity as it collapses the singular into an identity, a unity, called "red." Whereas the latter, even as it makes a connection or establishes a belonging, retains an ambiguity that resists absorption without remainder into a category or the reification of a connection into an identity.

Because language is integral to the life of singularities, it is also integral to the common, which is at the heart of the political practice of the coming community. Indeed, according to Agamben the common is language; it is the linguistic and communicative nature of human beings. To understand this point, we need to consider Agamben's account of the society of the spectacle.[82]

Building on Guy Debord's work,[83] Agamben notes that capitalism in its current form presents itself as an immense accumulation of spectacles or images, images not only associated with the media but images as the currency of human sociality itself. Under the contemporary capitalist regime, the real world is transformed into an image, and the image becomes reality. Think of "reality TV," "Facebook," the ubiquity of "spin," the phenomena of people maintaining dual virtual lives, political campaigns and the spectacle of celebrity to name just a few egregious examples.[84] All that was lived directly is distanced or mediated via representation. As Debord puts it, "The spectacle corresponds to the historical moment at which the commodity completes its colonization of social life."[85]

How does this pertain to the common and the possibilities for a new democracy? According to Agamben, the spectacle is language, the very communicativity or linguistic being of humanity that has been alienated and expropriated by capital. As a consequence of this capture, that which united human beings—language—is now used to separate them by means of the transformation of collective perception, social memory and social communication into spectacular commodities, which as infinitely fungible, are then manipulated for capitalist ends.[86]

---

81. Agamben, *Coming Community*, 10.

82. Ibid., 93, 80; Agamben, *Means Without End*, 115.

83. Debord, *The Society of the Spectacle*.

84. Consider as well the comment made by one TV announcer during the opening ceremony of the 2008 Olympics that with this spectacle, China was hoping to replace one image of itself with another or the proliferation of virtual churches, where even the transcendent is being captured by the spectacular logic of capital.

85. Debord, *Society of the Spectacle*, 29.

86. Agamben, *Coming Community*, 80.

But there is a positive dimension to this development, one that contains the possibility of a new politics, a new democracy, a new community. About this new possibility Agamben says, "For the first time it is possible for humans to experience their own linguistic being—not this or that content of language, but language *itself*, not this or that true proposition, but the very fact that one speaks."[87] In other words, the spectacular regime has succeeded in deterritorializing language, unhinging and emptying traditions and beliefs, ideologies and religions, identities and communities.[88] It has also reterritorialized language as a commodity. Nevertheless, in the first stroke, in the deterritorializing of language, it has raised the possibility of humanity experiencing itself as linguistic being, constituted by *logos*, which is what Agamben means by the common.[89]

It is on this experience of the common that Agamben rests his hope for a new democracy. Rather, this discovery *is* the emergency of a new democracy. He writes,

> What is at stake in this experiment is not at all communication intended as destiny and specific goal of human being . . . What is really at stake, rather, is the only possible material experience of being-generic . . . What is in question in political experience is not a higher end but being-into-language itself as pure mediality, being-into-a-mean as an irreducible condition of human beings. *Politics is the exhibition of a mediality: it is the act of making a means visible as such.*[90]

It is the experiment, the experience, the means itself that is the new democracy.

The new politics, the democracy that is beyond sovereignty, is the common experience of language. It is the experience of humanity's common being-in-language, its communicativity. And it is democratic because as an experience of the same that is freely available to all it constitutes a common life and a community without identity, a community of co-belonging without any representable condition of belonging.[91] The coming community is a non-representable community that by means of this non-representable, common experience or event of language forecloses any possibility of exclusion.[92]

87. Ibid., 83.
88. Ibid.
89. Ibid., 80.
90. Agamben, *Means Without End*, 116. Italics in original.
91. Agamben, *Coming Community*, 86.
92. See Wall, *Radical Passivity*, 154.

At first glance, this might appear to be a rather thin reed on which to erect a new politics, akin, perhaps, to suggesting that the common experience of breathing, of respiration, is sufficient ground for a new kind of community. Such an interpretation of Agamben's work, however, would be a terrible mistake, failing to appreciate either the nature of being-in-language or the force of his claim that politics is the exhibition of mediality, the sphere of pure means.[93]

Breaking with the means/ends antinomy that he suggests has paralyzed Western political thought, Agamben asserts that politics should be conceived of neither as a means to an end nor as an end in itself. Rather, following through on a possibility first broached by Aristotle, he holds that human beings as such are "without a function" and that politics corresponds to this "essential inoperability" of humankind.[94] In other words, politics is the space and time that is available not for the realization of any particular or pre-given end but for the becoming actual of potentialities and possibilities. Politics is an indeterminate space; the space of possibilities becoming actual, the experience of potentialities (and vice versa). It is a space permeated with the suggestive glow (what he calls "gesturality"[95]) of halos, not the hard finality of stone. Recalling the ontological significance of language in Agamben's work, we might say that politics is the space where the whatever being of singularities shows itself (instead of representing identities) by being called in language. Language is the stuff of politics; politics is the event of being-called in language.

This linguistic politics is pregnant with democratic potential insofar as it construes politics as the sphere of the becoming of singularities, of their continuous individuation by the actuation of possibilities in being-called in language. It is because this experience of being-called in language is common and because this politics is always haunted by the halo of possibilities—recall that individuation is not once-for-all but a fluid, ceaseless shuttling between potential and actual—no possibility or person can be excluded.

Before moving on, it is worth asking how Agamben's account of the coming community and the common connects to the apparently unrelated treatment of sovereignty, the state of exception, bare life and the refugee. Some, such as Negri, see little connection, suggesting that Agamben's earlier promising work on the coming community has been eclipsed by his later

---

93. Agamben, *Means Without End*, 60.
94. Ibid., 140. See Aristotle, *Nicomachean Ethics*, 1.7.
95. On the gesture and gesturality, see Agamben, *Means Without End*, 49–60.

"The Fragile Brilliance of Glass"   155

and decidedly less promising work on the state of exception and so forth.[96] Such a conclusion, however, reflects a failure to grasp the persistent concern in Agamben's work for the political task of reconnecting life and language in a form of life where happiness, love, and joy are possible. This is a task to which he contributes by means of the work of disenchantment, exposing how sovereignty captures life and language, creating the bare life of *homo sacer* and the anesthetizing image of the spectacle. And it is his hope that in this exposed empty space of language, of the refugee, of the common a new politics will arrive.

The Fragility of Hope

Faced with a sovereign power that produces bare life, that exposes life to the naked, unmediated power of death, Hardt, Negri, and Agamben all find hope in the constitutive power of singularities. Specifically, they see in these singularities the potential for a new politics, one based not on sovereign dominion and the exclusionary force of the state of exception but on free, open, democratic collaboration in the production of the common.

At this point we may ask if these visions sparkle with anything more than the fragile brilliance of glass. Are the multitude, the common, and so forth capable of sustaining this hope for a new democratic politics beyond sovereign dominion? Do they truly gesture toward a democratic form of life capable of resurrecting the *homo sacer* from the camp that is the current global capitalist order?

There are several reasons to think that they do not. Already it has been noted that biopolitical accounts of power and politics are not infrequently critiqued for supposedly diminishing the possibilities of resistance. Such criticisms, as I have already suggested, are misplaced, for Hardt and Negri as well as Agamben seek to expand democratic opportunities and resistance. The problem with their efforts lies elsewhere, in what might be called the modesty and even impossibility of their hope.

To begin with the problem of the modesty of their hope, other radical theorists of democracy who share much with Hardt, Negri, and Agamben suggest that the best that this new democratic politics can hope for is to be fugitive, episodic, on the run and generally overwhelmed by greater forces.[97] Agamben sounds a similar note when he writes, "Wherever these singularities peacefully manifest their being-in-common, there will be another Ti-

---

96. Negri, "Political Subject and Absolute Immanence," 236.

97. Coles, "Of Tension and Tricksters," 307. Coles is referring to Wolin, *Politics and Vision*, 601–2.

ananmen and, sooner or later, the tanks will appear again."[98] So conceived, what they name as hope appears more like a Sisyphean determination than the expectation that another world truly is possible.

Certainly this is a modest hope, a hope not so much for the victory of this new democracy—for the end of the agony of strife and struggle in the (active) rest of a common life—as it is for the endurance of strife and struggle. At best it would seem that theirs is a vision of what Sheldon Wolin calls "fugitive democracy."[99] Granted, endurance may well be preferable to mere resignation and a fugitive democracy is certainly better than an uninterrupted state of exception, but both remain some distance from a genuinely peaceful politics where humans connect and collaborate in networks of love and joy unabated and unchecked.

The modesty of their democratic hope is reinforced by the ateleological, aleatory character of the multitude and the coming community. Recall that there is no natural, historical, or theological *telos* that inspires this new democracy. The singularities are not inclined in any particular direction. Accordingly, their hope for this new democracy is a modest one insofar as the emergence of this democracy is essentially arbitrary, random. We cannot guess, much less know, when or if it will emerge; all we know is that it might emerge.

This conclusion is not contradicted by reference to a "materialist teleology" or "something that humans are and have to be." Such teleological language notwithstanding, they are not implying a determinate direction of movement but are merely recognizing the sheer possibility or potential to move. Specifically, Hardt and Negri associate the will with a Spinozan *conatus*, a will or desire that is innovative, creative, generative.[100] Agamben describes it in terms of "whatever being" and the continuous shuttling of singularities between possibilities and actualities.[101] In both cases what is meant is the power of movement prior to the will's absolutely free choice of direction.[102] Which means that the birth of this new democracy is entirely

---

98. Agamben, *Means Without End*, 89.

99. Wolin, "Fugitive Democracy," 31–45; Wolin, *Politics and Vision*, 601–2.

100. Negri, "Political Subject and Absolute Immanence," 233.

101. Negri criticizes Agamben on this point, arguing that his ontology fails to account for the productive, innovative force of life. Again, this criticism misses the mark for failing to recognize that the generative force of singularities is implicit in the shuttling on the line of individuation back and forth between the potential and the actual. See ibid., 235.

102. Recall the previous quotation (referenced by note 72 above) from Agamben where he distinguishes his account from both nihilism and decisionism. He associates nihilism with the choice not to move while decisionism is the choice to accept a pregiven destiny.

at the mercy of the whim of the indeterminate and therefore indifferent will of the singularities. Its advent is finally utterly arbitrary.

And so hope recedes. Even if we grant the less than self-evidently true claim that innovation and creativity are necessarily liberative, will these ontological possibilities cross the threshold to actualize this democracy? There is no telling; it is a throw of the dice. As Hardt and Negri write, democracy is not the end of history. What it is, and always is, is a possibility. Granted, they are hopeful that this democracy will appear; they recognize opportunities and possibilities in the current political situation; they look for a "strong event," a "radical insurrectional demand," a "real political act of love" that will move us forward out from under the shadow of Empire.[103] But there is neither a divine call nor historical vocation nurturing the hope that such an event will occur. It (always) might happen, but it (always) might not. And, as Agamben suggests, even when it does, the tanks are not far behind.

If the fugitive and aleatory character of their democracy diminishes hope, other elements of their thought threaten to eclipse it altogether. This is to say, there are certain features of their thought that suggest their hope is not merely modest but impossible, unfounded. The first concerns the ontology on which their vision of singularities is founded. Both oppose the transcendental sovereignty that collapses difference, forecloses possibility, and captures being in the prison house of unity, identity, destiny by means of the state-form, deity, and biopower. In opposition to such, both articulate a democratic vision whereby singularities are free to express themselves. For Hardt and Negri this is a matter of singularities giving expression to the intrinsically generative power of being and in the process of doing so, collaborating with other singularities in the production of a new democratic political subjectivity that is the multitude. For Agamben, it is a matter of singularities experimenting with their possibilities and in so doing discovering the linguistic common that is shared with all.

Moreover, Hardt and Negri as well as Agamben describe these productive collaborations and expressive experiments in terms such as "love" and joy" and it is clear as well that the social relations resulting from such encounters are understood to be peaceable. In other words, the coming democratic politics is one of affinity, of love, joy, and peace.

The difficulty with such a democratic vision is that the univocal ontology on which their respective visions rests precludes such affinity. This is the case because while the singularities that these thinkers celebrate may well be social (is it possible to be anything else?), they are not and cannot be related, in the sense of sharing an affinity that exceeds the usefulness of

---

103. Hardt and Negri, *Multitude*, 358.

contract or the dominion of war. In other words, their ontology is more inclined toward a variant of liberal democracy[104] than it is to a genuinely novel and radical democracy. In fact, their ontology rules out open, democratic, receptive relations.

That this is the case is evident in subtle and not so subtle ways in their work. For example, even as they speak of love and joy, they consistently distance what they mean by those terms from the kinds of social relations that are typically associated with them. Thus, Hardt and Negri reject any desire for community, unity, bond and body. Likewise, Agamben's coming community is impersonal, established and sustained on the basis not of any *particular* relation but on relation in general, generic, anonymous being, human communicability.[105] We are left wondering what kind of love and joy this is.

The answer is the only kind that is available to univocal being, namely, contract or conquest.[106] This is the case insofar as both visions are rooted in a univocal ontology that they trace backward through Spinoza to Duns Scotus and the medieval nominalists. The appeal of nominalism—particularly as it passes through Spinoza—is that its account of singularities preserves difference while its univocal extension of power from the divine to the material paves the way for a pure productive immanence or materialist vitality that allows them to jettison transcendence without thereby consigning humanity to the furnace of nihilism.

The difficulty arises with regard to the kinds of relations that univocity is capable of sustaining, specifically the way univocal being preserves difference. Because being is univocal, difference can only be preserved by maintaining a kind of distance between singularities, whether that is construed in terms of a differential of desire/power/intensity or in terms of the particular, contingent configurations of actualized potentialities that individuate singularities. The distance between singularities must be preserved, lest drawing too near, they are lost in the generic anonymity of univocal being. As a consequence, effectively singularities can relate in only one of two modes, or a hybrid thereof: use/contract and capture/war. On one hand, singularities can draw near (but not too near) and collaborate for the sake of a common project. This is to say, there is a relation

---

104. Liberal democracy understood here in terms of a politics of choice associated with the development of human capacities that takes the specific form of market/contractual relations mediating the competitive interaction of intrinsically disparate interests. See Macpherson, *The Real World of Democracy*.

105. Wall, *Radical Passivity*, 162.

106. For this understanding of univocity of being, see Alliez, *Capital Time*; Pickstock, *After Writing*; Schmitz, "Is Liberalism Good Enough?," 86–104.

of mutual usefulness whereby singularities relate as means/instruments/opportunities for potentiality's presentation, for creative expression. On the other hand, the presence of other singularities is always already an implicit threat—either by drawing too close so that the differences that differentiate disappear in the sameness of univocal being or by refusing to collaborate, thereby obstructing creative expression. In such a circumstance, the relation of singularities is one of conflict and war, either defensive or for the sake of conquest and control.

It would be uncharitable to suggest that Agamben, Hart, and Negri underwrite warfare and conquest. When they speak of love and joy, clearly this is not what they have in mind. Nevertheless, their visions remain circumscribed by the second pole of univocal relations. So constrained, what they mean by love and joy cannot be the fruit of the kinds of sharing, intimacy, and participation that might unite human beings in a communion, a body, a friendship deeper than mere use that nevertheless does not efface but preserves real differences. And a love and joy so constrained, so impoverished, are not love and joy at all, or are only a pale distortion. Hence the impossibility of their hope for a novel democracy; it is foreclosed by their univocal ontology, which simply cannot accommodate the bonds of love, which are the wellspring of joy and peace.

The second aspect of their work that raises questions about the credibility of their democratic hope concerns what could be called the problem of "anthropodicy." The problem, put simply, is this: If humanity is an instantiation of a productive immanence or materialist vitality, then how could empire and the camps come to pass? Why are we not already and completely immersed in a radically democratic life? For all the insights they offer about empire, sovereignty and the state of exception, they offer no explanation for how this condition could arise in the first place. Whence cometh that which they seek to overcome?

One could offer a Manichean answer—there are two forces inherent in matter—but they do not. Sovereign power is not a different power than the productive power of life but its capture and distortion. Likewise, they could borrow from Christian orthodoxy and suggest that this "fall" is a surd or even from a nominalist inclined Protestantism and suggest it is just willful disregard. But they do not do this either. Instead, they say nothing. As a result we are left with an ontology that suggests human relations should be marked by joyous conviviality and from this we are to draw hope. Yet we are surrounded by abundant evidence that humanity is *not* constituted by a productive, generative love. Instead, we see the production of death.

In light of their dismissal of divinity, transcendence, and any natural or historical *telos* coupled with the aleatory or contingent character of expressive singularities, the answer to this anthropodicy would appear to be simply "bad luck." Such is the throw of the dice. But this is hardly grounds for hope insofar as it suggests the eternal return of the same. There is no reason to expect that tomorrow might be different from today. The flux of aleatory singularities is constant. It cannot be otherwise. The eternal now. Sooner or later the tanks will always show up. That is the luck of the draw. And hope becomes a kind of valiant resignation to this indeterminate fate.

At one point, Agamben reflects on the theological notion of limbo, using it as a kind of trope for the purely immanent, ateleological world of singularities he envisions.[107] About the inhabitants of this world, he says that abandoned by God, they feel no pain. Deprived of the vision of God, they fully enjoy their natural perfection. Neither blessed nor damned, without destination they are infused with joy. Yet how do these singularities, full of the natural joy that arises in the wake of divine abandon, call out the tanks, and where is the joy in always facing them? And does not getting run over by them hurt?

A cloak of invisibility seems to be cast over human complicity with the power that creates the *homo sacer*, the state of exception. The structures of law, of the spectacle, the processes of biopower and sovereignty are exposed with steady brilliance, yet the persons behind the screen, the singularities that guard the camps and compose and impose the laws and exclude from them remain invisible. We are presented with a powerful account of how things happen to us, but left unsaid is how we who are ontologically constituted by a vital joy and love can do horrible things to each other.

As a consequence, the hope they offer collapses. The ontology of productive immanence or materialist vitality cannot support the weight of this democratic hope because there is a credibility gap, a deafening silence that separates that ontology from the hope that would rest upon it. It is the silence regarding how the productive power of joy and love can erect the camps and how, having erected the camps, it might return to joy and love.

We are encouraged to take hope in the very power that has been turned against us (and that we turn against others) in the first place with no reason to think that it will not be turned against us (or that we will turn it against others) again; indeed with plenty of reasons to think that it will. Sooner or later the tanks always show up, driven by singularities constituted by the same generative power of love as are we. How can we expect, how can we hope for anything else?

---

107. Agamben, *Coming Community*, 5.

The Elusiveness of Democracy

Hardt and Negri are forthright in claiming to be about the task of theorizing a new global democracy emerging in the common work of the multitude. In contrast, Agamben does not name the new politics "democracy." Nevertheless, his account of singularities, the common, and the coming community bear a family resemblance, at least, to Hardt and Negri's democracy of the multitude.

The previous section, however, suggested that their hopes for this democracy are diminished if not destroyed by certain features of their thought. As a transition to the Augustinian political theology of democracy that follows, I want to suggest that their hope for democracy falters because their vision of democracy is insufficiently democratic. As my starting point I take the claim, implicit in Hardt, Negri, and Agamben and explicit in various proponents of radical democracy today, that democracy is a politics of inclusion, of participation, of the broadest solidarity and engagement.

It is on this point that Hardt, Negri, and Agamben falter, for even as they conceive of democracy inclusively, as a matter of solidarity in the production of the common, they exclude the dead as well as the holy Trinity. And in this way their hope is enervated, because their truncated vision of democracy cuts them off from important resources of hope, for it is precisely the holy Trinity and the dead known as the communion of saints that provide a better hope. A hope for more than a fugitive democracy and a hope that is more than the throw of the dice. A hope for a love that is more than carefully maintained and guarded distance and a hope for the power that interrupts the eternal return and makes all things genuinely new.

With regard for the exclusion of the dead, and its effect on the hope for resisting the current order, the exclusion of the dead, who in the church are known as the communion of the saints, from this new democratic politics is implicit in the rejection of divinity. Yet Hardt, Negri as well as Agamben make this exclusion known as they endorse and praise the voracious deterritorializing of capitalism. The destruction of particularisms, the transgression of customs and boundaries, the uprooting of the local are all positive effects of global capitalism, according to Hardt and Negri.[108] In a similar vein, Agamben affirms the capitalist deterritorialization of the body, which emancipates it from its theological, biological, and biographical chains.[109] He also lifts up the petty bourgeoisie as exemplary of the kind of deracinated, identity-less singularity that he envisions inhabiting the coming com-

---

108. Hardt and Negri, *Empire*, 43, 47–48, 52, 363.
109. Agamben, *Coming Community*, 46.

munity. Recall, as well, his positive assessment of the spectacle's liberation of language. He writes with admiration of the way the spectacle "all over the planet unhinges and empties traditions and beliefs, ideologies and religions, identities and communities" and argues that citizens of the coming community will continue and complete this process.[110] Like a tornado that uproots everything in its path and accelerates it, so capitalism frees singularities from every location, every community and identity that preempts volition and restores mobility. This includes the dead, the communion of saints, and the manifold ways they contribute to the present by means of the tradition, which in the memorable words of Chesterton is "the democracy of the dead."[111] After all, the indeterminate singularities that populate the present must not be constrained by the dead and their traditions. Indeed, even the individual body's biology and biography are infringements upon the liberty of these singularities.

By truncating democracy in this way, they would deliver us into the maw of capitalism. And so we discover one source of the deficiency of their hope. Their hope is not a hope for democracy but a hope for capitalism insofar as it hopes for singularities who relate to the past (and each other) like the petite bourgeoisie—as a rootless [identity-less], accidental [mobile] tourist or consumer [nomad]. Their hope is not a hope for democracy insofar as by cutting us off from the communion of saints they deprive us of the wisdom and the habits that would aid us in resistance.

As for the exclusion of God, like the pagans whom Augustine suggested could not be just because they failed to render to God what was due, so Hardt, Negri, and Agamben are not democrats insofar as their political vision excludes divinity.

And it is this exclusion, this failure of democratic vision that wrecks their hope on the shoals of the eternal now, where resistance always may emerge but where its emergence is always met, sooner or later, by the tanks. This exclusion devastates their hope precisely because it is nothing less than the exclusion of the possibility of the arrival of the novel, of the genuinely creative moment that permanently interrupts the static flux, the endless return of the same, the eternal now, with the unexpected possibility of another world, another way of life, where the festive sounds of democratic celebration is not always, sooner or later, mixed with the heavy metallic noise of tanks and the cries of victims.

Granted these thinkers would object strenuously to this characterization of their work. Each believes that theirs is a vision of the possibility of

---

110. Ibid., 83.
111. Chesterton, *Orthodoxy*, 48.

the novel, the creative. Yet as I have suggested above it is not at all clear that they really offer anything more than perpetual conflict.

The problem I identified as "anthropodicy" highlights this. For all the emphasis on creativity and novelty, they do not account for the first "novelty," that is, how it is possible that love and joy could fashion weapons and erect camps in the first place. And once we find ourselves in such a world, the deficiencies of their hope suggest, we are unable—on their terms—to look forward to a world that is truly different.

This is the case because their pure immanence has excluded any supplementation. They embrace univocity because they believe that it alone is capable of recognizing human creativity and the positive, generative power of being. Yet, as I have suggested, this ontological capture imposed its own limitations on human creativity. For one thing, it reduces human sociality to a continuum delimited by contract and conquest. Furthermore, by excluding divinity, it also abandons us to our own resources, which, it is clear from the current political situation, are not sufficient to the task of bringing a world of love, joy, and peace to pass. The most it can offer is a fugitive democracy. In other words, it too shines with the fragile brilliance of glass.

What is needed to make this democracy more than fugitive is a broader, more inclusive vision. What is needed is a democracy that includes the dead in its conversations, seeing in them and seeking from them not chains but life-lines of wisdom and the habits to which we might cling when battered by capitalism or dragged toward the camps. What is needed is a democracy that includes the Trinity in its conversations—present and active not as a sovereign power that imposes and conquers but that makes it possible for humanity to draw near to one another in love and joy, living and acting in genuinely new ways, ways that exceed our own possibilities but do so in a manner that does not curtail the freedom of our wills but enhances it. To this more excellent way, this better democracy, we now turn.

III. A Democratic Augustinian Church

The church has always understood itself to be about the announcement of the good news that the seemingly permanent state of exception created by sin has been interrupted. In Christ, it claims, something genuinely new has arrived and as a result, bare life is redeemed and renewed as the joyous, peaceful, flow of conviviality that is love. Implicit in this announcement is the recognition that sovereign power, the exercise of dominion that produces the *homo sacer*, is unnatural, a contingent aspect of the tragic moment that is sin.[112]

112. While the tradition has differed over whether "political" life is natural or not,

Moreover, the church has also claimed that as the body of Christ it is the site of this novel and redemptive interruption. As such, the church claims to be the coming community; it is the advent of a democratic politics that is capable of sustaining hope for a common life, a communion, of joy, love, and peace open to and shared by all.

To support the claim that the church instantiates a democratic politics, I turn to the work of Saint Augustine, for in an Augustinian political ecclesiology we can trace the line of a politics that is non-statist and democratic, simultaneously refusing to organize its life internally by means of sovereign power while welcoming the contributions of outsiders.

Of course, at first glance the suggestion that Christianity, particularly in its Augustinian inflection, might embody a democratic hope strikes one as patently absurd. After all, is not Augustine the theologian of empire, the stenographer if not the architect of the "Constantinian settlement" that enabled the church to embrace sovereign power with a clear conscience? Is not the church in his wake authoritarian, statist, deeply invested in sovereign power, and jealously guarding (sometimes with great cruelty) exclusionary boundaries established by means of dogmatic creeds and confessions that foreclose democratic conversation internally while discounting the voices and contributions of others externally?

Certainly it would be absurd to deny that the church has been and continues to be guilty as charged. Moreover, I do not mean to suggest that Augustine himself got this exactly right. Even if we set aside the long history of misreading to which Augustine has been subjected, there remain elements in his thought that suspend the democratic trajectory of this theology. For example, although there may be ways that his treatment of women, the Jews, and the use of coercion against heretics and pagans can be mitigated, those (and other?) undemocratic features of his thought cannot be erased entirely.

Acknowledging these difficulties, I will show how a broadly Augustinian political ecclesiology points to the possibility of a democratic politics. Previously it was suggested that Hardt, Negri, and Agamben are insufficiently democratic insofar far as they exclude the dead and the deity from their coming communities. Insofar as Christianity includes both the dead—by means of its recognition of the communion of saints as well as the respect given to the apostolic tradition—and the deity in the conversation about its form of life, it is in this respect more democratic.

However, it is precisely these inclusions that raise doubts concerning the democratic potential of the church. Specifically, they prompt questions

---

it has agreed that coercive power of sovereign dominion is a tragic consequence of the fall. For an introduction to Augustine's view and the medieval debates on this point, see Markus, "Two Conceptions of Political Authority," 14–15.

about the extent to which the church can break with sovereignty and be open to the contributions of outsiders. After all, does not God exercise sovereign dominion and has not the church copied this by embracing the state? And does not apostolic tradition doubly resist outside supplementation, first by its fullness rendering supplementation unnecessary and second by its dogmatic rigidity making it impossible? In defense of Christian democracy, we begin with the charge of sanctioning sovereign power by embracing the state.

The City of God amid the Earthly Cities

Hardt, Negri, and Agamben argue that state-democracy is finished and that the coming democratic politics will be decidedly non-statist in form. His imperial reputation notwithstanding, Augustine's vision of the church is precisely that of a church not wedded to the state. Indeed, as Stanley Hauerwas suggests, the church of Augustine's time was a democratic interruption of the late Roman Empire.[113] Hence, Augustine's *City of God* is rightly read as a sustained critique of empire in the face of the charge leveled by pagans that the advent of the church contributed to the downfall of the Roman state.

What is particularly telling in Augustine's defense of the church is that in the course of making it he actually heightens the offense. While he denies the church's role in Rome's imminent demise, his more fundamental argument is that Rome did not really constitute a commonwealth in the first place. Not only is this tantamount to putting salt on a wound, but his defense amounts to an odd admission of guilt insofar as beside the church, earthly cities such as Rome, built as they are on the sovereign power of *dominium*, are revealed to be, which is to say made, something less than a genuine commonwealth, something less than authentically political.

Hence it should be unsurprising that, as Robert Marcus[114] rightly recognized but wrongly interpreted, Augustine's vision did not seek or result in a church more tightly joined to sovereign power; rather, just the opposite. Augustine's genealogy of the Roman empire resulted in the reduction of sovereign authority. The result is a church untied from the *dominium* of earthly cities, a church that is a polity, a politics in its own right, albeit one marked not by sovereign *dominium*. And if we were not unduly influenced by a variety of mostly Protestant narratives about the fall of the church linked to the age of Constantine and Augustine, we might see that Augustine contrib-

---

113. Hauerwas, "Democratic Time," 547.
114. Markus, *Saeculum*.

uted to a 1,200+ year struggle of the church against the sovereign claims of the earthly cities. (Indeed, Augustine was well aware that the attention and service of kings to the church was not a mark of glory but "a more perilous and sorer temptation."[115])

Furthermore, in spite of the way he has been frequently misused, not only is Augustine's vision of the church non-statist, but he does not even offer a theory of the state as such. *The City of God* is not an essay in political theory that espouses a general account of political institutions and states. Augustine neither has nor offers a theory of the state. Thus the "earthly city" is not properly equated with the modern state or even any singular form of ancient polity or ensemble of institutions. Rather, it is but a trope for the condition of order, or perhaps, peculiar disorder that is life distorted by sin. Moreover, this earthly city does not have a characteristic space or set of goods and responsibilities that belong to it alone—the city of God traverses the same space and is concerned with the same goods and responsibilities—although it does have a distinctive mode of existence characterized by love of self and the lust for dominion.

If anything, *The City of God* narrates a kind of political ecclesiology, although even this characterization has its limits insofar as the city of God is greater than the church on pilgrimage through this world. At the outset Augustine notes, "The glorious city of God is my theme in this work"[116] and he then proceeds to juxtapose the two cities, not as two distinct and autonomous sets of institutions, certainly not as a theory of church and state, but as two spiritualities, two rules flowing from two loves. As Augustine puts it, "Two cities have been formed by two loves: the earthly by the love of self, even to the contempt of God; the heavenly by the love of God, even to the contempt of self. The former, in a word, glories in itself, the latter in the Lord."[117] Thus, we have a political cartography of a single space, including a variety of institutions and formations—among them are the church and what are typically called governing apparatuses—that is simultaneously the site of two different modes of existence or performances of life.[118]

Of course, to modern eyes, this way of conceiving a "city" is highly irregular. As a consequence, Augustine's refusal to neatly sort out these two cities, to reify these two rules, by means of clear and distinct institutional and territorial identifications and boundaries (e.g., church and state, spiritual and material, etc.) has led those who came after him to do precisely

---

115. Augustine, *Concerning Man's Perfection in Righteousness*, chapter 15.35.
116. Augustine, *City of God*, Preface.
117. Ibid., 14.28.
118. See Cavanaugh, "From One City to Two," 299–321.

that. Typically, his failure to draw the institutional and territorial distinctions we expect has provoked the suggestion that he was joining the church to the state (the imperial Augustine) or that he has removed them entirely from conflict (the proto-liberal Augustine). Yet both of these miss the mark. By insisting that he be read in accord with the strictures of modern, statist visions of politics, the non-statist and indeed democratic features of Augustine's political theology are effaced.

Thus far my argument that Augustine's political vision was non-statist has been largely negative: he attacked the Roman Empire; he did not have a theory of the state. But a negative argument will not suffice. After all, as the work of Markus proves, merely reminding us that Augustine was not modern—and so did not share a Weberian vision of politics as statecraft—does not mean that his thought is not amenable to such a construal.

Moreover, if Agamben is correct and modern sovereign power, which Weber defined in terms of a monopoly on violence within a set of geographical boundaries and which Foucault's account of biopolitics refines but does not fundamentally overturn, is but an intensification and modulation of a sovereign power reaching back at least as far as the Roman figure of the *homo sacer*, then even pre-modern politics such as Augustine's, if all he is is pre-modern, do not really escape the statist, sovereign political logic of modernity.

But Augustine's distance from the state-form is not merely that of a pre-modern *prolepsis* or anticipation. Rather, his is the distance of the refugee, or, in more biblical and theological terms, of exile, diaspora, or pilgrimage. This is perhaps seen no more clearly than in a passage from *The City of God* that, ironically, has fueled the aforementioned confusion regarding the character of his politics:

> Miserable, therefore, is the people which is alienated from God. Yet even this people has a peace that is not to be lightly esteemed, though, indeed, it shall not in the end enjoy it, because it makes no good use of it before the end. *But it is our interest that it enjoy this peace meanwhile in this life; for as long as the two cities are commingled, we also enjoy the peace of Babylon* . . .[119]

Augustine goes on to say that the people of God are sojourners among the earthly cities. As he does so, he obviously has in mind here the words of the prophet Jeremiah to the Jews in Babylonian exile: "But seek the welfare of the city where I have sent you into exile, and pray to the LORD on its behalf, for in its welfare you will find your welfare" (Jer 29:7 NRSV).

---

119. Augustine, *City of God*, 19.26.

Within the parameters of modern statist politics, for Jeremiah and Augustine to exhort the people of God to make a home and participate in the welfare of a foreign nation can only be heard as a kind of resigned surrender, the loss of a distinct political form, first of Israel and then of the church, and subsequent absorption into the state.

Such a reading, though, reflects a forgetfulness of the fact that Augustine defines these cities not in terms of borders and boundaries or a monopoly on the use of force, but in terms of loves. So accustomed are we moderns to thinking of the church and state as disparate *territories* (spiritual versus material) that we fail to perceive that for Augustine, like much of medieval Christianity after him, it was a point of debate as to whether one could even conceive of a space outside the church.[120] Thus, his endorsement of exile, of diaspora, of pilgrimage is not in any way a loss of political vitality.

On the contrary, it is the articulation of a different kind of politics, one that does not advance by means of sovereign dominion and the state of exception. (Although it might be argued that it is a kind of positive state of exception, a different kind of camp, akin perhaps to a revival or frontier camp meeting.) The city of God is on pilgrimage in this world and while it certainly occupies space, it does not capture space in the modern sense of establishing stable borders or barriers to ward off an unwelcome or hostile outside. (Indeed, as was just suggested, the status or existence of a territory designated "the outside" is uncertain. We will return to this later.)

And this is in keeping with the democratic pulse of Augustine's vision, that desires to see the circle of communion extended until all space is no longer broken by trenches and battle lines, by fences, borders, and barriers, but instead is become the smooth space of fraternity that perfectly echoes in a non-identical repetition the joyous sounds of divine-human conviviality.

In other words, when Augustine advocates the intermingling of the two cities, he is not watering down the rigors of discipleship so that it is amenable with imperial ambition. Nor is he suggesting that Christianity is really spiritual and not political. Instead, he is merely following the logical outcome of this pilgrim politics; he is declaring the inclusive reach of Jesus. The earthly and heavenly cities are purposefully entangled in this world; the citizens of the heavenly city are properly found in the company of the citizens of all earthly cities as refuges, exiles, sojourners, and pilgrims. That they are such is a reflection of the heavenly city's desire for and means of accomplishing universal filiation—the renewal and extension of human communion, without exclusion, "to the ends of the earth." That the city of

---

120. See Chroust, "The Corporate Ideal and the Body Politic in the Middle Ages," 423–52; Ladner, "Aspects of Mediaeval Thought on Church and State," 403–22.

God does not have a fixed geographical location or armed boundaries is not a deficiency; it is a consequence of its impotent strength. It is mobile, able to move like the wind, transgressing every boundary, appearing wherever two or three are gathered, for the sake of expanding the democracy of love, joy, peace to all.

A Democratic Church: The Lordship of Christ and the Common Good

The second charge against the church as a democratic politics amounts to the claim that certain features of its life preclude the possibility for democracy internally. In particular, it would appear that the lordship of Christ, as well as the church's adherence to the common good, suggests a kind of sovereign eclipse of the human volition and creativity that distinguish a genuinely democratic politics.

With regard to the lordship of Christ, already in Scripture we have clues that Christ does not exercise sovereign dominion over his followers. For example, Christ renounces the master-servant relation, instead calling his disciples friends (John 15:15) and he likewise instructs his disciples not to emulate the tyrannical dominion of the Gentile rulers (Mark 10:42). In the high Middle Ages, the non-coercive, non-restrictive lordship or rule of Christ over the church and world was spelled out in terms of analogical being. In other words, when Hardt, Negri, and Agamben embrace univocity as a means of safeguarding human vitality and creativity, they fail to see that analogy can do the same.

Indeed, given the problems with univocal being noted previously, being understood analogically is actually superior to univocal being in this regard, for it permits precisely the kinds of intimacy and participation that forestall conflict and exceed mere use and contract, which is crucial to the flourishing of a genuine sociality of joy, love and peace.

But this is to jump ahead in the story, for Augustine pre-dates the medieval discussions of univocity and analogy. Nevertheless, within his theology there lies the sensibility that will later be expressed in the analogy of being. Specifically, he articulates a non-sovereign lordship of Christ. This is perhaps most succinctly articulated in his observation that God is closer to us than we are to ourselves[121] and it is reflected as well in claims like, "Christ is our knowledge, and the same Christ is also our wisdom. He Himself implants in us faith concerning temporal things, He Himself shows forth the

---

121. Augustine, *Confessions* 3.6.

truth concerning eternal things. Through Him we reach on to [Him]."[122] Of course, at first glance, this might be construed as the pinnacle of sovereign biopower, completely and utterly obliterating any sense of human agency and, in particular, freedom of the will. Yet Augustine maintains the freedom of the will. In fact, the significance he gives the will in the Christian moral psychology is one of his contributions to the tradition.

How is it, then, that the lordship of Christ can coexist with human freedom, creativity, and volition? The answer, which is not available to a univocal ontology, can be found in Augustine's account of the freedom of the will.[123] To begin with, according to Augustine the will is not absolutely or radically indeterminate after the manner of Hardt, Negri, and Agamben's singularities. Such a radically indeterminate will could only gaze upon objects indifferently, viewing the choice of any of them as a mere fungible "option." As David Schindler notes, when the will is conceived as radically indeterminate, "the world in general is reduced to a series of options, none of which can be any more compelling than any other for the simple reason that none of them can be compelling at all."[124] The operation of such a radically indeterminate will could only be arbitrary and so susceptible to the difficulties that cripple Hardt, Negri, and Agamben's accounts. Not to mention that such a world of gray indifference hardly portends the joyous conviviality to which Hardt and company aspire.

Instead of an indeterminate, ateleological will, Augustine offers an account of the will that is not radically indeterminate yet still free. His account begins with identifying the will with love. "A righteous will," writes Augustine, "is a good love... [L]ove striving to possess what it loves is desire; love possessing and enjoying what it loves is joy."[125] The will is not indifferent, arbitrary movement. It is movement that is moved; it is movement toward that which is loved; it is a movement toward a *telos*.

The question is, when Christ exercises lordship, is Christ dominating the will, coercing this movement toward himself and so violating the voluntary character of the will? Answering "yes" would amount to establishing sovereignty in the heart of the church.[126] And for univocal being, "yes" is the

---

122. Augustine, *On the Trinity* 13.19.24.

123. What follows is drawn primarily from Schindler, "Freedom beyond Our Choosing," 67–98. Note that although I use the language of "freedom," the focus of this point is not freedom—understood by Augustine as the ability to enjoy the good—but agency, that is, the voluntary nature of the will's acts.

124. Schindler, "Freedom beyond Our Choosing," 73.

125. Augustine, *City of God Against the Pagans*, 14.7.

126. At least once in his writing, Augustine answers "yes," arguing that Christ used force on Paul to get him to "long for light in his heart." See Augustine, *Political Writings*, 187.

only answer that can be given. The necessity of maintaining a distance between beings in order to preserve individuation that is inherent in univocal being means that influence exerted on an agent can only be extrinsic. Thus, with the arrival of nominalism we see also the advent of legalism.[127] Morality and the law, and for that matter any teleology, become external forces that confront the will with a naked demand to surrender its indeterminate freedom to choose. Law and morality become, by definition, moments of sovereign power, power that coerces the will to the extent that it curtails the will's liberty of indifference.

Understanding how Christ can be Lord and not coerce the movement of the will toward himself is an answer that comes in two parts in Augustine. To begin with, first, consider how the will attains its object. The will is an act of movement toward an object, but for this movement to take place, the will must engage all the human faculties involved in perceiving, pursuing, and enjoying an object. And each of these other faculties, in enabling the will to achieve its own acts, does not intrude upon, interfere with, or diminish the freedom of the will. To the contrary, as Schindler puts it, "whatever enables the will to achieve its own acts enters *intrinsically* into its operation rather than intruding upon it from the outside."[128] At this point we are not far from imagining how Christ could exercise a lordship that does not impinge upon the liberty and creativity of those who would follow him. For example, centuries later Aquinas will make precisely this point, arguing that God can move others without thereby diminishing the voluntary nature of the acts that result.[129] Such an activity can only be imagined by conceiving of being in terms of analogy, whereby the agency of God and humanity do not compete on the same plane in a kind of zero-sum competition.[130] As Augustine says, God is closer to us than we are to ourselves. Or in another striking turn of phrase that makes the same point, when speaking of his sin in the *Confessions*, he writes, "You were within, and I was outside."[131] In other words, Christ does not work on the will externally, overriding the will and forcing it in a direction contrary to itself, but internally.

How God works internally constitutes the second part of the answer we seek. Not only does Christ's lordship preserve the voluntary nature of the will because God is closer to us than we are to ourselves but the integrity

---

127. Westberg, "Reason, Will, and Legalism," 431–36.
128. Schindler, "Freedom beyond Our Choosing," 77.
129. Aquinas, *Summa Theologica*, 1.83.1.
130. See Placher, *Domestication of Transcendence*, 27–31.
131. Augustine, *Confessions*, 10.27.38. Quoted in Cary, "United Inwardly by Love," 11.

of the will is preserved precisely insofar as Christ's rule engenders delight. According to Augustine, certain objects attract the movement of the will; they are so appealing that in a sense the will out runs the object's pull or attraction in its eagerness to attain that object. This eagerness Augustine calls *delectatio*, delight or enjoyment. About this he writes:

> The human will is so divinely aided in being made just, that (beyond man's being created with a free will and beyond the teaching by which he is instructed how he ought to live) he receives the Holy Spirit, by whom there is formed in his mind a *delight* in, and a *love* of, that supreme and unchangeable good which is God ... in order that ... he may conceive an ardent desire to inhere in his maker, and may burn to enter upon the participation in that true light.[132]

Thus, Christ does not coerce, does not force or suppress the will. Rather, Christ attracts and delights. The earthly city is ruled by a sovereign power that coerces the will by means of the fear of death while the city of God is ruled by the love that delights the heart and so elicits a response, that is, draws it near.[133]

In addition to Christ's exercise of lordship, the church's commitment to the common good may foster skepticism regarding its ability to envision and enact a genuinely open democratic politics. In this regard, it is perhaps understandable that the prominence given to creeds and confessions and, for that matter, offices such as the episcopacy are thought to work against democratic engagement in the church.

Again Scripture points the way beyond this static vision of the common good and the life that is ordered toward it, as Paul writes, "we know only in part, and we prophesy only in part ... for now we see in a mirror, dimly" (1 Cor 13:9, 12 NRSV). The common good or common love that orders the church's life is provisional, in the sense of still being communally discerned and articulated (see 1 Cor 12:1–11). Rowan Williams puts this as well as anyone when he writes, "The church proclaims that there is one human destiny and that it is found in relation to one focal figure, Jesus; but also that what this human destiny means cannot be worked out without

---

132. Augustine, *On the Spirit and the Letter*, 3.5 cited in Hanby, "Democracy and Its Demons," 461.

133. For an account of obedience that comports with Augustine and is in stark contrast with the legalism and *dominium* of nominalism, see McCabe, *God Matters*, 226–34, the central point of which is "A totally obedient community would be one in which no one was ever compelled to do anything" (229).

'communion', a relation of profound and costly involvement with each other and receiving from each other."[134]

Notwithstanding the way Augustine has come to be identified in some quarters with a rigid and inflexible orthodoxy, such a provisional and hence open understanding of the common good is entirely in keeping with an Augustinian ecclesiology. Consider, for example, Augustine's engagement with the Donatists.[135] Was an Augustinian ecclesiology closed and rigid, one might expect Augustine to have *joined* the Donatists, the purported upholders of the true faith and pure practice. Conversely, having condemned them, one might expect him to have approved of their departure from the church and then refused to recognize their sacraments, should they seek to return. But he does neither. While he thinks that they are indeed in error, he does not think that they should have divided the church and departed. In fact, it is their very act of division and not their differences regarding the sacraments and the purity of the church that merits their condemnation. Likewise, even having divided the church, their sacraments are not simply to be rejected as invalid, *tout court*. In effect, Augustine's argument with the Donatists is precisely about the open character of the church. He takes issue with the Donatists for quitting the argument, failing to trust that the sacraments create the kind of relations where differences of conviction and confession can be engaged and even maintained without severing the communion.

Augustine's commitment to engagement, to the value of argument, as opposed to simply imposing conformity can be discerned in a comment regarding the benefits of engaging heretics. He writes,

> While the hot restlessness of heretics stirs questions about many articles of the catholic faith, the necessity of defending them forces us both to investigate them more accurately, to understand them more clearly, and to proclaim them more earnestly; and the question mooted by an adversary becomes the occasion for instruction.[136]

It is perhaps easy to miss the openness articulated in this passage because he begins from the conclusion that the interlocutor in question is a heretic. But alas, fourth-century Hippo was not Guantanamo Bay; as Richard Hanson has argued, the effort to achieve orthodoxy happened by means of trial and error, during which almost everyone—including Augustine; consider his *Retractions*—changed their ideas in some way.[137]

134. Williams, *Truce of God*, 27.
135. Here I draw from Milbank, *Theology and Social Theory*, 402–3.
136. Augustine, *City of God*, 16.2.
137. See Hanson, "Achievement of Orthodoxy," 151.

As the passage suggests, engaging heretics was not simply the exercise of a sovereign authority that demands submission or cuts off but was a matter of argument. And it was a matter of an argument that might well result in the church's growth and change. Thus Augustine mentions the possibility of the church's study, understanding, and proclamation of the faith being enhanced and corrected through such engagement.

In other words, orthodoxy is not rightly understood as a static template of thought or belief that is imposed on the mind by a sovereign authority. Rather, it is an argument. As Stanley Hauerwas writes, "'orthodoxy' is not the avoidance of argument. Orthodoxy is the naming of arguments across time that must take place if we are to be faithful to Jesus."[138] In spite of the various and sordid elements of *dominium* intertwined in it, the development of orthodoxy in the church is not devoid of this kind of vulnerable, open engagement.

Along these same lines, authority in the church is not rightly understood or exercised as a means of squelching differences or enforcing a narrow and suffocating conformity to a static rule. After all, it was the *bishop* Augustine who criticized the Donatists for quitting the argument and it is the bishop Augustine who embraced the mixed and diaspora character of the church. Again Hauerwas is helpful in making sense of this when he writes, "'Bishop' is the name of the office that God has given the church to ensure that the dead—who are not dead, but who live with God in the communion of the saints—get to continue in the debates that are the Christian tradition."[139] Bishops and others exercising authority have the responsibility to see that the voices of the saints, including those who went before us, are not excluded from our conversations about what it means to follow Jesus. In this regard, an Augustinian ecclesiology is not adverse to the kinds of democratic practice that John Howard Yoder names a "hermeneutic of peoplehood" or Terence Nichols calls a "participatory hierarchy."[140]

This sense of the church as an open space, a democratic space characterized, in Williams's words, by "profound and costly involvement with each other" is further exemplified in Augustine's insistence that the church is a *corpus permixtum*, a mixed body, made up of both believers and

---

138. Hauerwas and Coles, "Conversation," 324.

139. Ibid.

140. Yoder, *Priestly Kingdom*, 15–45; Nichols, *That All May Be One*. Yoder articulates a democratic church in terms of an open process of discernment guided by agents of direction (prophets), agents of memory (historians), agents of linguistic self-consciousness (teachers), and agents of order and due process (bishops). Nichols articulates what he calls a "participatory hierarchy" over against a command hierarchy that is synonymous with sovereign authority.

non-believers. While it is not uncommon to hear this interpreted as a sign of Augustine's capitulation to empire, the cost of the church's gaining a share of sovereign power, in light of what has already been said about Augustine's political cartography, such a conclusion cannot be sustained. As suggested earlier, the intermingling of the two cities is not a matter or regret or a sign of capitulation. Rather, it is a manifestation of the very heart of what the church is about in this time between the times. Thus, Augustine writes at length:

> Let this city bear in mind, that among her enemies lie hid those who are destined to be fellow-citizens, that she may not think it a fruitless labor to bear what they inflict as enemies until they become confessors of the faith. So, too, as long as she is a stranger in the world, the city of God has in her communion, and bound to her by the sacraments, some who shall not eternally dwell in the lot of the saints . . . But we have the less reason to despair of the reclamation even of such persons, if among our declared enemies there are now some, unknown to themselves, who are destined to become our friends.[141]

The mixed body, like the pilgrim church itself, is a manifestation of the church's openness, its desire to engage all, to exclude none. Granted this passage speaks of at least the possibility of the final exclusion of some from the lot of the saints, but even that points to the democratic openness of the church: There shall be no forced filiations; no sovereign power will be brought to bear on those who refuse what Christ offers. Put another way, Christ knocks on the door, but will not kick it down. In which case, it could be debated where the exclusion lies, a point to which we will return shortly.

Finally, pertaining to the democratic openness of the common good that orients the church's life, we can point to the pluralist character of the city of God to which Augustine draws attention in the midst of describing its missionary sojourn amongst the earthly cities:

> This heavenly city, then, while it sojourns on earth, calls citizens out of all nations and gathers together a society of pilgrims of all languages, not scrupling about diversities in manners, laws, and institutions whereby earthly peace is secured and maintained, but recognising that, however various these are, they all tend to one and the same end of earthly peace. It therefore is so far from rescinding and abolishing these diversities, that it even preserves and adapts them, so long only as no hindrance to the worship of the one supreme and true God is thus introduced.[142]

---

141. Augustine, *City of God*, 1.35.
142. Ibid., 19.17.

Here again we see that the church is not some fortress of rigid orthodoxy that forecloses on diversity and difference in the forms of its life. Indeed, here we see most clearly how the church is not in fact a single form of life but many, a multiplicity or Pentecost of Eucharistic sites dispersed like a network or rhizome across the social body, walking through walls for the sake of befriending all. In this regard, those with authority in the church are not only agents of memory, as suggested above, but primarily agents of communion, assisting in the articulation of the common as it emerges in the many forms of the life of this rhizomatic body of Christ. To cite Hauerwas one more time, "the bishop is the agent of unity, to ensure that one liturgical assembly does not isolate itself from other liturgical assemblies in such a manner that the complexity that is the gospel is lost . . ."[143]

A Church without Borders: Learning from Outsiders

The third suspicion leveled against the claim that an Augustinian ecclesiology holds forth the possibility of a democratic church concerns the church's relation to outsiders. Of course, the church desires to see outsiders become insiders; that is, after all the heart of the inclusive democratic impulse commonly called "evangelism." And insofar as both the church and Christ renounce sovereign power, this welcome extended to outsiders by the diaspora or pilgrim church will not be accompanied and accomplished by coercion. Yet the question remains, can this church welcome the insights and wisdom of outsiders? Does the provisionality and openness to supplementation that properly characterizes its life internally extend to relations with outsiders as well? Is it democratic in the sense of open to learning from the outsider? Is it possible to have a strong ecclesiology without simultaneously embracing an ecclesiocentrism that assumes there is nothing to be learned from outsiders that might enrich and enhance the project of its common life and worship?

Scripture again sets the precedent here insofar as it makes clear that the church cannot be understood (or exist) without the presence of the Jews. Likewise there are passages—such as Matthew 25:31–46—that point to Christ's being present outside the church in ways that make it imperative for the church to attend to outsiders. It is worth mentioning in this regard as well the "insider/outsider" dialectic present at various points in the gospels, points where it is made clear that the church's confession was frequently first uttered by those who were socially and/or theologically outsiders.

---

143. Hauerwas and Coles, "Conversation," 324–25.

The witness of Scripture notwithstanding, it remains to be seen if an Augustinian ecclesiology can be democratic in the sense of open to the insight of outsiders. After all, Augustine has been cast as the first master of oppression and his hostility to difference has been identified as "the Augustinian imperative."[144]

The first clue that such a characterization of Augustine is a mischaracterization can be found in the previously cited passage when Augustine notes the pluralist character of the church. At first glance one may be inclined to dismiss this on the grounds that such differences concern little more than what would later come to be called *adiaphora*, inessential or indifferent matters. But such a dismissal would be a mistake, for Augustine's point is not that such differences are to be tolerated and this on the grounds that they are inconsequential. Rather he notes and lauds the great diversity that enriches the church's life as it is on pilgrimage amongst the nations and peoples. He says that far from actively suppressing such diversity, the church actively preserves and adapts to it. Why? Because such differences contribute to the promotion and enjoyment of earthly peace, which, including as it does such mundane matters like acquiring the necessities of life, is of obvious importance to the city of God as it goes about its temporal tasks.

But this rather mundane example does not exhaust the ways in which the church needs the contributions of outsiders. Beyond this, Augustine also encourages the church to be open to the knowledge and wisdom of outsiders, appealing to the Israelites' plundering the Egyptians at the outset of the Exodus as a figural precedent. He affirms the ways pagan institutions, knowledges, and arts can be useful to the church, even aiding it in understanding Scripture.[145] In fact, Augustine goes so far in his openness as to affirm that "most excellent precepts of morality . . . and some truths in regard even to the worship of the One God are found among them."[146] Moreover, he attributes the pagans' possession of such gems to "the mines of God's providence which are *everywhere* scattered abroad."[147] Certainly this comports well with his own biography, for even as he is perhaps known best for some of his disagreements (with the Pelagians, Donatists, and Manicheans), the well-known influence of Platonic thought on his own ought to dispel the myth that there exists an "Augustinian imperative" to squelch differences and shun engagement. God's providence has seen fit to scatter

---

144. William Connolly, cited in Mathewes, *Theology of Public Life*, 108.
145. Augustine, *On Christian Doctrine*, 2.17–40.
146. Ibid., 2.40.
147. Ibid. Italics added.

divine wisdom widely; it would be foolish, then, for the church to hunker down in a stained glass bunker, rejecting *a priori* any word from the outside.

Taken as a whole, the image Augustine presents of the church is not that of an enclosed compound with thick borders, impervious to and without benefit from external supplementation. Rather, whether it is the characterization of the church not as a distinct territory set apart from the world but as the movement of love on pilgrimage across all space, the recognition of the mixed nature of the church—and of the earthly city as well, his criticism of opponents for quitting the argument, the embrace of diverse customs and cultures for the ways they contribute to the church's life, or the acknowledgment of even the theological wisdom of pagans, an Augustinian ecclesiology appears to be suspended from heaven, as it were, without borders, coextensive with all temporal space. Accordingly, there is no outside and no outsiders in the sense of a space or persons who are preemptively excluded from the conversation and so from contributing to the form of the church's common life.

In fact, insofar as the earthly city is ruled by a self-love that sanctions dominion, sovereign power, the state of exception, as a means of securing the self from the threat of others, it can be argued on Augustinian grounds that it is the earthly city and not the church that erects borders, that is exclusionary.

Conclusion

With the sovereign power of empire darkening the horizon of human life, Hardt, Negri, and Agamben see a ray of hope in the possibility of more radical modes of democratic practice, which they conceptualize as the multitude, the common, the coming community and so forth. While their hope is rightly placed—our hope for deliverance from the brutal state of exception in which we live and die does lie in a new democratic politics—their thought fails to sustain this hope because it is not democratic enough, because through its exclusion of the holy Trinity and the tradition of the saints, it cuts itself off from the possibility of the genuinely novel, of the possibility of persons drawing near to one another in love and without fear of loss, of the possibility of not only randomly and temporarily interrupting the state of exception but to actually defeating it.

The radical democrat Rom Coles, who likewise looks to the emergence of a new democratic practice as a source of hope, argues that this new, emergent democracy entails a kind of dual receptivity, which he articulates in terms of teleological and ateleological responsibilities.[148] What he calls teleological responsibilities are a matter of receptivity to the past: listening to and cultivating the wisdom and practices of the tradition, of those who have gone before us, for the sake of orienting further efforts to deepen democracy. On the other hand, ateleological responsibilities are a matter of receptivity to the beyond, to the future: being open and vulnerable to external supplementation. Listening to and learning from others and events beyond our tradition. Coles is insistent that a radically democratic practice entails both responsibilities. It entails living in the difficult tension created by these dual responsibilities.

Coles's conception of the problematic of democracy provides another way to frame the argument of this essay. The democratic visions of Hardt, Negri, and Agamben falter because they embrace the ateleological responsibilities of democracy to the exclusion of the teleological responsibilities. They have replaced the proper tensional relation between the teleological and the ateleological with the antagonistic and mutually exclusive disjunctive: either *telos* or freedom. As a result, their democracy is eternally fugitive and random.

The challenge for Augustine and an Augustinian political theology or ecclesiology is the opposite one of properly respecting the ateleological responsibilities that accompany the church's democratic vocation of inviting all into the communion of charity that is the divine life of the Trinity. Or, to put it a little differently, the challenge for the church is to accept that although it looks *forward* in faith and hope to the day when it will see clearly, face to face, and when it will know fully, in this time between the times, while it is on pilgrimage, it reflects the glory of God in broken, haphazard, and incomplete ways. In other words, while on pilgrimage, it too shines with the fragile brilliance of glass. While it may not be fugitive—the public character of its democratic vocation may ordinarily preclude such hiddenness—it is a refugee, in exile. Every foreign land is to it as its native country, and every native land is to it a land of strangers.[149]

While Augustine may have failed this challenge at certain points, which include but are not limited to his approval of coercive *dominium* as non-sinful,[150] an Augustinian political ecclesiology offers a vision of a

---

148. Coles, *Beyond Gated Politics*, xv.

149. See the *Epistle to Diognetus*, chapter 5.

150. See Milbank, *Theology and Social Theory*, 427–32. Milbank's point is that Augustine errs not by admitting the necessity of coercion in this time between the times, but in failing to grasp its character. Augustine failed to grasp how coercion is always tainted by sin and hence is a tragic risk.

church that is more democratic, open, responsive and collaborative than typically thought.

So long as the church is on pilgrimage, it must be open, receptive, vulnerable, democratic. Insofar as the church seeks to include all in a common life that *it* is still in the process of discerning and embodying, it is intrinsically open, receptive, democratic. So long as Christ continues to appear in the stranger, so long as God is faithful to the Jews, and so long as divine providence continues to scatter wisdom everywhere abroad, the church is open. So long as sin persists in its own life, so long as it is a *corpus permixtum*, it is open and vulnerable. So long as it is charged with the ministry of reconciliation, of communion, and there remains even one "outsider," even one who has not been invited or welcomed,[151] so long as there is time, the church will always have room for one more perspective, one more language, one more custom, one more voice, in its chorus of praise.

And even when the church concludes its pilgrimage and arrives at the heavenly banquet, it will remain open, receptive, democratic. For so long as its participation in the communion of the divine life is that of the finite with the infinite, its openness, its receptivity will continue as it delves ever deeper into the love and joy and peace that is without end.

---

151. See Luke 15:2–10; 1 Cor 15:29.

Bibliography

Agamben, Giorgio. *The Coming Community*. Translated by Michael Hardt. Minneapolis: University of Minnesota Press, 1993.

———. *Homo Sacer: Sovereign Power and Bare Life*. Translated by Daniel Heller-Roazen. Stanford: Stanford University Press, 1998.

———. *Means Without End: Notes on Politics*. Translated by Vincenzo Binetti and Cesare Casarino. Minneapolis: University of Minnesota Press, 2000.

———. *Potentialities: Collected Essays in Philosophy*. Translated by Daniel Heller-Roazen. Stanford: Stanford University Press, 1999.

———. *State of Exception*. Translated by Kevin Attell. Chicago: University of Chicago Press, 2005.

———. *The Time That Remains: A Commentary on the Letter to the Romans*. Translated by Patricia Dailey. Stanford: Stanford University Press, 2005.

Alliez, Éric. *Capital Times*. Translated by Georges Van Den Abbeele. Minneapolis: University of Minnesota Press, 1996.

Aquinas, Thomas. *Summa Theologica*. Translated by Fathers of the English Dominican Province. Allen, TX: Christian Classics, 1981.

Arendt, Hannah. *Eichmann in Jerusalem: A Report on the Banality of Evil*. New York: Penguin, 1994.

Aristotle. *Nicomachean Ethics*. Edited by Roger Crisp. New York: Cambridge University Press, 2000.

Augustine. *Augustine on Romans*. Text and translation by Paula Fredriksen Landes. Chico: Scholars, 1982.

———. *Augustine: Political Writings*. Edited by E. M. Atkins and R. J. Dodaro. Translated by Margaret Atkins. Cambridge: Cambridge University Press, 2001.

———. *The City of God*. Translated by Marcus Dods. New York: Modern Library, 1950.

———. *The City of God Against the Pagans*. Edited and translated by R. W. Dyson. New York: Cambridge University Press, 1998.

———. *The Confessions of St. Augustin*. In *Nicene and Post-Nicene Fathers*. First series. Edited by Philip Schaff. 1:27–207. Peabody, MA: Hendrickson, 1994.

———. "Eighth Homily: 1 John 4:12–16." In *Augustine: Later Works*, edited and translated by John Burnaby, 320–28. Philadelphia: Westminster, 1955.

———. *Homilies on the Gospel of St. John*. In *Nicene and Post-Nicene Fathers*. First Series. Translated by John Gibb. 7–452. Peabody, MA: Hendrickson, 1994.

——. *Of True Religion*. In *Augustine: Earlier Writings*, translated by John H. S. Burleigh, 218–83. Philadelphia: Westminster, 1953.

——. *On Christian Doctrine*. In *Nicene and Post-Nicene Fathers*. First series. Edited by Philip Schaff. 2:513–621. Peabody, MA: Hendrickson, 1994.

——. *On Free Will*. In *Augustine: Earlier Writings*, translated by John H. S. Burleigh, 102–217. Philadelphia: Westminster, 1953.

——. *On the Spirit and the Letter*. In *Nicene and Post-Nicene Fathers*. First Series. Translated by Peter Holmes and Robert Ernest Wallis. 5:79–114. Peabody, MA: Hendrickson, 1994.

——. *On the Trinity*. In *Nicene and Post-Nicene Fathers*. First Series. Translated by Arthur West Haddan. 3:1–228. Peabody, MA: Hendrickson, 1994.

——. "Second Homily: 1 John 2:12–17." In *Augustine: Later Works*, edited and translated by John Burnaby, 270–78. Philadelphia: Westminster, 1955.

——. *A Treatise Concerning Man's Perfection in Righteousness*. In *Nicene and Post-Nicene Fathers*. First Series. Translated by Peter Holmes and Robert Ernest Wallis. 5:153–76. Peabody, MA: Hendrickson, 1994.

Aulén, Gustaf. *Christus Victor*. Translated by A. G. Hebert. 1951. Reprint, Eugene, OR: Wipf and Stock, 1998.

Bader-Saye, Scott. *Church and Israel after Christendom*. Boulder, CO: Westview, 1999.

——. "Thomas Aquinas and the Culture of Fear." *Journal of the Society of Christian Ethics* 25 (2005) 95–108.

Badiou, Alain. *Being and Event*. Translated by Oliver Feltham. New York: Continuum, 2005.

——. *Deleuze: The Clamor of Being*. Translated by Louise Burchill. Minneapolis: University of Minnesota Press, 1999.

——. *Ethics: An Essay on the Understanding of Evil*. Translated by Peter Hallward. New York: Verso, 2001.

——. "Gilles Deleuze, 'The Fold: Leibniz and the Baroque.'" In *Gilles Deleuze and the Theater of Philosophy*, edited by Constantin Boundas and Dorothea Olkoski, 51–69. New York: Routledge, 1994.

——. *Infinite Thought: Truth and the Return of Philosophy*. Translated and edited by Oliver Feltham and Justin Clemens. New York: Continuum, 2005.

——. *Logics of Worlds*. Translated by Alberto Toscano. New York: Continuum, 2009.

——. *Manifesto for Philosophy*. Translated by Normam Madarasz. Albany: State University of New York Press, 1999.

——. "On a Finally Objectless Subject." In *Who Comes After the Subject?*, edited by Eduardo Cadava, et al., 24–32. New York: Routledge, 1991.

——. *Saint Paul: The Foundations of Universalism*. Translated by Ray Brassier. Stanford: Stanford University Press, 2003.

——. *Theory of the Subject*. Translated by Bruno Bosteels. New York: Continuum, 2009.

Balibar, Etienne. "Citizen Subject." In *Who Comes After the Subject?*, edited by Eduardo Cadava et al., 33–57. New York: Routledge, 1991.

Balthasar, Hans Urs von. *Explorations in Theology*. Vol. 1. San Francisco: Ignatius, 1989.

——. *The Glory of the Lord*. Vol. 2. San Francisco: Ignatius, 1984.

——. *A Theology of History*. San Francisco: Ignatius, 1994.

Becker, Ernest. *The Denial of Death*. New York: Free, 1997.

Bell, Daniel M., Jr. "Forgiveness and the End of Economy." *Studies in Christian Ethics* 20 (2007) 325–44.

———. "Justice and Liberation." In *The Blackwell Companion to Christian Ethics*, edited by Stanley Hauerwas and Sam Wells, 182–95. Malden, MA: Blackwell, 2003.

———. *Liberation Theology after the End of History: The Refusal to Cease Suffering.* New York: Routledge, 2001.

———. "Sacrifice and Suffering: Beyond Justice, Human Rights, and Capitalism." *Modern Theology* 18 (2002) 333–59.

Benhabib, Seyla, ed. *Democracy and Difference: Contesting the Boundaries of the Political.* Princeton: Princeton University Press, 1996.

Black, Antony. *Guild & State.* New Brunswick, NJ: Transaction Publishers, 2003.

Bornkamm, Günther. *Paul.* Translated by D. M. G. Stalker. New York: Harper & Row, 1971.

Broadman, James W. *Charity and Religion in Medieval Europe.* Washington, DC: Catholic University of America Press, 2009.

———. *Charity and Welfare: Hospitals and the Poor in Medieval Catalonia.* Philadelphia: University of Pennsylvania Press, 1998.

Brooks, David. "The Age of Conflict." *The Weekly Standard*, November 5, 2001, 19–23.

———. "Facing Up to Our Fears." *Newsweek*, October 22, 2001, 66–69.

Bruni, Luigino, and Stefano Zamagni. *Civil Economy: Efficiency, Equity, Public Happiness.* Translated by N. Michael Brennen. New York: P. Lang, 2007.

Bull, Malcolm. "The Limits of Multitude." *New Left Review* 25 (September-October 2005) 19–39.

Burchell, Graham. "Liberal Government and Techniques of the Self." *Economy and Society* 22 (1993) 267–82.

Burchell, Graham, Colin Gordon, and Peter Miller, eds. *The Foucault Effect: Studies in Governmentality.* Chicago: University of Chicago Press, 1991.

Byrne, Brendan. *Romans.* Collegeville, MN: Liturgical Press, 1996.

Cary, Phillip. "United Inwardly by Love: Augustine's Social Ontology." In *Augustine and Politics*, edited by John Doody, Kevin Hughes, and Kim Paffenroth, 3–34. Lanham, MD: Lexington, 2005.

Cavanaugh, William T. "From One City to Two: Christian Reimagining of Political Space." *Political Theology* 7 (2006) 299–321.

Chesterton, G. K. *Orthodoxy.* Garden City, NY: Doubleday, 1959.

Chroust, Anton-Herman. "The Corporate Ideal and the Body Politic in the Middle Ages." *The Review of Politics* 9 (1947) 423–52.

Coles, Romand. *Beyond Gated Politics: Reflections for the Possibility of Democracy.* Minneapolis: University of Minnesota Press, 2005.

———. "Of Tension and Tricksters: Grassroots Democracy between Theory and Practice." In *Christianity, Democracy and the Radical Ordinary: Conversations between a Radical Democrat and a Christian*, 277–308. Eugene, OR: Cascade, 2008.

Davies, W. D. *Jewish and Pauline Studies.* Minneapolis: Fortress, 1984.

Debord, Guy. *The Society of the Spectacle.* Translated by Donald Nicholson-Smith. New York: Zone, 1994.

Deleuze, Gilles. *Coldness and Cruelty.* In *Masochism: Coldness and Cruelty; Venus in Furs*, by Gilles Deleuze and Leopold von Sacher-Maoch, 7–142. Translated by Jean McNeil. New York: Zone, 1991.

———. *Difference and Repetition*. Translated by Paul Patton. New York: Columbia University Press, 1994.

———. *Essays Critical and Clinical*. Translated by Daniel W. Smith and Michael A. Greco. Minneapolis: University of Minnesota Press, 1997.

———. *Expressionism in Philosophy: Spinoza*. Translated by Martin Joughin. New York: Zone Books, 1992.

———. *Foucault*. Translated by Seán Hand. Minneapolis: University of Minnesota Press, 1988.

———. *Kant's Critical Philosophy: The Doctrine of the Faculties*. Translated by Hugh Tomlinson and Barbara Habberjam. Minneapolis: University of Minnesota Press, 1990.

———. *Nietzsche and Philosophy*. Translated by Hugh Tomlinson. New York: Columbia University Press, 1983.

———. *Spinoza: Practical Philosophy*. Translated by Robert Hurley. San Francisco: City Lights, 1988.

———. "Postscript on the Societies of Control." *October* 59 (1992) 3–7.

———. "Seminar Session on Scholasticism & Spinoza." Translated by Timothy S. Murphy. http://www.imaginet.fr/TXT/ENG/140174.html [August 6, 1999].

Deleuze, Gilles, and Félix Guattari. *Anti-Oedipus: Capitalism and Schizophrenia*. Translated by Robert Hurley, Mark Seem, and Helen R. Lane. Minneapolis: University of Minnesota Press, 1983.

———. *A Thousand Plateaus: Capitalism and Schizophrenia*. Translated by Brian Massumi. Minneapolis: University of Minnesota Press, 1987.

———. *What is Philosophy?* Translated by Hugh Tomlinson and Graham Burchell. New York: Columbia University Press, 1994.

Deleuze, Gilles, and Claire Parnet. *Dialogues*. Translated by Hugh Tomlinson and Barbara Habberjam. New York: Columbia University Press, 1987.

Depoortere, Frederiek. "The End of God's Transcendence? On Incarnation in the Work of Slavoj Žižek." *Modern Theology* 23 (2007) 497–523.

Derrida, Jacques. *Acts of Religion*. Edited by Gil Anidjar. New York: Routledge, 2002.

———. *Adieu to Emmanuel Levinas*. Translated by Pascale-Anne Brault and Michael Nass. Stanford: Stanford University Press, 1999.

———. *The Gift of Death*. Translated by David Wills. Chicago: University of Chicago Press, 1995.

———. *On Cosmopolitanism and Forgiveness*. Translated by Mark Dooley and Michael Hughes. New York: Routledge, 2001.

———. *Rogues: Two Essays on Reason*. Translated by Pascale-Anne Brault and Michael Nass. Stanford: Stanford University Press, 2005.

———. *Specters of Marx*. Edited by Bernd Magnus and Stephen Cullenberg. New York: Routledge, 1994.

de Vries, Hent. *Philosophy and the Turn to Religion*. Baltimore: Johns Hopkins University Press, 1999.

Epistle to Diognetus. In *Ante-Nicene Fathers*, edited by Alexander Roberts, James Donaldson, and Arthur Cleveland Coxe, 1:23–30. Peabody, MA: Hendrickson, 1994.

Foucault, Michel. "About the Beginning of the Hermeneutics of the Self: Two Lectures at Dartmouth." *Political Theory* 21 (1993) 198–227.

———. *The Order of Things: An Archaeology of the Human Sciences*. New York: Vintage, 1994.

———. "Preface." In *Anti-Oedipus: Capitalism and Schizophrenia*, by Gilles Deleuze and Félix Guattari, xi–xiv. Translated by Robert Hurley, Mark Seem, and Helen R. Lane. Minneapolis: University of Minnesota Press, 1977.

———. *"Society Must Be Defended": Lectures at the Collège de France, 1975–76*. Edited by Mauro Bertani and Alessandro Fontana. Translated by David Macey. New York: Picador, 2003.

Friedman, Milton. *Capitalism and Freedom*. Chicago: University of Chicago Press, 1982.

Fukuyama, Francis. "The End of History?" *National Interest* 16 (1989) 3–18.

———. *The End of History and the Last Man*. New York: Free, 1992.

———. *Trust: The Social Virtues and the Creation of Prosperity*. New York: Free Press, 1995.

Glassner, Barry. *The Culture of Fear*. New York: Basic, 1999.

Glynos, Jason. "'There Is No Other of the Other': Symptoms of a Decline in Symbolic Faith, or, Žižek's Anti-capitalism." *Paragraph* 24 (2001) 78–110.

Goodchild, Philip. *Deleuze and Guattari: An Introduction to the Politics of Desire*. Thousand Oaks, CA: Sage, 1996.

Hallward, Peter. *Badiou: A Subject to Truth*. Minneapolis: University of Minnesota Press, 2003.

Hanby, Michael. "Democracy and Its Demons." In *Augustine and Politics*, edited by John Doody, Kevin Hughes, and Kim Paffenroth, 117–44. Lanham, MD: Lexington, 2005.

Hanson, Richard. "The Achievement of Orthodoxy in the Fourth Century AD." In *The Making of Orthodoxy*, edited by Rowan Williams, 142–56. New York: Cambridge University Press, 1989.

Hardt, Michael. *Gilles Deleuze: An Apprenticeship in Philosophy*. Minneapolis: University of Minnesota Press, 1993.

Hardt, Michael, and Antonio Negri. *Empire*. Cambridge: Harvard University Press, 2000.

———. *Multitude: War and Democracy in the Age of Empire*. New York: Penguin, 2004.

Harink, Douglas. *Paul Among the Postliberals*. Grand Rapids: Brazos, 2003.

Hart, David Bentley. *The Beauty of the Infinite*. Grand Rapids: Eerdmans, 2003.

———. "A Gift Exceeding Every Debt: An Eastern Orthodox Appreciation of Anselm's *Cur Deus Homo*." *Pro Ecclesia* 7 (1993) 333–49.

Halivni, David. *Revelation Restored*. Boulder, CO: Westview, 1997.

Hauerwas, Stanley. "Democratic Time: Lessons Learned from Yoder and Wolin." *Cross Currents* 55 (2006) 534–52.

Hauerwas, Stanley, and Romand Coles. "A Conversation." In *Christianity, Democracy, and the Radical Ordinary: Conversations between a Radical Democrat and a Christian*, 322–46. Eugene, OR: Cascade, 2008.

Hayek, Friedrich A. *The Constitution of Liberty*. Chicago: University of Chicago Press, 1978.

———. *The Fatal Conceit: The Errors of Socialism*. Edited by W. W. Bartley III. Chicago: University of Chicago Press, 1988.

———. *Law, Legislation and Liberty*. Vol. 2, *The Mirage of Social Justice*. Chicago: University of Chicago Press, 1976.

Hays, Richard. *Echoes of Scripture in the Letters of Paul.* New Haven: Yale University Press, 1989.

———. *The Faith of Jesus Christ.* 2nd ed. Grand Rapids: Eerdmans, 2002.

Henderson, John. *Piety and Charity in Late Medieval Florence.* Chicago: University of Chicago Press, 1994.

Hütter, Reinhard. "The Twofold Center of Lutheran Ethics: Christian Freedom and God's Commands." In *The Promise of Lutheran Ethics*, edited by Karen L. Bloomquist and John R. Stumme, 31–54. Minneapolis: Fortress, 1998.

Ignatieff, Michael. *The Warrior's Honor.* New York: Metropolitan, 1997.

Johnson, Luke Timothy. *Rereading Romans.* Macon, GA: Smyth & Helwys, 2001.

Jones, L. Gregory. *Embodying Forgiveness.* Grand Rapids: Eerdmans, 1995.

Kafka, Franz. "In the Penal Colony." Translated by Willa Muir and Edwin Muir, 140–67. In *Franz Kafka: The Complete Stories.* Edited by Nahum N. Glatzer. New York: Schocken, 1995.

Keenan, James F. *The Works of Mercy.* Lanham, MD: Rowman & Littlefield, 2005.

Klein, Naomi. *The Shock Doctrine: The Rise of Disaster Capitalism.* New York: Picador, 2007.

Ladner, Gerhart B. "Aspects of Mediaeval Thought on Church and State." *The Review of Politics* 9 (1947) 403–22.

Lefebvre, Alexandre. "A New Image of Law: Deleuze and Jurisprudence." *Telos* 130 (2005) 103–26.

Leith, John H., ed. *Creeds of the Churches.* 3rd ed. Atlanta: John Knox, 1982.

Levering, Matthew. *Christ's Fulfillment of Torah and Temple: Salvation according to Thomas Aquinas.* Notre Dame: University of Notre Dame Press, 2002.

Lindbeck, George. "Postmodern Hermeneutics and Jewish-Christian Dialogue: A Case Study." In *Christianity in Jewish Terms*, edited by Tikva Frymer-Kensky et al., 106–14. Boulder, CO: Westview, 2000.

———. "What of the Future? A Christian Response." In *Christianity in Jewish Terms*, edited by Tikva Frymer-Kensky et al., 357–65. Boulder, CO: Westview, 2000.

Locke, John. *An Essay Concerning Human Understanding.* Edited by Peter H. Nidditch. Oxford: Clarendon, 1975.

Luther, Martin. "The Freedom of a Christian." In *Martin Luther: Selections from His Writings*, edited by John Dillenberger, 42–85. Chicago: Quadrangle, 1961.

MacIntyre, Alasdair. *After Virtue.* 2nd ed. Notre Dame: University of Notre Dame Press, 1981.

Malkin, Michelle. "Candidates Ignore 'Security Moms' at Their Peril." *USA Today*, July 21, 2004, 11A.

Marglin, Stephen A. *The Dismal Science: How Thinking Like an Economist Undermines Community.* Cambridge: Harvard University Press, 2008.

Markus, Robert A. *Saeculum: History and Society in the Theology of St. Augustine.* New York: Cambridge University Press, 1970.

———. "Two Conceptions of Political Authority: Augustine, *De Civitate Dei*, XIX. 14–15, and Some Thirteenth-Century Interpretations." In *The City of God: A Collection of Critical Essays*, edited by Dorothy F. Donnelly, 93–118. New York: P. Lang, 1995.

Marshall, Bruce. "Christ and Cultures: The Jewish People and Christian Theology." In *The Cambridge Companion to Christian Doctrine*, edited by Colin Gunton, 81–100. New York: Cambridge University Press, 1997.

Massumi, Brian. *A User's Guide to Capitalism and Schizophrenia: Deviations from Deleuze and Guattari*. Cambridge: MIT Press, 1992.
McCabe, Herbert. *God Matters*. London: G. Chapman, 1987.
Macpherson, C. B. *The Life and Times of Liberal Democracy*. New York: Oxford University Press, 1997.
———. *The Real World of Democracy*. New York: Oxford University Press, 1972.
Mathewes, Charles. *A Theology of Public Life*. New York: Cambridge University Press, 2007.
Milbank, John. *Being Reconciled*. New York: Routledge, 2003.
———. "Can a Gift Be Given? Prolegomena to a Future Trinitarian Metaphysic." *Modern Theology* 11 (1995) 119–61.
———. "The Double Glory, or Paradox versus Dialectics: On Not Quite Agreeing with Slavoj Žižek." In *The Monstrosity of Christ: Paradox or Dialectic?*, edited by Creston Davis, 110–233. Cambridge: MIT Press, 2009.
———. "Forgiveness and Incarnation." In *Questioning God*, edited by John D. Caputo, Mark Dooley, and Michael J. Scanlon, 92–128. Bloomington: Indiana University Press, 2001.
———. "Materialism and Transcendence." In *Theology and the Political*, edited by Creston Davis, John Milbank, and Slavoj Žižek, 393–426. Durham: Duke University Press, 2005.
———. "The Midwinter Sacrifice: A Sequel to 'Can Morality Be Christian?'" *Studies in Christian Ethics* 10 (1997) 13–38.
———. "On Theological Transgression." *Arachne* 2 (1995) 145–76.
———. "A Real Third Way." In *The Crisis of Global Capitalism*, edited by Adrian Pabst, 27–70. Eugene, OR: Cascade, 2011.
———. "Socialism of the Gift, Socialism by Grace." *New Blackfriars* 77/910 (1996) 532–48.
———. "Stories of Sacrifice." *Modern Theology* 12 (1996) 27–56.
———. *Theology and Social Theory*. Cambridge, MA: Blackwell, 1990.
Mollat, Michel. *The Poor in the Middle Ages: An Essay in Social History*. Translated by Arthur Goldhammer. New Haven: Yale University Press, 1986.
Negri, Antonio. "The Political Subject and Absolute Immanence." In *Theology and the Political: The New Debate*, edited by Creston Davis, John Milbank, and Slavoj Žižek. 231–39. Durham: Duke University Press, 2005.
Nichols, Terence. *That All May Be One: Hierarchy and Participation in the Church*. Collegeville, MN: Liturgical, 1997.
Novak, Michael. *The Spirit of Democratic Capitalism*. Lanham, MD: Madison, 1991.
Ochs, Peter. "Commentary." In *The Jewish-Christian Schism Revisited*, edited by Michael G. Cartwright and Peter Ochs. Grand Rapids: Eerdmans, 2003.
Orwell, George. *The Orwell Reader: Fiction, Essays and Reportage*. New York: Harcourt Brace, 1956.
Pabst, Adrian. "Modern Sovereignty in Question: Theology, Democracy and Capitalism." *Modern Theology* 26 (2010) 570–602.
Perelman, Michael. *The Invention of Capitalism*. Durham: Duke University Press, 2000.
Pickstock, Catherine. *After Writing: On the Liturgical Consummation of Philosophy*. Malden, MA: Blackwell, 1998.
Placher, William C. *The Domestication of Transcendence: How Modern Thinking about God Went Wrong*. Louisville: Westminster John Knox, 1996.

Rich, Frank. "The Day Before Tuesday." *New York Times*, September 15, 2001, A23.
Robin Corey. *Fear: The History of a Political Idea*. New York: Oxford University Press, 2004.
Sanders, E. P. *Paul and Palestinian Judaism*. Minneapolis: Fortress, 1977.
Schindler, David. "Freedom beyond Our Choosing: Augustine on the Will and Its Objects." In *Augustine and Politics*, edited by John Doody, Kevin Hughes, and Kim Paffenroth, 67–98. Lanham, MD: Lexington, 2005.
Schlabach, Gerald W. "'Love Is the Hand of the Soul': The Grammar of Continence in Augustine's Doctrine of Christian Love." *Journal of Early Christian Studies* 6 (1998) 59–91.
Schmidt, Carl. *Political Theology: Four Chapters on the Concept of Sovereignty*. Translated by George Schwab. Cambridge: MIT Press, 1985.
Schmitz, Kenneth. "Is Liberalism Good Enough?" In *Liberalism and the Good*, edited by R. Bruce Douglass, Gerald M. Mara, and Henry S. Richardson, 86–104. New York: Routledge, 1990.
Schnädelbach, Herbert. *Philosophy in Germany, 1831–1933*. Translated by Eric Matthews. New York: Cambridge University Press, 1986.
Sedgwick, Peter H. *The Market Economy and Christian Ethics*. New York: Cambridge University Press, 1999.
Shklar, Judith N. *Political Thought and Political Thinkers*. Edited by Stanley Hoffmann. Chicago: University of Chicago Press, 1998.
Siegel, Marc. *False Alarm: The Truth about the Epidemic of Fear*. Hoboken, NJ: J. Wiley, 2005.
Smith, Adam. *An Inquiry into the Nature and Causes of the Wealth of Nations*. Edited by Edwin Cannan. Chicago: University of Chicago Press, 1976.
Smith, Daniel W. "The Doctrine of Univocity: Deleuze's Ontology of Immanence." In *Deleuze and Religion*, edited by Mary Bryden, 167–83. New York: Routledge, 2001.
Smith, James K. A. *Jacques Derrida: Live Theory*. New York: Continuum, 2005.
Smith, Thomas W. "The Glory and Tragedy of Politics." In *Augustine and Politics*, edited by John Doody, Kevin Hughes, and Kim Paffenroth, 187–216. Lanham, MD: Lexington, 2005.
Sobrino, Jon. *The Principle of Mercy: Taking the Crucified People from the Cross*. Maryknoll, NY: Orbis, 1994.
Stendahl, Krister. *Paul Among Jews and Gentiles, and Other Essays*. Minneapolis: Fortress, 1976.
Surin, Kenneth. "Liberation." In *Critical Terms for Religious Studies*, edited by Mark C. Taylor, 173–85. Chicago: University of Chicago Press, 1998.
———. "The Undecidable and the Fugitive: Mille Plateaux and the State-Form." *SubStance* 66 (19991) 102–13.
Tamari, Meir. *The Challenge of Wealth: A Jewish Perspective on Earning and Spending Money*. Northvale, NJ: J. Aronson, 1995.
Tierney, Brian. *Medieval Poor Law*. Berkley: University of California Press, 1959.
Tillich, Paul. *Systematic Theology*. Vol. 2. Chicago: University of Chicago Press, 1957.
Tracy, David. *The Analogical Imagination*. New York: Crossroad, 1987.
Wall, Thomas Carl. *Radical Passivity: Levinas, Blanchot, and Agamben*. New York: State University of New York Press, 1999.

Wannenwetsch, Bernd. "The Desire of Desire: Commandment and Idolatry in Late Capitalist Societies." In *Idolatry*, edited by Stephen C. Barton, 315–30. New York: T. & T. Clark, 2007.
Westberg, Daniel. "Reason, Will and Legalism." *New Blackfriars* 68.809 (1987) 431–36.
Williams, Rowan. "Politics and the Soul: A Reading of *The City of God*." *Milltown Studies* 19/20 (1987) 55–72.
———. *The Truce of God: Peacemaking in Troubled Times*. Grand Rapids: Eerdmans, 2005.
Wolin, Sheldon. "Fugitive Democracy." In *Democracy and Difference: Contesting the Boundaries of the Political*, edited by Seyla Benhabib, 31–45. Princeton: Princeton University Press, 1996.
———. *Politics and Vision*. Expanded ed. Princeton: Princeton University Press, 2004.
Wood, Ellen Meiksins. *Empire of Capital*. New York: Verso, 2003.
Woodhead, Linda. "Love and Justice." *Studies in Christian Ethics* 5 (1992) 44–61.
Yeago, David. "Jesus of Nazareth and Cosmic Redemption: The Relevance of St. Maximus the Confessor." *Modern Theology* 12 (1996) 163–92.
———. "Martin Luther on Grace, Law, and Moral Life: Prolegomena to an Ecumenical Discussion of *Veritatis Splendor*." *The Thomist* 62 (1998) 163–91.
Yoder, John Howard. *The Jewish-Christian Schism Revisited*. Edited by Michael G. Cartwright and Peter Ochs. Grand Rapids: Eerdmans, 2003.
———. *The Priestly Kingdom*. Notre Dame: University of Notre Dame Press, 1984.
Young, Iris Marion. *Inclusion and Democracy*. New York: Oxford University Press, 2000.
Žižek, Slavoj. "Dialectical Clarity versus the Misty Conceit of Paradox." In *The Monstrosity of Christ: Paradox or Dialectic?*, edited by Creston Davis, 234–306. Cambridge: MIT Press, 2009.
———. "The Fear of Four Words: A Modest Pleas for the Hegelian Reading of Christianity." In *The Monstrosity of Christ: Paradox or Dialectic?*, edited by Creston Davis, 24–109. Cambridge: MIT Press, 2009.
———. *The Fragile Absolute—or, Why Is the Christian Legacy Worth Fighting for?* New York: Verso, 2000.
———. "From Democracy to Divine Violence." In *Democracy in What State?*, by Giorgio Agamben et al., 100–20. New York: Columbia University Press, 2011.
———. "Holding the Place." In *Contingency, Hegemony, Universality*, by Judith Butler, Ernesto Laclau, and Slavoj Žižek, 308–30. New York: Verso, 2000.
———. *Interrogating the Real*. Edited by Rex Butler and Scott Stephens. New York: Continuum, 2006.
———. "Neighbors and Other Monsters: A Plea for Ethical Violence." In *The Neighbor: Three Inquiries in Political Theology*, by Slavoj Žižek, Eric L. Santer, and Kenneth Reinhard, 134–90. Chicago: University of Chicago Press, 2005.
———. "On Alain Badiou and *Logiques des mondes*." http://www.lacan.com/zizbadman.htm.
———. *On Belief*. New York: Routledge, 2001.
———. *The Puppet and the Dwarf: The Perverse Core of Christianity*. Cambridge: MIT Press, 2003.
———. "Schelling-in-Itself: 'The Orgasm of Forces.'" In *The Žižek Reader*, edited by Elizabeth Wright and Edmond Wright, 251–65. Malden, MA: Blackwell, 1999.

———. "Thinking Backward: Predestination and Apocalypse." In *Paul's New Moment: Continental Philosophy and the Future of Christian Theology*, edited by John Milbank, Slavoj Žižek, and Creston Davis, 185–210. Grand Rapids: Brazos, 2010.

———. *The Ticklish Subject: The Absent Centre of Political Ontology*. New York: Verso, 2000.

———. *Welcome to the Desert of the Real! Five Essays on September 11 and Related Dates*. New York: Verso, 2002.

Index

Abraham, 57, 59, 62n35, 104–5
affirmation, xiii, 3, 14–16, 18–20, 23, 43, 50–51, 53, 63, 83, 151
Agamben, Giorgio, x, xiv, 103–4, 110–13, 121, 123, 127, 136–37, 140–47, 149–62, 164–65, 167, 169–70, 178–79
agency, 122, 170–71
analogical, xiv, 46n75, 57, 66, 69n150, 85, 94n53, 104, 128, 129, 169
analogy of being, 68, 69n153, 84, 92–94, 98–99, 169
anarchy, 110, 124
Anselm, Saint, 3, 15, 16, 87–88, 92, 94, 96, 98, 99
anti-Semitism, 42–44, 52, 57
antinomian, xiv, 60, 113, 115
Aquinas, Thomas, xiv, 15n24, 68–69, 88n41, 92–94, 98, 128–31, 134, 171
Arendt, Hannah, xii, 3–4, 9
atheism, 35, 45n73, 46–47, 65, 74
atonement, 3, 15–16, 18, 61, 66, 69–71, 87–89, 95–96, 98–99
Augustine, Saint, x, xiv, 3, 16, 17n28, 18n29, 20–27, 61n128, 93, 95–97, 100, 124, 130–32, 136, 145, 148, 162, 164–75, 177–79

Bader-Saye, Scott, 15n24, 57, 59n120, 64n141
Badiou, Alain, x, xiii, xiv, 2, 13, 14, 17, 19n30, 21, 24, 29–60, 62–63, 65–68, 70, 73, 104, 114–17, 119, 123, 127, 132, 151n80
Balthasar, Hans Urs von, 16n26, 67, 69n152, 87, 88n36, 88n38, 88n39, 89n41, 92, 94n55
being-for-death, 2, 13–14, 17–19, 35, 43, 53
being-for-life, xiii, 2, 13–14, 16–17, 19, 21, 28
Benjamin, Walter, 112, 134n150
biopower, 7–8, 121, 139, 157, 160, 170
Bornkam, Günter, 39n42, 57n114,
boundaries, 23, 27, 34, 138–40, 161, 164, 166–69
Bruni, Luigino, 134
Bull, Malcolm, 121, 133
Bultmann, Rudolf, 36n42, 57, 59,

camp, 128, 137, 140, 143–45, 155, 159–60, 163, 168,
capitalism, xii–xiv, 10–11, 30–33, 37, 52–53, 56, 70–77, 80–81, 83–86, 88, 96, 98–100, 103–4, 117, 120, 122–27, 129, 133, 139, 140n18, 152, 161163
Catholic, xiii, 6, 23, 45, 63, 173,
Cavanaugh, William, 166n18
Chalcedon, 66–67, 75, 90–94
chance, 36, 49, 55–56, 114, 116, 151n80
charity, 17, 23, 65, 69, 71–72, 88–90, 94, 97, 99–102, 104, 127, 129, 134, 179

Christ, Jesus, xiii, xiv, 2, 3, 13–20, 23, 28, 33–35, 37–39, 41–44, 46n75, 58n115, 60–62, 65–76, 82, 86–87, 89–92, 94–102, 110, 112, 115, 117n83, 119, 127, 129–30, 132–33, 163–64, 168–72, 174–75

Christianity, ix, xiv, 14–15, 21, 27, 33–34, 39, 44–45, 57–59, 60n124, 61n130, 62n132, 63, 64n138, 72, 82, 86, 97, 105, 108–110, 117n83, 119, 127, 130n138, 133, 164, 168

Chrysostom, John, 58

church, x–xi, xiv, 15, 22–23, 32, 64, 66, 69, 72, 90, 95–96, 101–2, 112, 130n138, 134, 136–37, 152n84, 161, 163–70, 172–80

City of God, 3, 21–23, 27, 95, 165–68, 172, 175, 177

Civil Society, 2, 4–12

Coles, Rom, 155n97, 174n138, 176n143, 178–79

Coming Community, xiv, 136, 145, 149–50, 152–54, 156, 158, 161–62, 164, 178

common, the, xi, xiv, 136, 146–55, 161, 178

common cood, 88n40, 126, 134, 169, 172–73, 175

communion, 13, 20, 24, 26–28, 88, 94–96, 129–30, 134, 159, 164, 168, 173, 175–76, 179–80

communion of the saints 22–24, 161–62, 164, 174

concrete universal, xiii, 32, 56, 65, 67, 92, 94, 118,

contract, 6, 61n131, 84–85, 105, 113n58, 122, 125, 142, 158, 163, 169

count, the, 30, 36n31, 45, 47, 115, 123–24, 151n80

covenantal nomism, 61–62, 64

cross, 3, 15–19, 34, 70–72, 87, 89, 95, 100, 117n83, 113

cruelty, 76, 80, 82–83, 88, 90, 94, 97, 102, 117, 164

Davies, W. D., 57, 58n119, 60, 61n127,

de Vries, Hent, ix–x

death, xii–xiii, 2–6, 13–24, 26–28, 31n8, 35, 42–43, 45, 50, 53, 62n132, 66, 70–72, 75, 85–87, 89, 92, 96, 98, 100, 105–7, 109–110, 115, 117n83, 127–28, 142–43, 146, 155, 159, 172

Debord, Guy, 152

debt, xii, 16, 69–72, 82, 86–90, 95–98, 100, 102, 105, 109–110, 128

deconstruction, 21, 104, 107,

Deleuze, Gilles, ix, xi, xiii–xiv, 2, 4, 9–12, 16, 35, 36n27, 36n31, 41n57, 69n150, 75–87, 89–92, 94, 96–97, 99, 104, 107–110, 114, 122–24, 127–28, 151n80,

democracy, xii, xiv, 76, 105n4, 107n20, 111, 117, 136–37, 144, 147–48, 152–53, 155–59, 161–3, 165, 169, 178–79,

Derrida, Jacques, xiv, 103n2, 104–7, 123, 125–26, 129,

desire, xiii, 2–3, 5, 9–12, 17, 22, 24, 26, 32, 42, 47, 50n91, 72, 76–86, 90, 92, 94, 98, 100, 107–8, 110, 115, 116n80, 118, 120, 123–24, 126, 129, 131n143, 132n147, 145–46, 149, 156, 158, 168, 170, 172, 175

deterritorializing, 52–53, 81, 123, 127, 138, 153, 161

diaspora, xii, 167–68, 174, 176

dice-throw, 36, 49, 132, 151, 157, 160–61

difference, 30–31, 38–42, 44, 50–55, 62–68 69n153, 78–79, 84–85, 90–94, 97–99, 114–15, 119, 138, 140n19, 147–50, 157–59, 174, 176–77

disciplines, 7–9, 139, 141, 144

dominion, 6, 23–24, 27, 55, 72, 76–77, 80, 83, 100, 103, 155, 158, 163, 164n112, 165–66, 168–69, 178,

Donatists, 173–74, 177

double bind of law, 104, 106, 107n20, 126

ecclesiology, xiv, 136, 164, 166, 173–74, 176–79

economy, xii, 10, 31n8, 46, 71–72, 78, 79n15, 88–89, 96–101, 104, 127, 133–35
egalitarian, 38, 40, 42
election of the Jews, xii–xiii, 57–67, 70–71
Elshtain, Jean Bethke, 3
empire, xi–xii, xiv, 14, 21, 38, 136–40, 159, 164, 175
eschatology, 26n57, 29, 106, 147
Eucharist, 95–96, 98, 176
event, xiii, 2–3, 13–15, 17–20, 23, 28, 30, 32–44, 46–50, 53–54, 57, 65, 73–74, 95, 112, 114–18, 123, 127, 133, 141, 151n80, 153–54, 157
evil, 3–4, 9, 19, 3, 47–49, 107, 110, 115
excess, xiv, 36n28, 103, 105n4, 115, 117, 142–43,
exile, 167–68, 179,

faith, x, 15, 18, 32, 37, 42–43, 45, 59–60, 65, 70–71, 73, 87, 89, 99, 101, 116, 120, 169, 173–75, 179–80
fear, xii–xiii, 1–6, 8–16, 18–24, 26–28, 72, 99, 100, 132, 172, 178
fidelity, 3, 7, 15, 18–19, 33, 35–38, 40, 42–44, 46–49, 54, 57, 65, 70, 116, 123, 133,
filiation, 14, 20, 24, 27, 63, 66, 168, 175
finite, 48, 67–69, 75, 78, 82–83, 85, 87, 89, 90–93, 94n53, 94n56, 96–98, 102, 180
forgiveness, 82, 88, 97
Foucault, Michel, xiii, 2, 4, 6–10, 11n17, 27, 74n1, 77, 86, 90, 97, 111, 121, 139, 141, 144, 167
Freud, Sigmund, 74
Friedman, Milton, 120, 122, 123n112, 124
fugitive, 81, 102, 155–57, 161, 163, 179

Gentiles, 29, 34, 38, 58, 60, 63–64, 66, 70
gift, 3, 15–20, 26, 28, 46n75, 61, 62n132, 63, 65, 71, 72, 75, 88–90, 99–100, m 125n123, 131–32

Glassner, Barry, 1, 11n16
globalization, 137–38, 145–47
God, x, xii, xiii, 15–19, 23, 25–28, 38, 44n68, 46n75, 58, 60–61, 62n132, 62n135, 66, 68–71, 74–79, 81–84, 86–98, 102, 104–6, 109–110, 117, 129, 132n147, 148, 160, 162, 165–69, 171–72, 174–75, 177, 179–80
good, 3, 5, 9, 11–13, 19–22, 24–25, 27, 31n8, 49, 55, 70, 85, 88, 95, 98, 100–101, 107–110, 115, 130–34, 139, 141, 166–67, 170n123, 172
gospel, good news 1, 13–14, 16, 21, 23, 28, 32–34 38–39, 43–44, 51–52, 56–57, 60, 65–66, 71, 73, 75, 100, 163, 176
governmentality, 6, 8–12, 27, 141n23
grace, 33, 36, 40, 42, 45n73, 48–49, 55, 57, 61, 71–72, 89, 93, 97, 100, 130n138, 132

Hallward, Peter, 45–46, 50, 51n92, 56n113
Hanson, Richard, 173
Hardt, Michael, 136–40, 141n23, 145, 147–49, 151, 155–58, 161–62, 164–65, 169–70, 178–79
Harink, Douglas, 57
Hart, David, 87, 89, 125n123, 159
Hauerwas, Stanley, xiv, 165, 174, 176
Hayek, Friedrich A., 121, 124–25
Hegel, G. W. F., 74, 116n80
Hobbes, Thomas, xiii, 2–6, 8–10, 13, 27, 55–56, 61n131, 71, 85, 99, 121, 142
Holy Spirit, 67, 95, 97–98, 130n138, 131n140, 132, 172
Homo Sacer, 142–44, 146, 155, 160, 163, 167,
hope, xi, xiii–xiv, 13, 17, 20, 26–28, 32, 45, 47–51, 55–59, 65–66, 70, 73–75, 80, 86, 90, 99, 102, 104, 136–37, 145, 153, 155–57, 159–64, 178–79

Index

hospitality, 72, 100–101, 105–6
humanity, xiv, 16–18, 24, 35, 55, 63, 66–71, 74, 78, 87–93, 102, 124, 129, 131, 152–53, 158–59, 163, 171

Ignatieff, Michael, 3, 9
immanence, xiii, 75–78, 80–81, 90–91, 94, 108, 158–60, 163
immortal, 22, 35, 43, 45, 49–50, 54, 68, 71
imperial, 8, 13, 28, 103, 121, 138–41, 145, 148, 165, 167–68
incarnation, xii, 66, 100
infinite, 41–42, 45, 48, 53, 68, 75, 78, 82, 86–92, 96–99, 102, 105, 109–110, 125, 129, 152, 180
Israel, 58–59, 63

joy, 22, 25, 28, 65, 72, 84–85, 100, 102, 123n114, 129, 136, 146, 148, 155–60, 163–64, 167–72, 177, 180
Judaism, the Jews, xiii–xiv, 35, 38, 41–44, 51–52, 56–64, 72, 105, 109, 119, 127n131, 130n138, 164, 167, 176, 180
judgment, xii–xiv, 16n25, 31, 43, 46n73, 47, 72, 74–76, 81–83, 85–90, 96–98, 100, 102, 107, 109–110, 128, 130–31
justice, xii, 16, 20, 70–71, 82–89, 97–98, 105–7, 114n59, 117, 120n106, 133–34

Kafka, Franz, 103
Kant, Immanuel, 25, 105, 108–9, 128
Kierkegaard, Søren, 129

law of love, xiv, 43, 53, 57, 103–4, 116, 119, 127, 133–34
law, xii, xiv, 11–12, 24, 30, 31n8, 34, 41–44, 51, 53, 57, 59–65, 70, 83, 97, 103–116, 119–34, 142–44, 151n79, 160, 171, 175
legalism, 171, 172n133
Levinas, Emmanuel, 105, 117, 120n106, 125n123

liberalism, xiii, 2–8, 12–13, 21–22, 27–28
liberation, xiv, 19, 32, 74–76, 81, 98, 101, 122, 127, 145–46, 162
Locke, John, 3, 9
love, xiv, 14–15, 17, 19–28, 32, 43, 45, 48, 50–53, 56–57, 65, 70–73, 83–86, 89, 94, 98–100, 102–4, 107, 115–16, 119–20, 127, 132–34, 155–61, 163–64, 166, 168–70, 172, 178, 180

Machiavelli, Niccolò, 5
madness, 76, 80–81, 83–84, 86, 94, 99, 102, 103
market, xi–xii, 9, 12, 19, 30, 72, 77, 81, 83, 85–86, 98, 100–101, 121–22, 123–27, 133–34, 138–40, 158n104
Markus, R. A., 164n112, 167
Martyr, Justin, 57, 58n115
Marx, Karl, 74, 104n2
Marxism, 79, 104n2, 122, 147
materialism, 74, 78
mathematics, 36, 41n57, 45–46, 48–49, 54
McCabe, Herbert, 132, 172n133
mediality, pure means, 113, 124, 127, 153–54
Messiah, 43, 56, 58, 60–62, 65–67, 70–71, 106, 112–13, 129, 130n138
metaphysics, xii, 75–6
micropolitics, 78
Milbank, John, 48n83, 61n131, 62n132, 71n156, 88n138, 89n42, 132n148, 134, 179n150
militant, x, 14, 35, 43–45, 49, 51–53
modernity, ix–xiii, 19, 31, 46–47, 73–75, 78, 81, 98, 108, 139, 141, 167
Montesquieu, Charles de, 3–4, 12
multiplicity, 41n57, 78, 114–15, 118, 120, 124–25, 148, 176
multitude, xiv, 42, 96, 102, 120–23, 125, 127, 129, 133–34, 136, 145–49, 155–57, 161, 178

Negation, 3, 14–21, 40, 115–16, 119

Negri, Antonio, xiv, 136–40, 141n23, 145, 147–49, 151, 154–59, 161–62, 164–65, 169–70, 178–79
neoliberal, 104, 120, 122, 124
Nichols, Terence, 174
Nietzsche, Friedrich, 78, 82
nihilism, 13–14, 22, 31, 83, 102, 146, 150, 156n102, 158
nomad, 81, 102, 162
nominalism, 85, 104, 108, 128–30, 132, 158–59, 171, 172n133
Novak, Michael, 125–26

Ockham, William of, 128
ontology, xiii, 19, 36, 41n57, 45n73, 46, 48, 52–54, 56, 66, 74–78, 79n15, 80–81, 83, 86, 90, 97, 119, 140n19, 150, 156n101, 157–60, 170
orthodoxy, 91, 159, 173–74, 176
Orwell, George, 11

Pabst, Adrian, 121, 133
participation, 17–18, 26, 42, 62n132, 66–67, 69–72, 84–85, 88–89, 93, 94n56, 99–100, 104, 128–34, 147, 159, 161, 169, 172, 174, 180
particularity, xi, 30, 33, 40, 43–44, 51–52, 54–55, 57–59, 63–65, 117n89
Pascal, Blaise, 32, 37
Paul, Saint, xiii–xiv, 2, 13–17, 24, 28, 29–35, 37–48, 51–53, 56–71, 73, 90, 109–115, 119, 130–32, 170n126, 172
peace, 9, 11, 19–20, 50, 55–56, 65–68, 69n153, 89, 91–92, 94, 102, 118, 155–57, 159, 163–64, 167, 169, 175, 177, 180
pilgrim, xii, xiv, 23, 137, 166–68, 175–80
Plato, 41, 47, 108, 177
politics, x, xii–xiv, 1–3, 5, 8, 11–16, 19–24, 26–28, 29–30, 32, 37–38, 42, 45–46, 50, 52, 74–78, 80, 83n28, 105–6, 110, 114, 116, 136–37, 141–44, 146–47, 149–51, 153–57, 158n104, 161, 164–65, 167–69, 172, 178

Pope Benedict XVI, 134
postmodern, ix, xi–xii, xiv, 22, 27, 29, 99, 102, 103, 121–22, 125–26, 136–39
potentiality, 110–11, 113, 116, 140n19, 150–51, 159
power, xii–xiii, 1, 4, 6–11, 17, 28, 36, 43, 47–50, 53, 68–69, 72, 74–80, 82–83, 85, 88, 93–94, 100, 103, 107, 109, 111, 113, 115–17, 121, 123, 127, 131, 137–46, 148, 155–61, 163–65, 167, 170–72, 175–76, 178
Protestantism, 51, 57–59, 159, 165

Rand, Ayn, 98
redemption, xiv, 14, 18–19, 57, 62n135, 63, 67, 70, 75, 91–92, 96, 119
refugee, 123n114, 144, 147, 154–55, 167–68, 179
repetition, 30n6, 42, 96, 107–8, 114–15, 168
responsibility, 7, 21, 27, 104–7, 117, 126, 174
resurrection, xiii, 3, 15–17, 20–23, 26–28, 29, 35, 37, 39, 44, 46, 66, 70–71, 92, 99, 115
revolution, 38, 50, 74, 76–78, 80–81, 83, 86, 141
Rorty, Richard, 3

sacrifice, xi–xii, 11, 14–16, 19–21, 23, 28, 39, 69, 71–72, 87–90, 94–100, 102, 104, 142–44
Sanders, E. P., 57, 60, 62n132
scarcity, 71–72, 89, 97–98, 100,
Schlabach, Gerald, 26
Scotus, Duns, 78, 83, 84n30, 128, 158
Shklar, Judith, 3, 6, 9, 12, 21
singularity, xi, 30, 32–33, 36–40, 42, 44–45, 47, 50–51, 53–54, 56, 59n122, 68, 79, 84, 103, 105–111, 113–14, 117n89, 122, 125–27, 138, 147–52, 154–62, 166, 170
Smith, Adam, 72, 101, 124, 125n124

sovereignty, xi–xii, xiv, 5–8, 10, 31, 103–4, 107n20, 111–12, 113n58, 118n89, 120–22, 127–29, 131, 133, 136–49, 153–55, 157, 159–60, 163–72, 174–76, 178
spectacle, 149, 152–53, 155, 160, 162
Spinoza, Baruch, 61n131, 78n11, 121, 156, 158
state of exception, 11, 111–13, 118n89, 121–22, 133, 134n150, 137, 140, 142–46, 154–56, 159–60, 163, 168, 178
state, xii, 5–12, 19, 24, 77, 80, 85, 98, 107n20, 112, 120–23, 127, 133–34, 138, 141, 143–44, 146–47, 157, 165–68, 178
Stendahl, Krister, 61
Suarez, Francisco, 128, 131n143
subject, xiv, 6–7, 14, 21, 25, 31–44, 45n73, 46–55, 57, 59–62, 65, 68, 72, 75n3, 76, 79–80, 104, 108, 114–17, 123n114, 125, 127, 130–33, 137–38, 147–48, 157
subjectivation, 33–35, 42–43, 48, 57, 59–62, 68
subsumption, 10, 139, 141, 146
subtraction, xiii, 17, 33, 35, 42, 57, 62, 114–16, 119
suffering, 3, 14–19, 70, 88
supercessionism, 62
supplement, 48, 54, 83, 92, 111, 134, 139, 141, 163, 165, 176, 178–79

technologies of the self, 7–9, 12, 121, 144
teleology, 85, 124, 148, 156, 160, 170–71, 179
territorializing, 11, 52–53, 81, 86, 109, 123–24, 127, 138, 153, 161
terror, xiii, 1–4, 8, 11–13, 20, 22–24, 27–28, 47, 55, 74, 84–85, 88, 114n59, 117, 120, 136
Tillich, Paul, 39n42
Tocqueville, Alexis de, 3–4
totality, 36n39, 44n68, 67, 91, 96, 114, 150–51

transcendence, xi, 33, 35, 46–47, 63, 67, 69n150, 74–75, 78, 82, 84–85, 90–92, 94n53, 96, 105, 108–9, 117, 148, 152n84, 157–59
Trinity, x, 17, 23, 67, 70–71, 89, 92, 99, 129, 161, 163, 178–79
truth, x, xiii, 2–3, 12–15, 17, 19, 23, 28, 30–57, 65, 67, 114, 116–18, 170, 177
turn to religion, ix–x, 107, 109

universalism, xi, xiii, 9–11, 14, 24, 27, 30–33, 36n28, 37–47, 51–54, 56–60, 62–65, 67, 92–95, 104–5, 108–9, 114, 117n89, 118, 120–21, 150, 168
univocity, xiv, 36, 46n75, 52, 54–57, 66, 68–69, 78–79, 83–86, 90–94, 97, 99, 151n80, 157–59, 163, 169–71

violence, xii, 5, 83–85, 89–90, 98, 106–7, 113, 117n89, 118, 127, 128, 131, 142, 144, 167
vitalism, 35–36, 107
void, 17, 34, 36, 40n49, 52, 56, 114, 117–18, 123n14, 150

war, xi, xii, 1, 5, 7, 11, 13, 20–24, 26, 28, 55, 63, 69, 80–81, 85–86, 117, 126, 133, 140, 143, 158–59
Weber, Max, 23, 71, 99, 167
Westberg, Daniel, 128, 131n143
will, 47, 54, 68, 69n152, 83, 85, 93, 94n55, 104, 110, 116–17, 120, 122, 125–34, 151, 156–57, 163, 170–72
Williams, Rowan, 172, 174
works of mercy, 28, 72, 95, 100–101, 134

Yoder, John Howard, 57, 58n115, 58n117, 174

Zamagni, Stefano, 134
Žižek, Slavoj, ix, x, xiv, 29, 45–46, 51n93, 104, 116–20, 123–24, 125n123, 126, 129, 133

www.ingramcontent.com/pod-product-compliance
Lightning Source LLC
Chambersburg PA
CBHW021730220426
43662CB00008B/780